Adult Interactive Style Intervention and Participatory Research Designs in Autism

"Writing up research done for a PhD in a way that will appeal to more general readers is a real challenge. This book reflects the author's passion to communicate the findings from her ground-breaking doctoral research in a way that is accessible and practically useful for a range of professionals. I hope that teachers and others are excited by the changes which Lila and the staff she worked with saw in the communication of some very hard to reach children, and inspired to try the methods she has developed for themselves. Lila has certainly provided all the information which anyone who wants to try out Adult Interactive Style Intervention for themselves will need. I thoroughly recommend this book to anyone who is concerned to increase the communication of children with learning difficulties and autism."

—*Jean Ware*, Reader in Education
(Special Educational Needs) at Bangor University

Regardless of their cognitive and linguistic abilities, people with autism can often find it difficult to develop the basic communicative skills necessary to gain full control over their environment and maintain their independence. Building on the author's own cutting-edge research, *Adult Interactive Style Intervention and Participatory Research Designs in Autism* examines the impact that the interactive style of neurotypical individuals can have on the spontaneous communication of children with autism.

This book provides clear and detailed guidance on how to conduct research into autism in real-world settings such as schools and homes. Kossyvaki critically evaluates a wealth of relevant case studies and focuses on a number of methodological issues that researchers are likely to face when carrying out research of this complex nature. The author walks the reader through present literature on the importance of spontaneous communication and the atypical way that this tends to develop in autism, before bringing the results of her own research to bear on the question of how the interactive styles of neurotypical individuals can have an impact upon the spontaneous communication of people with autism.

Adult Interactive Style Intervention and Participatory Research Designs in Autism is essential reading for academics, researchers and postgraduate students in the fields of special educational needs, inclusion, autism, research methods and educational and clinical psychology.

Lila Kossyvaki is Lecturer in Severe Profound and Multiple Learning Difficulties at the University of Birmingham, UK. She has conducted extensive research on how school- and home-based interventions can be used to promote social communication and play skills in children with autism and learning difficulties.

Routledge Research in Special Education Needs

This series provides a forum for established and emerging scholars to discuss the latest debates, research and practice in the evolving field of Special Educational Needs.

Books in the series include

Adult Interactive Style Intervention and Participatory Research Designs in Autism
Bridging the Gap between Academic Research and Practice
Lila Kossyvaki

The Global Convergence of Vocational and Special Education
Mass Schooling and Modern Educability
John G. Richardson, Jinting Wu, and Douglas M. Judge

Adult Interactive Style Intervention and Participatory Research Designs in Autism

Bridging the Gap between Academic Research and Practice

Lila Kossyvaki

Routledge
Taylor & Francis Group

LONDON AND NEW YORK

First published 2018
by Routledge

2 Park Square, Milton Park, Abingdon, Oxfordshire OX14 4RN

52 Vanderbilt Avenue, New York, NY 10017

Routledge is an imprint of the Taylor & Francis Group, an informa business

First issued in paperback 2019

Copyright © 2018 Lila Kossyvaki

The right of Lila Kossyvaki to be identified as author of this work has been asserted by her in accordance with sections 77 and 78 of the Copyright, Designs and Patents Act 1988.

All rights reserved. No part of this book may be reprinted or reproduced or utilised in any form or by any electronic, mechanical, or other means, now known or hereafter invented, including photocopying and recording, or in any information storage or retrieval system, without permission in writing from the publishers.

Notice:
Product or corporate names may be trademarks or registered trademarks, and are used only for identification and explanation without intent to infringe.

British Library Cataloguing-in-Publication Data
A catalogue record for this book is available from the British Library

Library of Congress Cataloging-in-Publication Data
A catalog record for this book has been requested

ISBN: 978-1-138-85669-1 (hbk)
ISBN: 978-0-367-23275-7 (pbk)

Typeset in Galliard
by Apex CoVantage, LLC

Printed in the United Kingdom
by Henry Ling Limited

I would like to dedicate this book to two beloved people who sadly left us in the years the book was being written and for whom I will always keep very fond memories in my mind:

to my friend Fotini Papaioanou who left very early
and
to my grandmother Katerini Kossyvaki who closed an era with her passing.

Contents

List of abbreviations viii
Foreword x

1 Introduction 1

2 Autism and spontaneous communication 6

3 Reviewing the literature on adult interactive style to inform practice 23

4 Adult interactive style at school and at home 46

5 The research project 65

6 Analysing and discussing the findings 93

7 Participatory research designs: implications for practitioners and parents 120

8 Participatory research designs: implications for research 145

9 Conclusions 166

Appendix 1: Questionnaire for Determining Spontaneous Communication in Children 173
Appendix 2: AISI protocol 176
References 180
Index 209

Abbreviations

AAC	Augmentative and Alternative Communication
ABA	Applied Behavior Analysis
ADI-R	Autism Diagnostic Interview-Revised
ADOS	Autism Diagnostic Observation Schedule
AISCC	Adult Interactive Style Coding Checklist
AISI	Adult Interactive Style Intervention
APA	American Psychiatric Association
AS	Asperger's syndrome
AVIGUK	Association for Video Interaction Guidance UK
BAMT	British Association for Music Therapy
BPS	British Psychological Society
CARS	Childhood Autism Rating Scale
CB	Challenging Behaviour
CICCA	Checklist for the Initiation of Communication in Children with Autism
DARL	Development in Areas Related to Learning
DD	Developmental Delay
DIR	Developmental, Individual difference, Relationship-based model
DISN	(Department of) Disability Inclusion and Special Needs
DSM	Diagnostic and Statistical Manual of Mental Disorders
DTT	Discrete Trial Teaching/Training
EHCP	Education, Health and Care Plan
EIBI	Early Intensive Behavior Intervention
EPSRC	Engineering and Physical Sciences Research Council
ES	Effect Size
ESRC	Economic and Social Research Council
GD	Group Design
ICD	International Classification of Diseases and Related Health Problems
NICE	National Institute for Health and Care Excellence
NT	Neurotypical
OT	Occupational Therapist

PACT	Preschool Autism Communication Trial
PAR	Participatory Action Research
PECS	Picture Exchange Communication System
PLASN-R	Pan-London Autism Schools Network – Research
PMLD	Profound and Multiple Learning Difficulties
PRT	Pivotal Response Training
QDSCC	Questionnaire for Determining Spontaneous Communication in Children
RCT	Randomised Control Trial
RIT	Reciprocal Imitation Training
RPMT	Responsive Education and Prelinguistic Milieu Teaching
S/PMLD SPMLD	Severe, Profound and Multiple Learning Difficulties
SAACA	Single Attention and Associated Cognition in Autism
SCERTS	Social Communication Emotional Regulation Transactional Support
SD	Standard deviation
SEN	Special Educational Needs
SEND	Special Educational Needs and Disabilities (SEND)
SLD	Severe Learning Difficulties
SLT	Speech and Language Therapist
SPELL	Structure Positive Empathy Low arousal Links
SPT	Symbolic Play Test
SSD	Single Subject Design
TA	Teaching Assistant
TAC	Team Around the Child
TAE	Transform Autism Education
TD	Typically Developing
TEACCH	Treatment and Education of Autistic and related Communication handicapped Children
VERP	Video Enhanced Reflective Practice
VIG	Video Interaction Guidance

Foreword

As Lila's doctoral supervisor, I witnessed first-hand how she worked successfully and developed a close working relationship with school staff where her study took place. Coming from Greece into an unfamiliar education system and curriculum, this was no mean feat and when her fieldwork was finished, she was invited to work at the school as a teaching assistant and asked to coach other staff.

As the title states, this book seeks to encourage researchers and practitioners to work more closely together where each informs and is involved in the work of the other. In schools, for example, teaching staff, parents and children may be involved as participants but rarely as part of the research team that decides on the key questions and methods. The author uses her own doctoral research to illustrate how the gap can be bridged and the issues which may arise.

The author's other main concern highlighted within the book is that much research in autism focuses on intellectually able people and rarely on those with autism and severe, profound and multiple learning difficulties (SLD/PMLD). She argues that interventions designed for those with SLD/PMLD who are not autistic often need to be adapted to be effective for children with autism and SLD/PMLD.

Her two main theoretical perspectives are taken from the social model of disability and a transactional view of child development. In practice this means that instead of trying to 'fix' the individual, one makes adjustments to how other people interact and communicate with the individual and takes account of the social, sensory and physical demands within a given situation or setting.

The book first reviews the literature on the development of spontaneous communication in autistic children and how adults might effect this, describing the aims and rationale of specific behavioural/naturalistic and developmental/relationship-based approaches. Lila's own research focused on how teaching staff might facilitate communication for children with autism and SLD/PMLD within a special school setting. Based on the literature, she developed a set of principles which she named AISI (Adult Interactive Style Intervention) to be used at school or home.

AISI consists of 13 general principles which relate to the adults' body language, speech and timing and 8 communicative opportunities which suggest situations which adults can set up to increase the likelihood of the child communicating spontaneously. Some of these are illustrated by the use of drawings taken from stills of the video recordings made during the author's research.

The aims and methods of her own action research study are described. Video recordings were made of the children's interactions with staff and Video Interaction Guidance (Kennedy, 2011) was adapted to feed back information to the staff on their use of AISI. Focus groups were arranged with the staff and the changes in the children's communication were analysed from the video recordings. The findings of the study are presented in Chapter 6. Chapter 7 focuses on implications for practice for practitioners and parents and Chapter 8 explores the implications for future research, suggesting ways in which research and practice can be bridged. The final chapter summarises the main points raised in each of the chapters.

This book will be of great interest and value to many different audiences and as such creates the foundations of a bridge to link different personnel effectively. Professionals in education, health and social care, researchers, parents, carers and autistic children and adults alike are all likely to find sections of this book of interest. There are many helpful suggestions both on doing research and on reflecting on practice, in addition to ideas on how one might facilitate communication with children with autism and SLD/PMLD.

The ultimate aim of the book is to enhance the lives of autistic children and their families and to enable professionals involved to choose interventions which can be used in real-world settings and in which parents and the children want to be engaged. Where cooperation is established and skills shared, all the time, effort and resources spent by professionals, parents and researchers will yield the greatest gains in terms of what is learned and how it is then implemented.

Dr Glenys Jones
University of Birmingham
February 2017

1 Introduction

1.1 The origins and significance of the book

Both academics and the wider society (which includes stakeholders such as practitioners, parents and people with autism) have identified a gap between academic research and everyday practice in real-world settings. McIntyre (2005), for example, focuses on the need to bridge the existing gap between academic research and school practice whereas David Mitchel in Higashida's (2013) book very eloquently claims:

> [. . .] often the gap between the theory and what's unravelling on your kitchen floor is too wide to bridge.
>
> (p. 6)

As an academic and practitioner myself, I have witnessed that University knowledge reaches real-world settings after considerable delay (if it ever does reach them). Moreover, good practice at school and even more at home is rarely disseminated beyond the specific setting. Therefore, the primary aim of this book is to take a small step towards bridging the gap between academic research and practice at school and at home, and in particular, to highlight this as a bi-directional journey. I take my doctoral thesis on enhancing spontaneous communication in children with autism as the starting point. This is further enriched by knowledge, thoughts, experiences and discussions on relevant topics throughout my professional career to date (pre- and post-PhD).

It has always been my philosophy to conduct research with ecological validity and societal impact. In short, I have always wanted to carry out research which directly transforms people's lives. My PhD supervisor, Dr Glenys Jones, advised me that in order to achieve this, my work has to be presented in an 'accessible for all' manner. More specifically, she remarked that if what I say or write is not understandable by everybody 'it is not good enough'. Following a presentation on my PhD topic I gave for Autism West Midlands in August 2014, an attendee commented on Twitter,

> The presentation was the best example I've seen yet of an academic ensuring work is accessible for a lay audience.

This was the best compliment I have received about my work, and it is a driving force which keeps me energised and focused on the above goal. Since then, I was lucky enough to have been often receiving similar comments when working with practitioners and parents. Nowadays, there is a demand from universities and research councils for research with impact (i.e. research which contributes to understanding of the world and promotes applicable solution to real-world problems) and public engagement. This last consists of experts working alongside and sharing knowledge with non-experts. This will, hopefully, encourage more academics in the field of education and social sciences to build partnerships with schools, parent organisations and the wider community.

Although autism is a whole spectrum including individuals of different abilities and needs (Wing, 2012), the focus of this book is on children and individuals with autism and additional severe, profound and multiple learning difficulties (SPMLD) for two main reasons. Firstly, this field has been largely under-researched, with limited literature available on the topic. To date, most studies have focused on individuals with autism without learning difficulties or individuals with SPMLD without autism. From lengthy discussions with colleagues in schools and in academia as well as parents, I realised the necessity of conducting research and exploring 'best practice' for people with autism and SLD/PMLD such as Baggs (2007), Fleischmann (2012) and Higashida (2013). It is encouraging that there are examples of books either authored or co-authored by people with autism and learning difficulties, which provide authentic insight on how it feels to be autistic or live with autism (e.g. Higashida, 2013; Gallardo and Gallardo, n.d.). Nonetheless, more needs to be done in this field in the form of a more holistic but also hands-on approach (e.g. general guidelines but also individualised strategies to understand behaviours, teach a number of skills). Secondly, this is an area of great interest for me and a topic I feel passionate about.

1.2 Theoretical frameworks

The main study presented in Chapters 5 and 6 of this book and much of the research I have been involved in so far draw upon two theoretical frameworks widely used in disability research and developmental psychology. These are the social model of disability and the transactional model of child development. I will summarise them in this section.

In order to explain the social model of disability, I will start by outlining the medical or deficit model of disability, still currently predominant. The latter assumes that society is set and pre-determined and the person should be adapted or 'treated' (Rieser and Mason, 1990). Llaneza's et al. (2010) article provides an example of using the medical model to interpret autism. This article compares autism prevalence to that of paediatric cancer, diabetes and AIDS and concludes that funding for autism research should continue, hoping that a cure will be yielded. Many individuals with autism are vehemently against the also so-called medical tragedy model. For example, Luke Jackson (2002), a person with autism, highlights that *'looking for a cure for autism can be linked to Hitler trying to create an Aryan race'* (p. 77).

On the contrary, the social model of disability asserts that the problems are often socially constructed and reside outside the individuals themselves (Rieser and Mason, 1990; Tregaskis, 2002). Society should, therefore, provide the support that people need to access their physical, sensory and educational environment. According to Thomas (1999, cited in Reeve, 2004) social disablism can take two forms: (i) structural (e.g. people being excluded from physical environments because they cannot access buildings) and (ii) psycho-emotional (e.g. the emotional cost of being excluded from certain aspects of life such as the impact of looks of disapproval or pity). Reeve (2004) has very successfully pointed out that considerably more emphasis has been given to the structural component whereas far less attention has been paid to the psycho-emotional dimension. The Adult Interactive Style Intervention (AISI) study, my doctoral research, explores the extent to which staff provide children with autism with the reasons why they need to initiate communication at school, and the methods for doing this. It also addresses the psycho-emotional dimension as in school, children feel accepted as they are, adults being the ones who have to adjust their interactive style and not vice versa. Additionally, the social model of disability promotes self-advocacy by people with autism. This was greatly respected in the AISI study. For the development of AISI, personal accounts written by individuals with autism (e.g. Grandin, 1984; Sinclair, 1992; Lawson, 1998; Gerland, 2000; Jackson, 2002; Sainsbury, 2009) were considered. AISI also has been supported by two PhD students (now graduates) with autism who attended doctoral student conferences at the University of Birmingham, where the intervention and the initial findings of the study were presented (Kossyvaki, 2010; Kossyvaki 2011).

According to the transactional model of child development, adults' behaviour may influence and shape children's development (Wetherby and Prizant, 2000). Since communication is '*a continuous dynamic interplay*' (p. 2), neurotypical (NT) adults bear the same responsibility with children, if not more, when communication breaks down (Aldred et al., 2001; Willis and Robinson, 2011). Developmental/relationship-based approaches which were used as a basis to develop AISI (see Chapter 3, 'Reviewing the Literature on Adult Interactive Style to Inform Practice for More Details') embrace the transactional developmental perspective. If, for example, adults speak too much or do not wait long enough, the child is very unlikely to initiate communication, not because they cannot do so but because the adults do not give them the time to do so. Similarly, if the adults do not respond to the child's 'inappropriate' initiations, this might discourage the child from initiating again.

There has been limited evidence of the impact of these two models specifically on individuals with autism and SPMLD. Some people might even challenge the ability of individuals with SPMLD to experience psycho-emotional disablism. Echoing Shakespeare's (2004) point that people with learning difficulties have been largely marginalised in the disability movement which has been dominated by people with physical and sensory disabilities, I would argue here that the impact of the aforementioned theoretical models needs to be further explored on the former population.

1.3 A note on terminology and the target readership of this book

I have always believed that actions should speak louder than words and I consider debates on terminology of secondary importance, especially when these take place at the expense of more 'hands-on' and solution-focused debates and research projects (e.g. should 2nd April be called 'autism awareness' or 'autism acceptance' day?; is 'severe learning difficulties' or 'severe learning disabilities' a more appropriate term to use?). I also believe that it is beyond my knowledge and expertise to decide upon terminology. Nonetheless, I would like to provide some clarifications here regarding the terminology used in this book. These are provided in order to avoid misunderstandings and feelings of offence for readers for whom terminology might be a sensitive issue.

The term '*autism*' is used throughout the book in order to describe people from the whole autism spectrum (e.g. Kanner's autism, Asperger's syndrome, Pervasive Developmental Disorder) following *The Diagnostic and Statistical Manual of Mental Disorders* (DSM-V) (APA, 2013) according to which autism spectrum disorder (ASD) is now the only diagnostic label for all people from across the spectrum. The terms '*children/individuals with autism*' (i.e. people first language) and '*autistic children/individuals*' (i.e. condition first language) are used interchangeably as there is no unanimously preferred way. The terms '*Challenging Behaviour (CB)*', '*behaviours of concern*' or '*inappropriate behaviours*' are also mutually used to denote behaviours which might put the individual or people around them at risk of being physically hurt of losing their dignity. The terms '*severe, profound and multiple learning difficulties (SLD/PMLD, S/PMLD, SPMLD)*' will be used throughout this book to denote people with substantial intellectual and cognitive disabilities. Sometimes the equivalent generic term '*complex needs*' might be used too. More specifically, the term '*SLD*' refers to people with significant intellectual difficulties, difficulties in mobility, coordination, communication and self-help skills and need for support in all areas of the curriculum whereas the term '*PMLD*' includes individuals with more complex learning needs, other significant physical or sensory disabilities or a severe medical condition requiring a high level of adult support both for their learning needs and for their personal care. It is beyond the scope of this book to deal with specific learning difficulties such as dyslexia, dysgraphia, dyscalculia and dyspraxia. The more generic terms '*special needs*' or '*special educational needs (SEN)*' are often used (as opposed to the medical term '*disability*') to describe individuals with different types of disabilities including autism and SLD/PMLD but not exclusively these. The terms '*real world*' and '*naturalistic*' settings are used as synonyms. Last but not least, I refer to myself using the personal pronoun '*I*' as this book is a reflection on my personal professional journey and using terms such as '*the author*' or '*the researcher*' would have made the book look distant and foreign.

I started writing this book as a Research Fellow and school practitioner, having a range of readers in mind. I want it to be relevant to a number of people who live, work and do research with individuals with autism and SPMLD. Addressing successfully and meaningfully a number of audiences from very different contexts (e.g. school, home, university) and countries has been a challenge. Pitching it in the best manner has been challenging (different people and audiences may be in favour of certain research approaches-qualitative or quantitative, some countries consider the use of the word 'autistic' insulting). Therefore, I decided to keep the rigour of academic writing (e.g. systematic literature review on covered topics, provide evidence for all claims I make, explain why certain decisions were made, acknowledge limitations) but avoid jargon as much as possible, explaining terms for lay audiences where necessary, and giving examples from and for practice beyond academia.

Half way through the writing of the book (July 2015), I obtained a lecturer's post at the University of Birmingham. Part of my role involves the supervision of undergraduate and postgraduate students (primarily teachers, TAs, therapists and parents of children or adults with SPMLD) in the collection of empirical data in order to evidence good practice or improve their skills and settings. I then realised the importance of such a book in helping to support students with limited research knowledge to collect data in real-world settings on top of, in most cases, a demanding full-time job. Therefore, I undertook to make this book of interest to part-time students in education and social science departments who are asked to conduct naturalistic research, while being employed full-time. I hope that the book makes sense to all audiences it is geared towards, and I have taken some small steps towards bridging the gap between academic research and practice at school, home and wider community when it comes to autism and learning difficulties – or more generally, SEN.

1.4 The layout of the book

This book consists of nine chapters (including Chapter 1 'Introduction', and Chapter 9, 'Conclusions'), structured in three sections. The first section (Chapters 2–4) begins by presenting literature on the importance of spontaneous communication and the atypical way this tends to develop in autism. It also examines the impact NT individuals may have on autistic people's spontaneous communication, and suggests a set of principles that school staff, parents and other people can use to increase spontaneous communication in individuals with autism and S/PMLD. The second section (Chapters 5 and 6) describes a part of my doctoral study on the effect of adult interactive style on the spontaneous communication of young children with autism at school. Specifically, it focuses on a number of methodological issues researchers are likely to face when doing research in naturalistic settings. It also presents and discusses some of the findings of the study (both quantitative and qualitative). The third part of the book (Chapters 7 and 8) outlines some lessons learnt from carrying out real-world research with autistic participants with S/PMLD and the people living and working with them. Additional practical advice on how to enhance practice is provided to parents and school staff, together with topics and ideas for future real-world research.

2 Autism and spontaneous communication

2.1 Introduction

One aim of this book is to explore the effect of adult interactive style on the spontaneous communication of children with autism. This chapter, the first of three reviewing the relevant literature, starts by defining social communication, a term which features heavily in the literature on child development. Following this, the chapter explores the differences between Typically Developing (TD) children's social communication and that of children with autism, with a particular focus on intentional spontaneous communication and issues in initiating communication in autism. The next section provides a number of cognitive/psychological and sensory processing theories which attempt to explain communication difficulties in autism; these theories need to be taken into consideration when trying to enhance adult interactive style. The chapter closes with a review of naturalistic studies, mostly school-based, which focus on communicative functions, methods and partners, as well as activities which are likely to elicit spontaneous communication in children with autism.

2.2 Social communication

Social communication skills are vitally important, as they enable children to have control over their social and emotional environment and to relate to other people (Jarvis and Lamb, 2001; Buckley, 2003). There are a number of different definitions of social communication. Webster's Collegiate Dictionary (1988) defines communication as

> a process by which information is exchanged between individuals through a common system of symbols, signs or behaviour.

The Chambers Dictionary (1998) defines communication as

> the conveyance of one's meaning to others.

Schlosser et al. (2003) describe communication as an interaction, which involves at least two people. In essence, the definitions of communication involve the transfer of information between at least two persons by verbal or non-verbal means. There are two types of communication depending on whether information is transmitted or received; these are expressive or receptive communication, respectively. Bogdashina (2005, pp. 21–22) argues that for an act to be communicative, there needs to be

- something to communicate about (the message);
- a sender;
- a receiver;
- a medium of transmission; and
- communicative intent.

Individuals may communicate for many reasons and using several media for transmitting their information. Communicative acts may serve several functions, which fall under three major categories (Prizant et al., 2000):

- behaviour regulation (e.g. request and protest);
- joint attention (e.g. comment and provide information); and
- social interaction (e.g. request social games or routines, greet and call others).

Means of communication can be split into two broad categories: linguistic means (e.g. spoken, written, sign language) and non-linguistic means (e.g. body language, facial expressions, gestures, pictures or symbols) (Bogdashina, 2005). Messages can be conveyed using a combination of these. It is important to note here that communication does not always involve intention (Messer, 1994). Intentionality and how this is defined in the AISI study is discussed later in this chapter.

Social communication is a term which needs to be clarified. In this book it is used as a joint term for communication and social interaction. This is in accordance with the revised criteria for *The Diagnostic and Statistical Manual of mental Disorders*, 5th Edition (DSM-V) (APA, 2013). According to this, difficulties in emotional reciprocity, verbal and non-verbal communication, social interaction and developing and maintaining relationships, all fall under the umbrella term, social communication. Many other recent studies in the field also use the term social communication (Drew et al., 2007; Murdock et al., 2007; Wetherby et al., 2007; Clifford et al., 2010).

Social communication is defined by Prizant et al. (2006) as

> a child's ability to understand social events, and to participate and communicate as a competent, confident, and active participant in social activities using both verbal and/or nonverbal skills.
>
> (p. 315)

Having defined the term social communication and presented its main components, it is worth exploring social communication in children with TD and in children with autism. This will show how social communication develops through different pathways in each group.

2.3 Social communication in typical development (TD)

The social communication development of TD children provides a context within which to analyse the social communication skills of children with autism. This is limited to a discussion of development from birth to 5 years old as individuals with autism and S/PMLD rarely master the social communication milestones beyond that age.

Child development is a dynamic process based on both biological and environmental factors: the rate of achieving each developmental milestone is attributed to both inherent characteristics and personal experiences (Sheridan, 2008). As a result, there is a great variability in the patterns that TD children develop. In this section, an overview of the average child's social communication development is presented, based on Sheridan's (2008) work, the *Early Support Developmental Journal* (DCSF, 2008a) and the Early Years Foundation Stage Pack (DCSF, 2008b).

Even from the *first days following their birth*, infants try to establish emotional ties with their carers and interact with them through eye contact and facial expressions. *By the first month*, they may turn towards a soothing human voice, smile socially, respond to a carer's vocalisations and regard a nearby speaker's face. *At the age of six months*, infants may vocalise to others, respond differently to different tones of other voices and maintain eye contact during interaction with a familiar person. They can also show emotions in response to other people's emotions and react enthusiastically to often repeated games and rough and tumble play. *At nine months*, infants may babble deliberately to communicate and shout to gain attention. They can respond when their name is called, imitate hand clapping and wave in context and respond differently to facial expressions of happiness and sadness in others.

At 12 months, infants understand simple instructions if accompanied by gestures, follow an adult's eye gaze, point to an object and look back to the adult for the purpose of requesting or commenting. They also demonstrate affection to familiars, begin to imitate sounds produced by others, show awareness of other children and display more sophisticated emotions (e.g. joy fear, anger, surprise). Their babbling gets increasingly speech-like (combination of consonants and vowels). *At the age of 2 years*, toddlers can use 50 or more recognisable words appropriately and understand many more and can put two or more words together to form simple sentences. They refer to self by name, use echolalia, use names of objects and people, demand carers' attention, wait for their turn or go signal at 'ready, steady, go' games, join in nursery rhymes and may have a tantrum when frustrated or misunderstood.

By the third year of age, toddlers usually have a large vocabulary, which is understandable even to strangers, use personal pronouns correctly, ask many questions beginning with 'what', 'where' and 'who' and can defer satisfaction of wishes to the future. *At the age of 4*, children's speech is grammatically correct and completely intelligible and their talk is mainly related to 'here and now'. They have some awareness of immediate past and future (e.g. before, later), use others as a source of information, are aware that some reactions can hurt others, show sympathy for peers in distress and demonstrate pride in own achievements. *By the time they turn 5*, children use fluent speech, which is grammatically conventional and phonetically correct and understand time and sequence concepts such as 'first-then'. They play imaginatively and cooperatively with peers, show care and concern for others, respond to simple instructions and talk about things they see, and about past and future events.

There is broad consensus in the literature that the development of communication requires a partnership between the child and the environment and that the most significant part of that environment is the adult (e.g. parent, carer, practitioner). Many studies indicate that parents positively influence their child's communication (Scherer and Olswang, 1984; Olson et al., 1986). More specifically, studies on parent-child interactions have shown that parents' prompt responsiveness to their children's initiations can foster the development of the latter's social communication (Salter-Ainsworth and Bell, 1974; Jarvis and Lamb, 2001). On the other hand, it has been reported that children being raised by depressed parents or in their absence may experience social communication difficulties. Mothers who suffer from depression and show flat affection to their children may affect their children's social communication skills (Wetherby and Prizant, 2002). In a study of social deprivation in orphanages in Romania, Rutter et al. (1999) found that 6% of 111 children who were adopted by English families showed autistic-like features. Children were exposed to extremely poor conditions while at the orphanages: remaining in cots all day, having to feed themselves through bottles with large teats, lacking personalised care and with very limited interaction with caregivers. Although the quasi-autistic patterns cannot be attributed only to the children's adverse experiences early in their lives, some inferences may be drawn. The extent to which the lack of early interactions may affect development is also shown in early studies conducted with primates. Monkeys raised in deprived environments of total isolation rocked and engaged in stereotyped behaviours (Floeter and Greenough, 1979). This literature review attempts to explore the impact of adults on children's communication and does not embrace past theories suggesting that poor interactions with parents or carers can cause autism (Bettelheim, 1967). To explore the differences of social communication between TD and autistic children, the next section presents the development of social communication in children with autism.

2.4 Social communication in autism

Kanner's (1943) first article on autism refers to problems of communication and useful language. Most of the 11 children with autism he first observed had little or no communicative ability. Qualitative impairments in communication are still one of the main diagnostic criteria for autism in the International Classification of Diseases and Related Health Problems (ICD-10) (World Health Organisation-WHO, 1993) and DSM-V (APA, 2013). Difficulties in social communication are very common in people with autism (Baron-Cohen, 1995; Kasari, 2002) regardless of their language abilities (Jordan, 1999). Both verbal and non-verbal communication might be affected (Koegel, 2000). Up to 50% may never develop functional verbal communication (National Research Council-NRC, 2001). But even pupils with competent speech and language skills often initiate very little communication (Koegel, 2000; Jones, 2002) or have problems with the prosody, semantics, syntax and pragmatics (Bogdashina, 2005). It is important to note that many young children with autism may not see the need to communicate in a verbal manner (Wall, 2004). Sinclair (1992), an able man diagnosed with autism, remembers he started using language to communicate late as a child because

> learning how to talk follows why to talk-and until [he] learned that words have meanings, there was no reason to go to the trouble of learning to pronounce them as sounds.
>
> (p. 296)

Similarly, Temple Grandin (1984), a professor at Colorado State University diagnosed with AS, recalls,

> I remember being able to understand everything that people said to me, but I could not speak back [. . .] I did not learn to speak until I was 3 1/2.
>
> (pp. 145–145)

She also mentions that even as a grown up when she is frustrated she often reverts to one word speech. Blackburn (2011), another very eloquent adult woman with autism, sees her ability to use speech drop dramatically when she is upset.

Difficulties in social communication can be evident as early as 12 months of age and children with autism have a distinguishable profile of social communication before they even reach the second year of life. Some of these difficulties can be shared with children with developmental delay (DD) and some others are unique to autism. Wetherby et al. (2007) conducted a relevant study to examine social communication profiles from videotapes being captured between 18 and 24 months of age in three groups of children (50 with autism, 23 with DD and 50 with TD) and found that children with autism performed considerably lower than the age-matched children in the TD group on all social communication measures and scored significantly lower on five social communication measures (i.e. gaze shifts, gaze/point follow, rate of communicating, acts of joint attention and inventory for conventional gestures) when compared to children with DD matched on age and developmental level.

Many other studies comparing children with autism and TD children or children with DD show differences in their social communication skills. McGee et al. (1997), comparing 3- and 4-year-old children with autism with their TD peers, found that the former focus less on other children and adults, vocalise less and are less likely to be close to other children. Murdock et al. (2007) compared the social communication skills of 16 children with autism (6 to 11 years old) with 16 age-matched TD peers and found that the former exhibit from 40% to 57% fewer verbal initiations, verbal responses, joint attention and non-verbal communicative attempts than their peers.

There is some controversy about whether the difficulty regarding effective communication for children with autism is weighted more heavily towards their expressive or their receptive language abilities. Some authors report that expressive language is often more advanced than receptive language (Pelios and Lund, 2001). More precisely, Hudry et al. (2010) researched 152 preschoolers with autism via the use of clinicians' assessments and parents' reports, and found that receptive language was relatively more problematic than expressive ability for at least one-third of the sample. On the other hand, there are studies claiming that expressive language can present more difficulties than receptive language. For example, Chan et al. (2005) explored the receptive and expressive language abilities of 46 5 to 6 year-old Chinese children and found that 63% of the children with autism in their sample demonstrated language difficulties; 42% had both expressive and receptive language difficulties, and 21% demonstrated difficulties in expressive language. It should be noted here that general intelligence did not seem to have played a role as these findings were equally spread among participants across the spectrum regardless of cognitive, language and adaptive abilities. The finding that there is considerable heterogeneity in the way language and communication abilities can be problematic in autism means that staff at school should be sensitive to each individual child. For example, if a teacher overestimates a child's ability to initiate communication, when the child does not initiate this can be attributed to laziness or lack of interest rather than lack of understanding. Similarly, another teacher might overestimate a child's ability to process language, and overload them with verbal instructions which the child cannot process, leading to a tantrum. In autism, language and communication should always be treated with caution.

2.5 Intentional spontaneous social communication in autism

There are several issues in the way autistic children initiate social communication. Intentionality and spontaneity are two terms of great significance, as they both seem to be problematic for many children with autism. This section also presents a number of issues autistic children have in initiating communication such as echolalia, echopraxia, pronoun reversal, difficulties with deictic words (i.e. words relating to time and space, which vary depending on the context – for example, now, then, here, there), taking things literally, repetitive questioning, endless talking and poor intonation control.

2.5.1 Intentionality of communication

Broadly speaking, communication can be unintentional, pre-intentional and intentional (Ogletree et al., 2002). Intentionality can be difficult to attribute to people's actions (Messer, 1994). For example, when a baby cries, this does not necessarily mean that they are trying to get the adults' attention. Bruner (1981) claims that intentionality should be attributed only when there is persistence to reach a goal. Intentional communication can be hard for children with autism. It entails attributing thoughts, emotions and beliefs to the speaker and the listener, and thus it might be seriously affected in autism because of Theory of Mind difficulties (Baron-Cohen, 1995) and intersubjectivity difficulties (Hobson, 2002), which these children often experience. Theory of Mind difficulties are concerned with assigning thoughts and emotions to themselves and others whereas intersubjectivity difficulties are related to their awareness of themselves in the minds of others and the difficulty of discriminating between 'me-ness' and 'you-ness'.

There is no consensus on the definition of intentional communication. For Harding (1982), being an intentional communicator means learning about oneself and others and realising that one's behaviour can have an effect upon others. Wetherby et al. (2000) define communicative intent as

> the systematic use of conventional behaviors to deliberately affect another person.
>
> (p. 124)

Wetherby and Prizant (1989, cited in Potter and Whittaker, 2001) consider communication intentional when one of the following is observed:

- alternation of eye gaze between the goal and the listener;
- persistent signalling until the goal is achieved; and
- awaiting of a listener's response.

On a similar note, Grove et al. (2000) present some common ways people with SPMLD might use to show intention to communicate. These are: (i) alternating eye gaze, (ii) clear waiting for a response, (iii) active seeking of proximity, (iv) systematic variation in behaviour (i.e. the person elaborates or changes the behaviour) and v) persistence and intensity of behaviour (i.e. the person repeats the behaviour in different situations and with different people). However, young children with autism are likely to have eye gaze processing deficits (Pelphrey et al., 2005) and are unlikely to repeat a communication signal when there is a communication breakdown (Meadan et al., 2008) as they often show no awareness of communicative failures (Jordan, 1993).

2.5.2 Spontaneity of communication

Numerous definitions of spontaneous communication, ranging from strict and conservative definitions to more liberal ones, have been used in previous studies. Halle (1987) considers spontaneous to be every un-cued communication. For Watson et al. (1989) spontaneous communication is every communication cued by the environment, but not by prompts. Stone and Caro-Martinez (1990) define spontaneous communication as unelicited, child-initiated communication with the exclusion of responses to questions. Zanolli et al. (1996) see spontaneity as initiations that occur in the absence of any physical or verbal prompt from others. Potter and Whittaker (2001) define spontaneous communication as a child's attempt to transmit a message without being verbally prompted. This last definition puts the least demands on children and it is highly recommended to use when it comes to young autistic children with S/PMLD.

All the definitions above consider spontaneity in a binary 'all or nothing' way. According to these, if there is an antecedent to the communicative act, then it is not spontaneous. In contrast, if there is no antecedent, then the communicative act is spontaneous. However, spontaneity can also be seen across a continuum. In the continuum model, instead of spontaneous and non-spontaneous communicative acts, there is a degree of spontaneity for each communicative attempt based on the intrusiveness of the antecedent stimuli (Kaczmareck, 1990; Carter and Hotchkis, 2002). The less intrusive the stimulus, the more spontaneous the communicative attempt.

2.5.3 Issues for children with autism in initiating communication

After having explored the patterns of social communication development in TD children and some of the differences children with autism show, it is worth mentioning several issues the latter may have in initiating social communication. The list presented here is by no means exhaustive, but it reflects potential communicative methods young autistic children with SLD/PMLD may use.

Among other methods, echolalia may be used to initiate communication. Echolalia means the repetition of words or phrases previously heard. It can take different forms. When words and phrases are repeated just after being said, this is immediate echolalia, whereas when words and phrases heard in the past are repeated, this is delayed echolalia (Bogdashina, 2005). Roberts (1989) identifies one more type, that of mitigated echolalia, in which phrases are repeated in slightly modified form. All types of echolalia can be used to initiate communication. The main reasons individuals with autism might initiate echolalia are to request, protest, label, provide information, give directions and call (Prizant and Duchan, 1981; Prizant and Rydell, 1984). Echolalia is common among TD children in the course of developing language but in autism this might last much longer and even continue into adulthood (Bogdashina, 2005). Echolalia often appears as a precursor of language development and it should be encouraged (Prizant et al., 2006). Therefore when a child uses echolalia to request an object, adults should provide the object.

Echopraxia is the equivalent of echolalia in sign language (Carr, 1982) and it can be used to initiate communication by children with autism whose preferred mode of communication is signing. Jordan (1993) defines echopraxia as

> the slavish imitation of sequence of actions without taking account of the new role or situation of the person imitating.
>
> (p. 244)

To my knowledge, the relationship between echopraxia and spontaneous communication has not been widely researched. This is possibly because fewer and fewer children with autism use sign language or other signing programmes (e.g. Makaton, Paget-Gorman) due to their difficulties with gesture and the limited number of people who can understand the signs. Another problem with signs is that some people with autism cannot go beyond the literal understanding of the signing gesture. For them, signing can be as abstract as language. For example, Donna Williams, a woman with autism, questions the connection between signing the squeezing of cows teats and asking for milk (Williams, 1996). The extent to which individuals with autism use echopraxia should be examined alongside the imitation difficulties this population is reported to have. It is found that imitation problems are affected by children's learning and motor difficulties (Vanvuchelen et al., 2011). Therefore, signing might not be preferred by children with autism and additional complex needs. Imitation difficulties are more apparent at younger age groups (Williams et al., 2004) and this might explain why older children with autism tend to use signing more. However, Rogers et al. (2003) found that children with autism have difficulties in facial and procedural imitation but not in gestural imitation when compared to chronological and mental age-matched, non-autistic controls, which shows that signing programmes might work for some of them.

Children with autism might use personal pronouns, deictic words (e.g. here, there, then, now) and verb tenses incorrectly when initiating communication. The complexities in the use of pronouns can last into adulthood (Bogdashina, 2005). Since Kanner's first studies (1946), it was noted that the speech of autistic children showed pronominal reversal referring to themselves as 'you' and to the person they were speaking to as 'I'. They often use names to refer to themselves or others (Bogdashina, 2005). There are many cases of children with autism asking '*Do you want to go out?*' when they want to go for a walk or say '*Hello [their own name]*' when they want to be greeted by a passer-by. The main reason for the errors in using the pronouns 'I/me', 'you' and 'she/he' lies in their deictic nature; they change according to the situation, instead of being permanent labels for people (Bogdashina, 2005). On a similar note, verbal children with autism might also have difficulty with deictic words such as 'yesterday', 'today', 'tomorrow', 'here', 'there', 'this', 'that' and verb tenses as their meaning depends on one's position in space or time (Noens and Van Berckelaer-Onnes, 2004). Hence, adults have to accept a child using people's names instead of pronouns (Jordan, 2001) and expect mistakes in deictic words and verb tenses.

The language of autistic people can be extremely literal (Kanner, 1946). Humour, sarcasm, irony, idioms and polite modes of expression are difficult for young children with autism and SPMLD to understand. These may confuse them and result in 'inappropriate' behaviours. For example, people with autism often say exactly what they see and feel without realising that they may be considered rude (e.g. they are very likely to respond 'yes' to the question 'do I look fat?' if the person who poses the question is carrying extra weight). Similarly, they misinterpret others' instructions (e.g. *'paint the child next to you'*). A reason which might account for their extreme literalness is their difficulty in understanding the pragmatics of the language as children with autism focus on what the words mean, without paying attention to the social situation (Bogdashina, 2005). Moreover, many children with autism use neologisms, giving new names to objects, people and activities which can only be understood by them and sometimes their parents (Bogdashina, 2005). These idiosyncratic words are often based on unique associations (Frith, 2003), which can be impossible to guess making it even more difficult for them to be understood. Similarly, non-verbal children with autism are likely to use idiosyncratic communication signals. In my practice at schools I have often noticed children using unconventional motor actions (e.g. hair twisting, hand flapping) to ask for a preferred activity to start or continue. This is impossible for a new member of staff to guess. Therefore, adults should respond, if possible, to idiosyncratic words and communication signals but teach children more conventional ways of communication so that they can avoid future frustration resulting from communication breakdowns.

Repetitive questioning, talking endlessly about special interests and poor intonation can also affect the way children with autism initiate communication. Sometimes, they may repeat the same question again and again not necessarily because they do not know the answer but for the sake of the predictable reaction they are going to get (Bogdashina, 2005). As a response to that, adults can provide reassurance by giving them the message that they were heard. Repetitive questioning can also occur non-verbally, as, for instance, when children try to exchange the same picture/symbol again and again. The more verbally able children very often assume that their communicative partner shares their knowledge and passion about their special interests. Thus, they make long monologues with no joint reference to check whether others are following them (Lawson, 2001). Children with autism and S/PMLD might attempt to hold 'conversations' in the absence of a conversational partner (Jordan, 1999). In cases like these, it is recommended that adults should initially show interest in the child's talk and then gradually try to convert this into a turn-taking process. When adults notice children talking in absence of a communicative partner, they can get involved as if the talk was addressed to them. Finally, autistic children often have a monotonous, robot-like, flat voice without variations in their intonation (Bogdashina, 2005). A very typical example of this is Temple Grandin. Her voice is faster, louder and flatter than the voice of the average NT individual. However, this little interferes with understanding and it should be targeted only if it bothers the autistic individual.

Given the particular ways children with autism may initiate social communication, there is a need to understand why these differences emerge. A variety of cognitive/psychological and sensory processing theories have been suggested to answer this question. Knowing the reasons behind children's behaviours may affect adults' behaviour.

2.6 Cognitive, psychological and sensory processing theories in autism

A variety of cognitive, psychological and sensory processing theories have been suggested in an effort to explain the way children with autism use social communication. These theories should also be borne in mind when developing a facilitative adult interactive style. The theories which are discussed in this section are: (i) Theory of Mind (Baron-Cohen, 1995), (ii) Executive Functioning (Ozonoff et al., 1991; Hill, 2004), (iii) Central Coherence (Frith, 2003), (iv) monotropic attention (Lawson, 2001) and (v) sensory processing (Bogdashina, 2003).

2.6.1 Theory of Mind

Children with autism often fail to attribute mental states such as thoughts, emotions, beliefs and desires to themselves and others. This appears in the literature as poor Theory of Mind or 'mind-blindness' (Baron-Cohen, 1995) and can put autistic children at a great disadvantage when they have to predict the behaviour of others. A lack of awareness of one's own needs and the inability to read others' minds have an effect on understanding and using communication (Howlin et al., 1999). For a communicative act to be successful, the sender of the message has to recognise the listener's needs and desires as well as to monitor what they need to know or what they already know. If the sender is not aware of their desires, emotions and needs, or cannot 'read' the thoughts, emotions and intentions of the recipient, communication is unlikely to succeed. Clare Sainsbury (2009), a woman with autism, gives an example of how difficulties in Theory of Mind can interfere with communication. She explained that one day her mother dropped her off at school. Clare turned to her in panic and asked, '*Where's the frying pan?*' Everyone in the class had been asked to bring a frying pan and it did not occur to Clare that she had to share this information with her mother. However, this difficulty is not universal to all people with autism. Several studies (Dahlgren and Trillingsgaard, 1996; Roeyers et al., 2001) showed that autistic people can carry out Theory of Mind tasks when these are well explained to them.

2.6.2 Executive Functioning

The term Executive Functioning is used to define a set of higher-order functions which are necessary for flexible, goal-orientated behaviours, especially in novel circumstances. Executive Functioning is an umbrella term including functions such as planning, working memory, impulse control and mental flexibility (Ozonoff et al., 1991; Hill, 2004). Effective communication requires that children with autism are flexible, can adapt to new situations and know what to say or do in different contexts. So if a child has Executive Functioning problems, their communication will be severely affected. The difficulty with Executive Functioning is quite universal in people with autism (Pennington and Ozonoff, 1996). Poor Executive Functioning can account for difficulties in initiating social interactions. For example, if a child with autism can independently use the toilet at home, this does not mean that they will do the same when at school. This can be further exacerbated by the fact that autistic children may have extra difficulties in generalising learnt skills in new contexts (NRC, 2001). Only after reaching a point of self-awareness in which they are able to monitor their actions and act with volition can people with autism be regarded as competent communicators. Planning and sequencing difficulties are also common in children with autism. For example, a verbal child with autism may find it difficult to start, maintain and end a conversation. These difficulties are very likely to result in processing delays which make the fast-paced communication even more challenging.

2.6.3 Central Coherence

Whereas NT people tend to process information globally and in context, people with autism are likely to process information locally and in a fragmentary way (Frith, 2003). This tendency is known as weak Central Coherence. There is inconclusive evidence regarding the frequency with which this difficulty appears in people with autism. Some studies have shown that all people with autism display a local processing bias (Happe, 1997) but others failed to do so (Jarrold and Russell, 1997). Such a difficulty might affect the social interactions of people with autism who cannot make sense of a seemingly 'incoherent world' (Frith, 2003). Williams (1994) compared this difference in processing information between herself and NT people to '*a busy department store, which can open only one department at a time*' (p. 3). Communication is transient with functions, methods, partners changing all the time and making each communicative interaction different to the previous ones (Noens and Van Berckelaer-Onnes, 2004). Therefore, autistic children have to simultaneously keep in mind various fragmented information in order to communicate, making the process very challenging.

2.6.4 Monotropic Attention or Single Attention and Associated Cognition in Autism

Another theory to explain the behaviour of people with autism which is close to Central Coherence is that of having a Monotropic focus of Attention or Single Attention and Associated Cognition in Autism (SAACA) (Lawson, 2011). A monotropic individual is able to focus on one thing at a time or use only one channel (e.g. visual, auditory, tactile) to filter information (Lawson, 2001). Since his first description of early infantile autism, Kanner (1943) highlights the attention difficulties people with autism may experience. He notes for one of his patients that

> to get his attention almost requires one to break down a mental barrier between his inner consciousness and the outside world.
>
> (p. 218)

Mesibov (2007) compares the attention of people with autism to a torch beam meaning their attention is very intense but narrowly-focused. Grandin (1984) remembers how she was studying the sand at the beach as if she was '*a scientist looking at a specimen under the microscope*' (p. 156). Due to these attention issues, autistic people often fail to notice most of the features of the social environment (e.g. individuals' facial expressions, non-verbal signals and other information) unless they have an interest in them. As a result, they are likely to behave inappropriately and to 'stand out'. To add to this, Courchesne et al. (1994) note that people with autism might experience a severe attention-switching problem. This means that it may take them a long time to shift attention from one activity to another. Hence, their initiations to communicate requests or comments might be delayed and/or appear out of context.

2.6.5 Sensory processing differences

Most children with autism have different ways of processing sensory stimuli (Bogdashina, 2003). These differences are so universal among children with autism that hyper- or hyposensitivity to sensory input is added to the criteria in order to get an autism diagnosis in DSM-V (APA, 2013). There are seven sensory systems within the nervous system which may be hyper- or hyposensitive in autism (Myles et al., 2000). These systems are auditory (hearing), tactile (touch), visual (sight), gustatory (taste), olfactory (smell), vestibular (balance) and the proprioceptive (body awareness). Sensory processing differences in any of these systems may greatly influence the way children with autism initiate communication. For example, a child with hypersensitivity in the auditory system may avoid communicating with a loud person and a child with hyposensitivity in the visual system might get very close to people before initiating communication. Children's sensory processing patterns should be identified before starting any intervention programme with them (Dunn et al., 2002).

After exploring the literature on different ways in which children with autism might initiate social communication, and some theories that can explain why this might be happening, it seems useful to present the findings of several relevant studies in the field. The next section discusses studies on spontaneous communication and autism with a particular emphasis on communicative functions, methods and partners as well as the effect of school activities on spontaneous social communication.

2.7 Previous research on children's spontaneous communication

Several studies have been carried out to investigate spontaneous communication in children with autism. Some that focus on the functions of communication, the methods children use, the partners they address and school activities which elicit most initiations are presented here. The findings are illustrated by quotes from individuals with autism.

2.7.1 Communicative functions

In one of the first studies in the field, Stone and Caro-Martinez (1990) explored the patterns of spontaneous communication during activities at school. They observed 30 children with autism and found that the most common communicative actions were: getting attention, engaging in social interactions and requesting. Stone et al. (1997) compared 14 children with autism to 14 children with DD and/or language difficulties and found that the former requested more often and commented less often than controls. In a study of 18 young children with autism and minimal or no speech, Potter and Whittaker (2001) suggested that the purpose of the majority of children's communication acts were requests and rejects or protests. Exploring spontaneous communication in children and young adults with autism, Chiang and Lin (2008) and Chiang (2009) found that request was the most commonly used function. In another study, Chiang (2008a) looked at the communicative spontaneity of 32 autistic children and pre-adolescents using Carter and Hotchkis's (2002) continuum model to explain the nature of spontaneous communication in naturalistic settings. Communicative acts were judged along a continuum from low to high spontaneity and results revealed that the majority of spontaneous communicative acts were at the highest level of the continuum. The level of spontaneity in requesting and rejecting was higher than the other communicative functions. Agius (2009) investigated the patterns of spontaneous and intentional non-verbal communication in 11 children with autism and found that requests and protests were the most common. Drain and Engelhardt (2013) observed five non-verbal children with autism and found that the participants in their sample primarily initiated communication for requesting purposes.

The main reason people with autism may not request or reject objects and activities is that they are unaware of their needs. Blackburn said, in a lecture in 2011,

> autistics are prompt dependent; they find it extremely difficult to initiate communication, being at the mercy of other people around them.

She also gave an example of continuing to go horse riding even when she had stopped liking it. Only when her mother realised that she did not like it any more and asked her whether she wanted to stop, Blackburn answered yes.

2.7.2 Communicative methods

Most of the studies researching the functions of children's spontaneous communication looked also at the methods children tended to use. In Stone and Caro-Martinez's (1990) study, motoric acts were the most common method of initiating communication. Direct manipulation of the examiner's hand was the primary method children with autism used to communicate in Stone's et al. (1997) study. The use of physical manipulation and re-enactments were the most frequent means of communication in Potter and Whittaker's (2001) study. Chiang et al. (2008) studied 104 children and infants with autism, DD and TD and found that young children with autism displayed difficulties in initiating high-level skills of joint attention such as pointing, showing and extending objects towards the tester's face when compared to all control groups. In Chiang and Lin's (2008) and Chiang's (2009) studies children tended to use unaided Augmentative and Alternative Communication (AAC) such as gestures and motoric actions during spontaneous communication. In Agius's (2009) study, children mainly used vocalisations, eye contact and hand manipulation whereas in Drain and Engelhardt's (2013) study participants used physical forms of communication (e.g. gestures and sign language).

There is a growing body of literature on the communicative methods children with autism use. However, this chapter cannot cover the whole literature on this, and focuses on 'Challenging Behaviour' ('CB'), eye contact and pointing. 'CB' is an ambiguous term which has often received vigorous criticism with regard to who is being challenged; the child or the adult. Emerson (2001) defines 'CB' as a

> culturally abnormal behaviour of such an intensity, frequency or duration that the physical safety of the person or others is likely to be placed in serious jeopardy, or behaviour which is likely to seriously limit use of, or result in the person being denied access to, ordinary community facilities.
>
> (p. 3)

'CB' is found to be common among children with autism and closely associated with the degree of the child's communication difficulties (Sigafoos, 2000). Improvements in communication skills tend to decrease occurrences of 'CB'. However, verbally skilled adults with autism recall using such methods to communicate when they were younger. Blackburn (2011) used to hit children who were trying to be her friends, as hitting made them go away.

Eye contact as a method of initiating communication can be very difficult for many people with autism. John Elder Robison (2007), a man with AS who was diagnosed in his 40s, says,

> When I speak, I find visual input to be distracting . . . I usually look somewhere neutral – at the ground or off into the distance – when I'm talking to someone. Because speaking while watching things has always been difficult for me.
>
> (p. 3)

Jackson (2002) describes vividly his difficulty in looking somebody in the eyes by saying,

I feel as if their eyes are burning me and I really feel as if I am looking into the face of an alien.

(p. 70)

The difficulty individuals with autism may have in finding the right method to get their message across is described by Gerland (2000, cited in Sainsbury, 2009), a Swedish woman with AS. She illustrates how people with autism can worry about something without approaching anybody to share their problem just because it is difficult to ask something '*which you don't have words for*'.

Children with autism may find difficulties in both imperative and declarative pointing (Camaioni et al., 2003; Naoi et al., 2008). Imperative pointing is pointing to an object for requesting purposes whilst declarative pointing is pointing to share an object or event of interest (Wall, 2004). While declarative pointing is quite uncommon in autism, imperative pointing might be present (Baron-Cohen et al., 1992). The reason why this is happening may be that imperative pointing involves 'non-social' ends, whereas declarative pointing is an end in itself, which lack meaningfulness for some people with autism.

2.7.3 Communicative partners

Most of the studies looking at communicative functions and methods investigated the partners to whom children address their initiations. It is essential to note here that some children with autism completely lack the understanding that they need a partner to send their message to in order to communicate their needs (Jordan, 1999). As a result, I have witnessed in my practice cases of children pointing to out of reach toys in an empty room or holding photos in front of their eyes and expecting objects to 'magically' appear.

In Stone and Caro-Martinez's (1990) research, the teacher was found to be the most common target of communication. Adults were the most common communicative partner in Chiang and Lin's (2008) and Chiang's (2009) studies. Almost all of the communicative initiations were directed towards familiar adults in Potter and Whittaker's (2001) study and children preferred to communicate with adults than other peers in Agius's (2009) study too.

An interesting finding by Chiang (2008a) showed that there was a difference in the nature of spontaneous communication when this was addressed to adults as opposed to peers. She found that spontaneity was decreased when children addressed teachers and increased when they addressed peers. This suggests that children with autism tend to depend on prompts to initiate communication to adults but not to peers. This might be happening as adults tend to pre-empt the needs of children with autism to avoid tantrums (Potter and Whittaker, 2001) while peers can be more unpredictable. It is also interesting to note here that autistic children tend to communicate more often with their TD peers than peers with autism or other special needs (Bauminger et al., 2003). A possible explanation for this might be that, among these groups, TD peers are the easiest group to train in scaffolding children with autism. A number of studies have used TD children to teach social skills in children with autism (Barry et al., 2003; Thiemann and Goldstein, 2004; Tsao and Odom, 2006).

2.7.4 Activities and their effect on spontaneous social communication

There are only a few studies which reported differences in children's spontaneous communication across activities. Stone et al. (1997) found that children with autism initiate communication more often during unstructured activities. Drain and Engelhardt (2013), although they only observed their participants during fairly structured teacher-led activities, discussing their findings came to the conclusion that less-structured environments result in more spontaneous communicative acts. Quite inconsistent with the previous studies is Chiang's (2009) work, which showed that spontaneous communication occurred more often during academic activities rather than free time, morning circle or lunch time. It is interesting to note here that CB was more likely to occur in academic activities (Chiang, 2008b), which may have raised children's spontaneous communication during these times. Similar were the findings of O' Reilly et al. (2005) study, which reported that a child with severe autism was self-injuring mainly during academic demands to escape from the activity but not during play or no-interaction conditions. Potter and Whittaker (2001) found that most spontaneous communication occurred in 1:1 or small group (i.e. 1 adult: 3–4 children) sessions.

2.8 Reflection activities

- Take some time to think whether children with autism you work or live with really 'communicate' their desires, preferences and needs. Is there communicative intent in their actions? Do you tend to pre-empt their communication to save time, avoid tantrums or simply because you know what they want?
- Think of a temper tantrum of child with autism whom you know. Based on the knowledge you gained, can you attribute this tantrum to their difficulty in communicating? If so, can any of the cognitive, psychological and sensory processing theories presented in this chapter help you prevent similar tantrums in the future?

3 Reviewing the literature on adult interactive style to inform practice

3.1 Introduction

For communication to be successful, both partners need to work effectively together. Increasing attention is being given to how adults should interact with autistic children to encourage and facilitate their communication (Potter and Whittaker, 2001; Prizant et al., 2006; Kossyvaki et al., 2016). This chapter considers some interventions in autism which focus on developing communication. It pays particular attention to the advice given on how adults should modify their behaviour and communicative style. A set of principles derived from these is suggested. The term child (instead of the plural form children) is used in this chapter when describing facilitative adult interactive style, as most of the interventions presented here involve adults tending to work on a 1:1 basis with the children. Regarding adults, the plural form is preferred as there is usually more than one adult using the intervention with a child for skill generalisation purposes.

The chapter starts by classifying the approaches aiming to develop social communication in autism into two broad categories: behavioural/naturalistic and developmental/relationship-based approaches. It then discusses different interventions which belong to these categories and focuses on the advice they give for a facilitative adult interactive style. The third section presents past studies reporting changes in children's spontaneous communication as a result of implementing these interventions. Finally, studies exploring the impact of parents' and practitioners' interactive style on children's communication are illustrated. The ultimate aim of this chapter is to show the rationale and evidence base of effective adult interactive style as shown in a number of interventions in order to conclude with the relevant principles contained within the Adult Interactive Style Intervention (AISI). The next chapter employs a number of drawings and examples to explain in detail how the AISI principles can be used by parents and practitioners.

3.2 Approaches to developing social communication in autism

There are a variety of approaches aiming to develop social communication in children with autism. Classifying them into broad categories can be problematic as there are many different taxonomies, which can be based on subjective judgements which do not always agree with each other (Jordan et al., 1998; Simpson, 2005; Yoder and McDuffie, 2006; Ospina et al., 2008; Kalyva, 2011). This book follows Ingersoll and Dvortcsak's (2006) classification system, which has two categories: behavioural/naturalistic and developmental/relationship-based. Although these interventions have some similarities in the way they are implemented, they also differ greatly in their theoretical underpinnings. This section gives an overview for the main components of behavioural/naturalistic and developmental/relationship-based approaches, explores their similarities and differences and the characteristics of children who benefit more from each one of them.

Behavioural/naturalistic interventions are based on the assumption that new skills should be taught in an environment where the antecedent stimuli are clear and systematic reinforcement follows a correct response (Cooper et al., 2007). These approaches break the target communication skill into smaller steps such as greet in response to the arrival of an adult (Charlop and Trasowech, 1991) or say 'thank you' when being given a desired object (Matson et al., 1993). Teaching usually takes place in highly structured environments. The main argument against these approaches is that the learnt skills are context limited. It has also been argued that they address only the child's ability to achieve environmental ends (e.g. get an object) and not social ends (e.g. request social games). Additionally, they are accused of using pragmatically irrelevant reinforcers, which do not help the child to make the connection between communication and achieving social ends (Wetherby, 1986). However, behavioural interventions have been subjected to rigorous research and there is evidence of gains in children's cognitive, communication, adaptive and social skills (Couper and Sampson, 2003). In these approaches, adults use reinforcement, prompts, modelling and predictability. They also set up the environment to promote children's initiations and use time delay procedures.

Developmental/relationship-based approaches, on the other hand, are based on the assumption that children with autism follow the developmental trajectories of their TD peers and suggest going back to practice the milestones they missed (Greenspan and Wieder, 1998). Learning is achieved through strong affect-laden relationships between the child and the adults (Ingersoll et al., 2005). Developmental/relationship-based approaches share the following common characteristics (Ingersoll et al., 2005; Ingersoll, 2010a):

- adults follow the child's lead;
- the environment is set up to evoke initiations from the child;
- all the child's communicative attempts, even the unconventional and pre-intentional ones, are interpreted as intentional;
- affective and emotional interactions are emphasised; and
- language and social demands are adjusted to the child's developmental level.

In these approaches, adults pay great attention to their interactive style. They build strong relationships with the child through sharing mutual enjoyment of their in-between interaction. Adults are also responsive to the child, adjust language input, follow their pace, use multiple cues and foster initiations.

Originating from different theoretical backgrounds, behavioural/naturalistic and developmental/relationship-based approaches have several strategies in common but display crucial differences as well. Both teach to the child's focus of attention, create an environment which fosters opportunities for communication and provide natural consequences (Wilcox and Shannon, 1998). One main difference is that developmental/relationship-based approaches focus on promoting social communication skills without making a distinction between different specific communicative functions or methods, whereas behavioural/naturalistic approaches teach specific communication functions (e.g. ask for information) and methods (e.g. sign for 'more'). The second crucial difference is that in developmental/relationship-based approaches adults respond to all the child's attempts to communicate even the 'unconventional' and pre-intentional, while in behavioural/naturalistic interventions adults prompt the child for an elaborated response (Kaiser et al., 1992).

There is a debate with regard to which children benefit from each type of intervention. The relevant evidence appears inconclusive. For Sherer and Schreibman (2005) and Stoelb et al. (2004, both cited in Brunner and Seung, 2009), behavioural/naturalistic interventions appear to be more beneficial for more cognitively able children whereas developmental/relationship-based interventions work better for less cognitively able children. However, Yoder et al. (1995) argue the reverse, having found that children with lower language levels benefited more from the behavioural/naturalistic interventions whilst children with higher language skills responded better to developmental/relationship-based approaches. Further research is needed and it is always important to consider the approach that is most suited for the individual child.

AISI is mainly based on developmental/relationship-based approaches. This is in accordance with research stating that facilitative strategies are more appropriate for teaching initiation than prompting strategies, which are more effective with responding skills (Rydell and Mirenda, 1994; Salmon et al., 1998). Moreover, all these approaches put particular emphasis on adults' behaviour which can affect to a great extent the child's communication (Nind, 1999; Potter and Whittaker, 2001; Prizant et al., 2006). However, there is an argument against these approaches which should be taken into consideration. Most of the developmental/relationship-based approaches evidence their effectiveness based on studies which are not experimental and as a result the effect of sample maturation cannot be ruled out (Ingersoll, 2010a).

The next sections go into detail about specific interventions which belong to the two approaches to teaching social communication in autism. The main emphasis is on the advice these interventions give for adult style as this formed the basis for the development of AISI.

3.3 Behavioural/naturalistic interventions and the role of adult style

3.3.1 Early Intensive Behavior Intervention and Discrete Trial Teaching/Training

The structured individualised programmes of Early Intensive Behavior Intervention (EIBI) derive from the systematic application of Applied Behavior Analysis (ABA), which is based on Skinner's theory of Operant Conditioning (Kearney, 2008). According to Skinner's theory, changes in behaviour are the result of an individual's response to stimuli (i.e. events) that occur in the environment. EIBI is used as an umbrella term to signify a number of teaching approaches within the ABA paradigm. Discrete Trial Teaching/Training (DTT) is possibly the most well known of the EIBI approaches and the one which adheres the most to strict ABA principles. DTT is a highly structured programme in which the therapists present a stimulus to the child and react immediately according to their response (Lovaas, 1981). If the response is correct, the therapists praise and reward the child whereas if the response is incorrect, the therapists immediately prompt the child to respond appropriately. DTT is unlikely to develop spontaneous communication as the child gets intensive instruction and direct feedback for responding to the adults. A common misconception about EIBI is that it is just 'table work', confined to the DTT approach, which however is only one part of a comprehensive ABA programme (Keenan et al., 2006). Overall, some of the advice given in the broader EIBI approaches with regard to the adult interactive style can be used when facilitating spontaneous communication. For example, adults should be brief and specific, using a clear voice when giving the stimulus which should have a distinctive onset and offset (Richman, 2001). Adults are also advised to get the child's attention before presenting the stimulus (Richman, 2001).

EIBI therapists use a variety of prompts. These prompts can be either verbal or physical. Physical prompts are recommended as although they might seem more intrusive, they are easier to fade than verbal prompts (Richman, 2001). They can range from full hand-over-hand prompt to show the child how to perform an action or a slight tap on the shoulder to remind them to take action. The adults should gradually reduce the amount of physical prompt they provide. For example, they may start with hand-over-hand help and gradually relax their grip, guide the child by the wrist, tap them on the shoulder or point to the activity they are supposed to be doing.

Adults in EIBI use reinforcement. This can take two forms: positive and negative. Positive reinforcement is the addition of a desired stimulus (e.g. biscuits, '*Nice job*', toy car, tickles) to the environment whist negative reinforcement is the removal of an unpleasant stimulus (e.g. an activity the child dislikes) from the environment (Cooper et al., 2007; Kearney, 2008). Reinforcement should be used differentially as it then becomes more powerful (Cooper et al., 2007). This means that adults should save the most meaningful reinforcers for the most difficult tasks. For example, they should provide more reinforcement the less prompted the child's communicative attempt is. Special importance is placed on the adults' tone of voice when reinforcing. This should be done with an upbeat voice (Richman, 2001). To sum up advice given by EIBI regarding adult interactive style, therapists are asked to use a number of prompts and reinforcers. They are also expected to get the child's attention before addressing them and to use brief and specific language.

3.3.2 Some other naturalistic/behavioural approaches

Apart from the DTT, there are a number of other naturalistic behavioural interventions. These approaches, although being structured, are more child-directed and use naturally occurring stimuli from the child's environment. This section briefly discusses the facilitative adult interactive style proposed in several of these interventions.

3.3.2.1 Incidental Teaching

The rationale behind Incidental Teaching is that every situation throughout the day can be used as a teaching opportunity and adults' instructions should be based on the child's interests and motivation (McGee et al., 1994). Adults are also asked to arrange the environment in a way to promote the child's initiations (Richman, 2001). A commonly used technique is to put favourite toys or objects the child needs in sight but out of reach. Crayons are removed from the cupboard before it is time for the child to colour or the forks are not on the dinner table when it is time for dinner. Once the child initiates request, the adults encourage them to elaborate on the initiation. Additionally, adults should follow the child's lead, wait for initiations, indicate expectation through gestures and use prompts to complete the interaction (McGee et al., 1994).

3.3.2.2 Pivotal Response Training

Pivotal Response Training (PRT) is an approach using mainly ABA principles but also some developmental procedures targeting five pivotal areas which, when improved, have a collateral effect on other areas of functioning (Koegel et al., 2006). These are motivation, responsivity to multiple cues, self-management, self-initiations and empathy. PRT suggests that adults make environmental arrangements which promote frequent opportunities to communicate. Adults should identify motivating materials, put items in sight but out of reach and provide the child with opportunities which break a preferred activity down into smaller steps (e.g. one building block at a time instead of a box full of blocks, small amounts of juice). In this way additional opportunities for communication are created. Adults are also advised to follow the child's lead, respond to their interest (e.g. *'Do you want the ball?'* when looking at the ball) and immediately provide the preferred item contingent upon the child's attempt to respond. Daily routines should be broken down too. For example, when entering a dark room the adults should wait for the child to request that the light be on or instead of opening jars and containers they should provide the child with the opportunity to ask for it. A short time delay may clearly show to the child that the routine is broken. Adults should gain the child's attention before giving instructions, use concise and task-related language, combine verbal instructions with modelling and ensure that instructions have a clear beginning and ending (Fisher, 2006). Reinforcers are recommended too (Fisher, 2006). Reinforcers start from immediate and obvious and they gradually get more abstract (e.g. from a sticker to the task completion itself). Adults are advised to be predictable and prepare the child for changes ahead of time.

3.3.2.3 Early Start Denver Model

The Early Start Denver Model (ESDM) fosters development in a variety of areas known to be affected by autism (Rogers and Dawson, 2010). Each child's interest is taken into account while adults try to support their social communication using carefully behavioural teaching strategies. ESDM uses teaching practices from EIBI, PRT and the Denver model. Adults are advised to engage the child in positive emotional experiences in which the latter will have the chance to practise their knowledge. They also have to offer the child opportunities to request, protest, comment, ask for help and greet as frequently as every 10 seconds. Reinforcement is widely used but the goal is to make social engagement the reward. For this reason, social experiences are paired with non-social rewards such as favourite objects, which enhance the reward value of social experiences. Adults should get and maintain the child's attention as well as systematically use fading prompts so that behaviours are triggered in response to environmental cues rather than adult prompts. They are also asked to respond to the child's communicative cues giving them the message that they have been heard. The language used should be developmentally appropriate. The *one-up rule* is proposed. This means that the length of adults' utterances is approximately one word longer than the length of the child's utterances.

3.3.2.4 Milieu Teaching

Milieu Teaching states that prompting and cueing can be done during highly natural activities in which the child's reinforcement is the communication outcome itself (Fey, 1986). Adults are asked to observe the child, and when the latter shows interest in an object or an aspect of the environment, they should try to evoke a response. If the child responds correctly, they are verbally reinforced and given the object. If the response is incorrect, adults should use prompts. There are four types of milieu language prompts: (i) model, (ii) mand, (iii) questions and iv) time delay (Ingersoll, 2011). The following example explains how these prompts might work. A child playing with a toy car and a therapist interrupting the child's game to prompt them to say '*car*' or '*play car*' set the scene. When the child's play routine is interrupted, the therapist can model what the child should say (e.g. '*car*', 'more *car*'), mand (e.g. '*Tell me what you want*'), question (e.g. '*What do you want?*') or restrict access and give an expectant look.

3.3.2.5 Reciprocal Imitation Training

The goal of Reciprocal Imitation Training (RIT) is to teach young children with autism imitation through play (Ingersoll, 2010b). Ingersoll (2008), who founded RIT, argues that imitation plays a central role in developing other social communication skills and therefore it should be targeted in early interventions. Reciprocity is an integral part of the intervention. The therapists are trained to imitate the child's verbal and non-verbal actions, describe them using simplified language and expand on their utterances (Ingersoll and Schreibman, 2006; Ingersoll, 2010b). Therapists are also asked to model actions with toys (Ingersoll and Schreibman, 2006). Before modelling, they should get the child's attention by facing them or calling their name. Therapists have to model the actions up to three times and if the child does not imitate after the third time, the former physically prompt the child to complete the action and then give praise. Overall, therapists have to fulfil the child's requests and briefly acknowledge their comments (Ingersoll and Schreibman, 2006). In sum, in RIT therapists keep a balance between modelling actions and following the child's lead. Imitation of verbal and non-verbal behaviours, running commentaries on the child's play using simple language, getting the child's attention before modelling, prompting and praising them are its main components.

To conclude, naturalistic/behavioural approaches share a number of common adult style principles. Adults should be responsive to the child following their interests, use simple language, create environments which promote spontaneous communication and pause, showing an expectant look. Special attention is paid to the development of language and this is why adults are encouraged to elaborate on the child's communicative attempts.

3.3.3 Picture Exchange Communication System

Picture Exchange Communication System (PECS) is a picture-based programme to teach children with communication difficulties to initiate communication in a social exchange (Frost and Bondy, 2002). It prompts children to exchange a picture of a desired object for that object. The cornerstone of PECS is that it aims at spontaneous communication as there is no verbal pre-empting such as '*what do you want?*' or '*give me the picture*'. The adults have to wait for the child to initiate communication by handing over the picture. Its significance lies in the fact that unlike other AAC systems (e.g. pointing or signing which can be seen in the absence of a communicative partner) the child has to physically interact with a partner by giving them something. In initial PECS sessions, two adults are needed; adult one (the communicative partner) holds out an empty hand in front of the object while adult two (the physical prompter) physically guides the child to hand the picture to adult one. Once this stage is mastered, prompts are gradually eliminated and more distance between adult one and the child is created (Bondy and Frost, 2002).

Bondy and Frost (2002) suggest a number of communication enhancement strategies to develop the child's spontaneity. Adults are encouraged to place favourite items within view but out of reach, offer small portions of food and drink, consume a favourite food or drink in front of the child and create the need for assistance (e.g. wind-up toys, firmly closed containers). They are also asked to interrupt a favourite cooperative activity, offer the child something they do not like, hold out two favourite items and say nothing and violate the child's expectations. When these strategies are put in place, adults are reminded to pause and wait to increase the likelihood of spontaneous communication. Communicative partners are advised to wait for at least five seconds with an expectant look, raised shoulders and eyebrows and if despite that the child does not respond they are advised to use subtle prompts. These prompts can include pointing to the picture or object, saying the initial sound of the word or having a second person model the response.

Therefore, in PECS, adults have to set up environments which promote the child's initiations and then wait for them to take action. Adults are also encouraged to show with their body language that they are available for communication and if this does not work to use prompts. The prompts should be physical or visual, as verbal pre-empting is not recommended.

3.3.4 Treatment and Education of Autistic and related Communication handicapped CHildren

Treatment and Education of Autistic and related Communication handicapped CHildren (TEACCH) is a structured teaching approach developed at the University of North Carolina in 1972. Central to it is an understanding of the 'culture of autism' (Mesibov, 2007) and the needs of each individual so that they can be helped to function in a predictable environment which encourages independence and communication (Blubaugh and Kohlmann, 2006). TEACCH can provide some advice on facilitative adult style.

Visual structure and motivation (e.g. snacks, favourite activities) are crucial when teaching children with autism to communicate (Lord and Schopler, 1994). Adults need to be predictable and to give information top to bottom or left to right. Depending on the child's abilities, a number of visual cues (e.g. written words, photos or symbols with written words, photo or symbol cards and objects of reference) can be used. Adults should clarify beginnings and ends of activities. Social reinforcement such as a smile, a hug, a pat on the back, an '*I am proud of you*' or even a sticker should be used with caution as they might be meaningless for children with autism (Mesibov, 2007). It is the adults' job to find what a meaningful reinforcer is for every child. Moreover, adults need to give multiple communicative opportunities across settings such as school, home and community (Lord and Schopler, 1994). Mesibov (2007) stresses the fact that adults should not give children objects they want unless they ask for them.

Adults are also encouraged to get the child's attention before communicating and to use real choices (i.e. meaningful and accessible choices). The child's attention should gradually be sustained for longer periods of time. Adults can use colours and highlighting in the visual cues to engage the child's attention. Mesibov (2007) draws attention to the fact that adults have to give the child the chance to choose from objects and activities they really like and these choices should be supported by visual cues. Language should be kept to a minimum. In TEACCH, building on the child's strengths is also very important.

To conclude, TEACCH uses visual supports to make children independent communicators. Adults should use as many visual cues as possible supported by minimal speech. They also have to get the child's attention before communicating and provide them with many real choices.

3.3.5 Portage

Portage is a home-based programme for preschool children with additional support needs and their families (White and Cameron, 1987). It aims to support the development of play, communication, relationships and learning. Most of the strategies used come from the EIBI (e.g. chaining, shaping and task analysis). Central to Portage philosophy is that parents have an essential role in delivering the programme. Adults in Portage should use clear language speaking only about things which can be seen or heard (Willis and Robinson, 2011).

Smith (1999) adapted the generic Portage programme to meet the specific needs of children with autism and provided some specific advice as to how adults can encourage spontaneous communication. More specifically, she asks them to be very responsive to the child. Adults should watch the child intensively and respond as if the latter communicated by asking questions, commenting, reacting and repeating. Adults should also pause expectantly and wait, extend communicative attempts, imitate the child and use slow speech and simple sentences. Reinforcement, exaggerated tone, gestures and facial expressions as well as fun are recommended too. Therefore, responsivity to the child's initiations is very significant in Smith's (1999) adaptation of Portage programme.

3.4 Developmental/relationship-based interventions and the role of adult style

3.4.1 Intensive Interaction

Intensive Interaction is an approach for enabling social communication based on the model of caregiver-infant interaction and can be used with individuals of all ages (Nind and Powell, 2000). It builds upon the basic aspects of communication such as taking turns, sharing personal space, using and understanding eye contact, facial expressions and non-verbal communication (Nind, 1999). Adults are expected to be observant, tuned in and responsive while allowing pauses and letting the child lead (Nind and Hewett, 2001). It is a *'process oriented approach'*

(p. 101) with the interaction itself being the ultimate goal (Nind and Powell, 2000). It is based on the rationale that when adults change their interpersonal behaviours (e.g. facial expressions, body language, vocal and gaze behaviour) to become more interesting and meaningful, children are likely to increase their social communication (Nind, 1999).

Nind and Hewett (2001) advise adults to position themselves below the child's eye level before communicating. Nind and Hewett (1994) place great emphasis on physical contact when interacting with people with limited understanding. Adult availability is another important principle. Pausing and waiting are of particular value in Intensive Interaction as children with communication difficulties may process information at a slower pace (Nind and Powell, 2000). Adults should celebrate and acknowledge all the child's attempts to communicate (Nind and Hewett, 2001). Imitation is also important (Caldwell, 2006). The need for adults to slow down and use some variation in the pitch of their speech is highlighted too (Nind and Hewett, 2001).

To summarise, adults are expected to get close to the child, show them they are available for communication, follow their lead and imitate them. They are also encouraged to respond to all the child's attempts to communicate and pause and wait to give them a turn.

3.4.2 Social Communication Emotional Regulation Transactional Support

The Social Communication Emotional Regulation Transactional Support (SCERTS) framework is a multidisciplinary approach to support children with autism and adults who work or live with them (Prizant et al., 2006). It aims to support the child to become a competent, emotionally regulated communicator and has a focus on developing strategies for the adults as well as for the child. Interpersonal support is an integral component of SCERTS. Adults should be responsive and foster initiations. Responsiveness can be achieved in a number of ways such as following the child's focus of attention, attuning to their emotion and pace, responding appropriately to their signals and recognising signs of dysregulation and offering support. Adults can also be responsive by imitating the child, pausing in anticipation of a response from them and offering breaks when needed. Initiations can be encouraged by offering choices, waiting for initiations and adults intervening only when it becomes clear that the child is not going to initiate. Allowing children to initiate and terminate activities may further promote initiations.

Setting the stage for engagement and providing appropriate developmental support are also very significant components of SCERTS. To engage children, adults are advised to get close, physically down to their level, and secure their attention before communicating. Adults can provide developmental support by repairing communication breakdowns and expanding on the child's non-verbal communication. It is the adults' responsibility to clarify the meaning of unclear signals coming either from themselves or the child.

Adults are advised to adjust language input and to model appropriate behaviours. If, for example, a child does not understand words, adults should mostly use single words. If a child does understand some words, adults can use two- and three-word sentences. The use of non-verbal cues (e.g. gestures, facial expressions and intonation) to support understanding is highly recommended. Adults should also model appropriate non-verbal communication (e.g. gestures, pointing), a range of communicative functions (e.g. holding out an open palm to request an object, pointing to interesting events in the environment and waving to greet) and 'child-perspective' language considering the child's intentions and developmental level (e.g. if a child reaches for a toy car, adults might say *'car'*, or *'car down'*). SCERTS draws adults' attention to the sensory issues many children with autism may experience. In particular, adults should avoid being overly enthusiastic or speaking too loudly when communicating with children who are hypersensitive to sounds and they should avoid touching or hugging children with tactile hypersensitivity.

Overall, SCERTS encourages adults to be responsive to the child, to promote initiations, to get close to them and show availability, to use 'child-perspective' language and a range of non-verbal cues to support understanding. Adults should also be alerted to the child's potential sensory sensitivities which must affect the way each individual child is approached.

3.4.3 Developmental, Individual difference, Relationship-based model-Floortime

The Developmental, Individual difference, Relationship-based (DIR) model-Floortime is a developmental intervention which takes young children with autism to the very first milestones they missed and starts the developmental process from the beginning (Greenspan and Wieder, 1998; Greenspan and Wieder, 1999). Affective interactions with others are highly emphasised (Wieder and Greenspan, 2003). Its primary goal is to help children form a sense of themselves as intentional and interactive individuals through building a link between emotions, behaviour and eventually words (Greenspan and Wieder, 1998; Greenspan and Wieder, 1999). Establishing secure relationships is the cornerstone to promote development of the functional milestones. Adults should base their interactions on the child's interests, imitate them and respond to their initiations (Schertz and Odom, 2004). Adults are also encouraged to hold the child's attention through their senses (e.g. vocal gestures, touch and motor experiences) (Greenspan and Wieder, 1998). Great attention is paid to children's individual sensory differences (Schertz and Odom, 2004).

Based on DIR model-Floortime, Sonders (2003) developed her own approach of developing communication skills, the Giggle Time. In this approach, adults assign meaning to the child's ordinary actions by making this a turn-taking process. Sonders (2003) considers giggle games to be the basis for pre-conversational speech. To start the *Giggle Time* adults are advised to use one of the pragmatic pre-language skills (e.g. eye contact, gesture, movement, social smile, touch, proximity and vocalisations). The adults' turn should be of similar length of time to the child's to keep the latter's interest. Given the children's affinity for predictability, adults are advised to repeat their turns exactly the same way each time. Once a routine is established, the adults' turns can be modified. Animated facial expressions, body movements and voice volume should be used. People who might feel embarrassed to be animated can use puppets pretending that it is the puppets' voice which is animated (Greenspan and Wieder, 1998). Exaggeration is very important in *Giggle Time* as the adults should be more interesting than the child's object of desire to start the interaction and get it going. Additionally, adults are advised to create problems for the child to solve which may offer opportunities for communication (Greenspan and Wieder, 1998). For example, they can read a book upside down or put the socks on the child's hands while getting dressed.

Giggle Time pays a lot of attention to the last and the last but one turn of each game. The last but one turn is called *cue turn*. It is noticeably different from the previous turns (e.g. louder, quieter or slower). The last turn is called *reinforcing turn* and it can be tickles, spin or a favourite object to increase the likelihood of the child starting again. Adults should follow the child's lead, imitate them and exaggerate. They are also advised to wait for initiations (for 10–15 seconds to show the child it is their turn to do something), use rhymes and combine them with movement to engage the child. Sonders (2003) highlights the importance of incorporating vestibular movement into the joint action routines stating that the lower the staying power of the child, the more vestibular movement is needed. The ideal distance between the adult and the child is within 60 cm apart. When adults want to show the child it is their turn, they should adopt a freezing expression and posture (e.g. mouth, eyes and limbs in an exaggerated open position). A song broken into phrases to establish a turn-taking routine can work really effectively for most children with autism. A child's favourite action song in which the adults drop the end word or phrase can work well too. Adults can do the action and wait for the word and if the child does not respond they can prompt by whispering the word.

To conclude, the DIR-Floortime model suggests that adults follow the child's focus of attention, imitate them and respond to all their communicative attempts, even the unconventional ones. Close proximity between the child and the adult, stopping part way through a predictable routine and an exaggerated body language and tone of voice are essential components of this approach.

3.4.4 Musical Interaction/Music Therapy

Musical Interaction focuses on the need to 'tune in' to the child and start working with what they are able to do. Parents or school staff are involved in the process and they are asked to implement the intervention in other contexts too. They follow the child's lead by imitating their sounds as well as their movements and physical actions, use running commentary songs and short repetitive routines which build up anticipation (Christie et al., 2009). Spontaneous songs about what the child is doing are encouraged as it is argued that some children are more likely to take notice of the adult if the adult sings a response rather than just says it (Methley and Wimpory, 2010). When adults imitate what the child does, this gives them the idea of exchange and turn-taking. Adults are also asked to treat the child as if they are communicating long before they really are (Methley and Wimpory, 2010). For instance, if the child runs away, the adults treat this as if they meant to communicate, by starting a running song. The power of this approach lies in the fact that '*Music, even in its most basic form, holds a kind of magic that can be all*-embracing' (Corke, 2002, p. 8).

Music Therapy bears many similarities to Musical Interaction but the two interventions are also different in certain respects. To start with, Music Therapy enables social communication through the use of musical instruments and it is delivered by a trained therapist who has a three-year musical training and a Music Therapy postgraduate qualification (British Association for Music Therapy - BAMT, 2012). The therapist sees the child on a 1:1 basis once or twice a week and there is usually no involvement of other adults who can extend the principles to the child's everyday life. Music Therapy is described as

> attentive listening on the part of the therapist *[which]* is combined with shared musical improvisation using instruments and voices so that people can communicate in their own musical language, whatever their level of ability.
> (BAMT, 2012 – Online)

The therapist improvises songs around what the child is doing, they follow and support the child through their music (e.g. matching music to the child's hand beating on the floor), while providing them with time and space in which they can explore the instruments. Special attention is paid to silent moments. Music is both sound and silence, and silence should be actively experienced (Nordoff and Robbins, 1977). Other important characteristics of music are that it gives predictability in the adults' behaviour (e.g. crescendo for anticipation) and synchronises and supports the adults' and the child's turns. Music reflects what is happening (e.g. if the interaction goes faster the music has to go faster too) and eventually the child picks up that they can influence the music. An example of how Music Therapy works in practice with an autistic child is given by Warwick (2001), a leading British music therapist, who says that she was '*trying to meet him where he was*' (p. 202). When the boy tapped on the strings of the autoharp, she tapped on the guitar strings and when the boy responded by tapping on a drum, she replied on a different drum. Music Therapy proponents argue that every individual, regardless of learning and communication difficulties has an inherent musicality and can respond in one way or another to music (Trevarthen et al., 1996). To this end, Corke (2002) comments,

> Music appreciation requires no verbal understanding; it goes beyond intellect and therefore is accessible to all levels of intelligence.
> (p. 12)

In summary, Musical Interaction and Music Therapy use rhythm, musicality of speech and music to support what the child is doing. Adults are asked to either sing commentaries or to improvise on an instrument a melody to reflect what the child is doing. They are also advised to respond to every sign from the child, even if this is not clearly communicative, and to use imitation and pauses.

3.4.5 Son-Rise or Option Program

The Son-Rise or Option Program (Kaufman, 1994; Kaufman, 2002) is a child-centred approach developed by the parents of a child with autism. The rationale behind it is that '*the children show us the way in*' and then adults can show them the way to the NT world. Instead of trying to force a child to conform to a world that they do not understand or does not make sense to them, adults try to go with them. Once a mutual connection is established, the child learns with greater success, speed and ease. An effective way of developing a relationship with the child is via the three E's, which are Energy, Excitement and Enthusiasm (Autism Treatment Center of America, 2008). Kaufman (1994) notes,

> We had to make ourselves into the most beguiling [. . .] clowns of the universe so we would excite him and entice him to walk through seemingly impenetrable walls.
>
> (p. 63)

Adults in Son-Rise approach should honour vigorously every child's attempt to communicate and acknowledge even the ineffective efforts by saying '*nice try*' or '*that was so close*'.

Adults are trained to be the number one attraction and join in the child's repetitive behaviours (Kaufman, 1994). All the child's repetitive behaviours should be seen as a doorway to create a relationship with adults. The Kaufmans started imitating their son '*turning his 'isms' in an acceptable, joyful and communal event*' (Kaufman, 1994, p. 49). By 'isms' they define things children do repetitively and to the exclusion of everything else. For example, when Raun, Kaufmans' son, spun plates, rocked or flicked his fingers, the adult who was with him would follow his lead and do the same besides him. This was their way of being with him. Imitating Raun was proven effective, as he would watch his parents when they were involved in his rituals.

Kaufman (1994) gives some practical advice on how to increase spontaneous communication. The first thing adults should do is to observe what the child is doing. Then they should place themselves one metre away and do what the child does for at least 15 minutes. Some children will respond from the first moment, some others might need longer. It is important that adults position themselves in a way that it is easy to get eye contact from the child. Being in front of them either at eye level or slightly below is the ideal position. Achievements should be celebrated in animated ways such as big, whispered or sung cheers, arms thrown in the air, jumps up and down, a little dance. These celebrations should be sincere and from the heart as children with autism may detect the discomfort of people around and move away from them. A lot of physical contact such as hugging, stroking, tickling, tumbling and throwing into the air is recommended but adults should always allow children the freedom to back off when they need to. Finally, adults are advised to offer choices and encourage the child to initiate.

In sum, adults should get close to the child before communicating, respond to all their communicative attempts, even the unsuccessful ones, follow their interests and imitate their 'isms'. Throughout the sessions, adults have to be as animated as possible to get the child's attention.

3.4.6 Hanen or 'More than Words' approach

The Hanen or 'More than Words' approach trains parents to develop a facilitative interactive style with their children (Pennington and Thomson, 2007). Its main goal is to teach the child communication skills and increase their vocabulary. Parents are encouraged to take time to Observe, Wait and Listen (the OWL technique) (Manolson, 1992). Additionally, the child is allowed to lead while parents 'share the moment' and add language and experience (Manolson, 1992). Special attention is drawn upon teaching parents how to recognise their child's attempts to communicate, use simpler language and engineer situations for them to communicate (Pennington and Thomson, 2007). Imitation, interpretation of child's behaviour and child-perspective language are very important in the Hanen approach (Manolson, 1992). Parents should acknowledge all the child's attempts to communicate. They should respond to the child's messages even if they may get it wrong, as their response lets the child know that s/he has been heard. Parents are advised to use language which is appropriate for the child's level and to speak as the child would, if they could. Manolson (1992) highlights the importance of waiting while acknowledging how difficult this can be: often a silent moment might be felt as an empty moment. Parents are also advised to let their child problem solve (Manolson, 1992). Use of words to attract attention such as 'wheeee', musicality of speech, physical contact as fun, praise, smiles, laughter and expansions (i.e. building on the child's responses) are some other core strategies taught to parents (Sussman, 1999).

Overall, the Hanen approach suggests that parents should take a step back and observe their child before communicating with them. They are encouraged to wait for initiations, imitate the child, acknowledge all their attempts to communicate, expand on them and use child-perspective language.

3.4.7 Preschool Autism Communication Trial

Preschool Autism Communication Trial (PACT) is a parent-mediated video-aided intervention which aims to help parents adapt their communication style to their child's difficulties (Green et al., 2010). Therapists use video feedback to advise on parent-child interactions. There are six main stages of the programme described by Green and Aldred (2012).

1 Parents are encouraged to establish shared attention by observing the child's focus and inferring intentions.
2 Parents are advised to increase the synchronous communication with the child (e.g. comment, acknowledge and follow topic/focus) and adapt to the child's language processing.
3 The focus is on language input. Parents are expected to develop the child's comprehension and use of language; they should use language matched to the child's development and focus intentions.
4 Parents should establish predictable routines and anticipation. Repetitive language and generalisation of the learnt skills in daily life routines are recommended.
5 Parents are asked to increase the variety of their communicative functions (e.g. request, comment and seek attention). They are also asked to use communication teasers (e.g. disruptions, sabotage, mistakes and breaks in the flow) to elicit more communicative initiations by the child.
6 Parents should extend language and conversation; they should try to build on topics to develop syntax, vocabulary, narrative skills and reciprocal conversations.

To sum up, PACT teaches parents to be sensitive to their child by inferring the child's intentions, following what they are doing and commenting on it. Language should be tailored to the child's developmental level and extended by the adults. Communication teasers, which increase the opportunities for spontaneous communication, are recommended too.

3.4.8 Responsive Teaching

Responsive Teaching is an early intervention curriculum to be implemented by parents and other carers who spend significant time interacting with children with autism (Mahoney and MacDonald, 2007). A positive emotional relationship between the child and the therapist is an integral part of Responsive Teaching (Mahoney and Perales, 2003). The programme focuses on a number of pivotal behaviours that are the foundations for developmental learning, such as social play, initiation, problem solving, joint attention, conversation, trust, cooperation, persistence and feelings of competence (Mahoney and McDonald, 2007). At the same time, Responsive Teaching has several adult goals to address children's social communication. Getting into the child's world, observing their actions and imitating them are principles adults should follow. Communication should be accompanied by appropriate intonation, pointing and non-verbal gestures. Activities children enjoy should be repeated. Adults are also advised to interpret the child's behaviour as an indicator of interest, follow their attentional focus and be sensitive to their sensations. The rationale behind these strategies is threefold:

1 following the child's lead increases eye contact;
2 contingent responsiveness increases intentional communication; and
3 using multiple cues enables the child to follow adults' attentional focus.

To sum up, adults are advised to establish a strong emotional relationship with the child, observe them, follow their interests and interpret their behaviour as communicative. They should also imitate the child and use non-verbal supports.

After presenting a number of interventions giving direct or indirect advice on adult interactive style, there is need to investigate the impact of some of them on children's spontaneous communication. The next section reports past studies having showed a link between adult style and children's communication skills.

3.5 Past studies on interventions and social communication

A number of studies have examined the changes in children's social communication after the implementation of different interventions. This section presents the findings of some studies which showed changes in children's spontaneous communication as a result of an intervention with reference to the role of adult style. The studies are grouped into two categories following the theoretical foundations of the interventions they used (i.e. behavioural/naturalistic and developmental/relationship-based interventions) and are presented in chronological order. The last section explores a number of studies which did not fit in either of the two categories because they used elements of different types of interventions.

3.5.1 Behavioural/naturalistic interventions

Although behavioural/naturalistic interventions refer to facilitative adult interactive styles, few studies examined the impact of adult style on children's social communication. This can be explained to some extent by the fact that other variables such as IQ, adaptive behaviour and language are most commonly examined when behavioural/naturalistic interventions are used (Eikeseth et al., 2007; Remington et al., 2007). Charlop-Christy et al. (2002) taught three children with autism to use PECS. They found that the structured and concrete nature of physical exchange and the time delay procedures adults used increased children's social communicative behaviours such as requests and joint attention. Jones et al. (2006) used DTT and PRT to facilitate initiating and responding to joint attention in five children with autism aged 2–3 years. The training took place in the preschool classroom and lunch areas. Adults were asked to develop rapport with the children, follow their choices and preferences and pair themselves with a variety of reinforcers. The findings reported that the strategy was effective in developing both types of joint attention skills which were maintained beyond the intervention period. Ingersoll and Schreibman (2006) used a multiple baseline design across five young autistic children to assess the benefits of RIT. They found that participants increased not only their imitation skills but also the use of language, pretend play and joint attention.

3.5.2 Developmental/relationship-based interventions

One of the main goals of developmental/relationship-based interventions is to improve children's social communication and this is why relevant studies focus not only on children but also on adults' behaviour. In this way, changes in children's behaviour can be clearly attributed to the way adults interact with them. Sussman (1999) randomised 51 preschool children with suspected autism and their main carer to either a 'More than Words' programme or a control group. The programme had a significant effect on both parents' and children's communication skills and the children's development of vocabulary. Chandler et al. (2002) carried out an 18-month intervention with ten young children with autism and their parents. The intervention consisted of Musical Interaction therapy translated into home-based activities. At the end of the intervention, all children showed gains in social interaction and expressive communication (both gestural and verbal). Mahoney and Perales (2003) trained the mothers of 20 autistic children in the Responsive Teaching logic model. They found significant improvements in children's social communication competence and initiations. Aldred et al. (2004) randomly allocated 28 young children with autism to treatment and control groups in a preliminary study for the development of PACT. All children in the treatment group increased their initiation of social interaction.

3.5.3 Combined interventions

Some researchers attempted to combine elements of different types of interventions to check the impact on children's communication. Most of these studies showed improvements in social communication skills regardless of the type of intervention used.

Kasari et al. (2006) conducted a Randomised Control Trial (RCT) study with 58 young autistic children. Children were randomised to a joint attention intervention, a symbolic play intervention and a control group. The two interventions focused on adult interactive style combining elements of ABA (e.g. systematic prompting and reinforcement) and facilitative interactive methods (e.g. following the child's lead, talking about what they were doing, expanding on what they said, sitting close to them, making eye contact and imitating their actions on toys). Results showed that children following either of the interventions initiated more joint attention compared to the control group.

Yoder and Stone (2006) compared the effectiveness of PECS and Responsive Education and Prelinguistic Milieu Teaching (RPMT) on facilitating children's intentional communication. Thirty-six preschool children with autism participated in the study. Adults using PECS were taught to show availability, use prompts which gradually fade away and create communicative opportunities in the environment. Adults trained in RPMT were encouraged to be responsive to the child and to use motivational activities and prompts when needed. Results showed that RPMT encouraged more initiations of joint attention for children who had some joint attention skills and high levels of intentional communication pre-intervention. PECS, on the other hand, was more effective for children who had minimal joint attention skills and low levels of intentional communication pre-intervention. Ingersoll (2011) compared the effects of Milieu Teaching, Responsive Teaching and a combined intervention on the expressive language of two preschoolers with autism. Adults using the Milieu Teaching had to playfully interrupt the child's play and prompt the use of language to initiate request. When the correct response was given, the child was reinforced by getting access to the toy. Adults being trained in Responsive Teaching had to use simplified language to narrate the child's play and expand on any language used by the child. The combined intervention consisted of strategies from both Milieu Teaching and Responsive Teaching. Ingersoll (2011) reported that Milieu Teaching led to more requests while Responsive Teaching spurred more comments. The combined intervention showed similar increase in both variables.

Apart from these studies having explored the impact of well-known interventions on children's communication, there is some smaller scale research focusing exclusively on adult interactive style. Researchers inspired by one or more well-known interventions developed their own adult style interventions and tried them in practice or asked people's views on what they consider to be an optimal adult interactive style. These interventions do not claim clear association with a specific intervention and therefore they are discussed in a separate section.

3.6 Past studies on adult style and spontaneous communication

Since there is inconclusive evidence regarding which intervention is the most effective when teaching social communication in children with autism, many studies employ eclectic approaches, which is an integration of the principles of different approaches. The focus of this section is on changing the adults' style of interaction to increase children's spontaneous communication. The studies to be presented are classified into two groups based on the communicative partner they were developed for and are presented in chronological order. A section on parents' interactive style proceeds, followed by a section on school staff's interactive style. Most of the principles used in these studies originate from developmental/relationship-based approaches as in these, altering adult interactive style is one of the main objectives.

3.6.1 Studies on parents' interactive style

A number of studies investigated parents' interactive style while trying to teach communication to their children. It is suggested that parents of children with autism interact with them in different ways than parents of TD children. For example, some studies found that parents of children with autism tend to be more directive (Watson, 1998) or smile less in response to their children's smiles (Dawson et al., 1990). This triggers a chicken/egg scenario: is it the children's particular communicative profiles or the adults' behaviour which accounts for the former's limited spontaneous communication? This section gives an overview of how parents tend to interact with their autistic children and the impact of changing their interactive style on the latter's communication.

Watson (1998) and Doussard-Roosevelt et al. (2003) observed mothers' interactive style when dealing with their autistic children. Watson (1998) examined the extent to which mothers of preschool children use language while following their child's lead. She observed 14 children with autism and 14 TD children for 15 minutes of free play with their mothers. Mothers of children with autism were as likely to use language for something which was within their child's focus of attention as mothers of TD children. However, they were more likely to use language for something that was not within the child's focus of attention. Qualitative differences in mother-child interactions were also evidenced by Doussard-Roosevelt et al. (2003) who video recorded 24 preschool children with autism and 24 TD children in free play sessions with their mothers. They reported that mothers of children with autism used more physical contact and intensive behaviours but less language than the mothers of TD children.

Another group of studies looked at the extent to which children with autism were influenced when their parents were trained to change their interactive style. Escalona et al. (2001) found that their sample of 20 young children with autism showed more social relatedness after being massaged by their parents for 15 minutes before bed every night for a month. Siller and Sigman (2002) compared 25 children with autism, 18 children with DD and 18 TD children. They illustrated a clear link between parental sensitivity to the child's focus of attention and the child's development of joint attention and language. Doussard-Roosevelt et al. (2003) examined the interactions of 9 mothers with their autistic and non-autistic children and noticed that children with autism were more engaged when non-verbal behaviours were employed. Kashinath et al. (2006) conducted an intervention with 5 preschool children with autism and their mothers in the family's home. Modifying the environment to promote interaction, using reinforcement and time delay, imitating contingently, modelling and gestural and visual cueing were the strategies the mothers were taught. The intervention had positive effects on the children's communication skills. Drew et al. (2007) recruited 24 toddlers with autism and randomly allocated their parents to either the training group or the control group. Reinforcement, use of visual supports for spoken language, imitation, watch and wait, simple gestures such as simple action songs and Makaton nursery rhymes were used. The study showed that some of the children in the parent training group improved more their communication and language skills. Ruble et al. (2008) researched 35 children with autism and their carers while interacting in a free play activity and concluded that the carer's responsiveness was associated with the child's initiations of social interactions.

Overall, studies on parent or carer interactive style showed that an effective communication style might involve more physical contact and less language. When language is used, it is usually for things within the child's focus of attention. Parents who are responsive to their child and often expand on their language are likely to facilitate the latter's communication. Simple gestures, imitation, waiting, use of fun, songs and musicality of speech were also effective principles that parents used to enhance their children's communication.

3.6.2 Studies on school staff's interactive style

Although there is growing literature on training parents of children with autism in using a communication enabling interactive style, little is known about principles teaching staff might be trained in. This section presents studies which were conducted in a school setting. Some of them collected data on what was actually happening in practice and people's views on it whereas some others put in place an intervention and collected pre- and post-intervention data.

Potter and Whittaker (2001) carried out a qualitative key study on the way teaching staff interact with children at school and their influence on children's spontaneous communication. They involved 18 young children with autism, who had minimal or no speech, from autism specialist classes in 5 special schools. Children were video recorded during everyday school activities and some staff were interviewed about the optimum communication enabling environment. The findings confirmed that when staff adopted a minimal speech approach (e.g. one or two relevant concrete words), used long pauses and non-verbal methods of interaction (e.g. rough and tumble play, burst and pause, imitation) and offered frequent opportunities for communication, the children communicated more often.

Natt (2015) asked children with autism themselves in order to explore their views on the optimum adult interactive style at school. She interviewed 6 primary aged children with autism who attended a specialist provision attached to a mainstream primary school. In order to effectively conduct the interviews, she used verbal questioning, photographs, drawing and small world play. Most children in her sample expressed a preference to be spoken to 'in a nice way', with an upbeat tone of voice and for adults to use visual aids. Most of them also preferred interactions involving fewer people and several aspects of optimal adult behaviour raised were linked to concrete rewards (e.g. giving them food or water). Children expressed little interest in or awareness of adults' facial expressions as long as these were not perceived as negative.

Some researchers took this a step further and tried to train teaching staff in principles thought to promote children's social communication. They then explored differences pre- and post-intervention. Hwang and Hughes (2000) studied the early communicative skills of 3 non-verbal preschool children with autism when the class staff went through a social interactive training. They found that contingent imitation, naturally occurring reinforcement, expectant looks and environmental arrangement were associated with increased eye contact, joint attention and motor imitation. Ingersoll et al. (2005) implemented a Developmental, Social-Pragmatic approach with three boys with autism. This approach was adapted from developmental/relationship-based approaches such as DIR-Floortime, Hanen, SCERTS and Responsive Teaching. The main components of the intervention included following the child's lead, engineering opportunities for initiation, acknowledging all attempts as communicative, emphasising affect and using indirect language stimulation. Findings showed an increase in the children's use of spontaneous speech. McAteer and Wilkinson (2009) undertook a study in an all-age school for pupils with autism. They trained staff in a 'facilitative style of interaction' and following training, changes in both adults' and pupils' behaviour were noted. Adults were waiting for the child to start the communication, showing that they were listening by responding or repeating and commenting on what the child was doing and pupils initiated interaction more frequently.

To sum up, these studies showed that when teaching staff wait for longer, follow the child's lead, provide them with visual aids and more opportunities to communicate and use concrete language, the children are more likely to initiate interaction. The same happens when the teaching staff are responsive, show availability, imitate the child, acknowledge all their attempts as communicative and use an upbeat tone of voice.

3.7 The principles of adult interactive style intervention

This chapter closes with an outline of the principles of AISI emerging from reviewing the literature (see Table 3.1). The next chapter covers each one of these principles in detail in order to explain to parents and practitioners how to use them in practice. It also contains a critical evaluation of the links between theory and practice.

Table 3.1 The adult interactive style intervention principles

General principles
1. Gain the child's attention
2. Establish appropriate proximity or touch
3. Show availability
4. Wait for initiations
5. Respond to all communicative attempts
6. Assign meaning to random actions or sounds
7. Imitate the child
8. Follow the child's lead or focus of attention
9. Use exaggerated pitch, facial expression, gestures and body language
10. Use minimal speech
11. Provide time for the child to process the given information
12. Expand on communicative attempts
13. Use a range of non-verbal cues

Communicative opportunities

1. Offer choices
2. Stop part way
3. Give small portions
4. Make items inaccessible
5. Give material they will need help with
6. Contradict expectations
7. Give non-preferred items
8. 'Forget' something vital

3.8 Reflection activity

- Reflect on an intervention you have been trained in and you use in your everyday practice. First, think of its theoretical foundations and what is in there about the importance of fostering children's spontaneous communication. Is there any advice given on communication enabling adult interactive style?

4 Adult interactive style at school and at home

4.1 Introduction

This chapter describes in detail the AISI principles and their implications for natural settings such as school and home, these being of great interest to professionals and parents. The whole AISI reflects Gray's (2000) point that when NT people interact with individuals with autism the former *'hold more than half the solution'* to make this work. People with autism, especially those who are at very early stages of communication development need to be systematically supported to understand the 'why' and 'how' of communication. All principles are linked to the existing autism and general SEN literature, and a number of boxed text examples are used to make the principles clearer. Overall, AISI consists of 13 general principles which relate to adults' body language, speech and timing, and 8 communicative opportunities which stand for situations adults set up to increase the child's chances for spontaneous communication. The first two sections of this chapter explore each one of these principles thoroughly, while the last section presents some drawings on how AISI principles can be manifested in a school setting. As an overarching rule, parents and practitioners should bear in mind that they have to apply the following principles in a creative way, as if these are followed strictly 'by the book' or if they go unchanged for long they are very likely to become fossilised and ineffective. For NT people who might feel uncomfortable with using some of the AISI principles I would like to reiterate a powerful quote from Blackburn (2011): '*Do autism in your head and not in your gut*'. This means that NT people should have a good understanding of autism and bear in mind the different relevant cognitive, psychological and sensory processing theories when trying to support communication even if this means that they have to behave in unusual ways.

I totally embrace Ware's (2003) point that adults find it more difficult to create a responsive environment and get the interaction going when they have to interact with more than one child at a time. Although acknowledging that this cannot often be the case at school and might also be hard to achieve at home (when there are other siblings), the term child instead of its plural form children is used in this chapter (as previously when describing facilitative adult interactive style). In terms of adults, the plural form is preferred to refer to both parents and practitioners.

4.2 General adult interactive style intervention principles

4.2.1 Gaining the child's attention

Adults should make sure that they have secured the child's attention before attempting any communication. This can be done in a number of ways verbally or non-verbally. For example, they can call the child's name before addressing them or they may say or chant something like '*Hello xxxxx (child's name)*', '*Where is xxxxxx (child's name)?*' or '*xxxxx's (child's name) turn*'. They can alternatively touch the child lightly, take hold of their hand or blow gently on their cheek. The need to make sure that adults gain the child's attention before communicating with them is highlighted extensively in the autism literature. For example Higashida (2013), a non-verbal young man with autism who wrote a book about his experiences of being autistic, reports his difficulty in telling that somebody is talking to him unless this person uses his name first to get his attention. Christie et al. (2009) suggest that adults should cut down all distractions before attempting to communicate with the child; this might mean to turn off the radio or TV and get them to put down the toy they are playing with. Adults after addressing the child should pause for a moment so that the child knows that somebody is trying to communicate with them. Ware (2003) in her book 'Creating a responsive environment for people with profound and multiple learning difficulties (PMLD)' provides some advice which is applicable to pupils with autism too. She mentions the importance of picking an appropriate moment to get the child's attention; this is definitely not the time that they are fully engaged elsewhere. She concludes by suggesting that adults need to have a variety of strategies for catching and holding the child's attention. This is of particular importance in autism as strategies which work on one day might not work on another day due to certain psychological and perception profiles this population exhibits (see 2.6 'Cognitive, Psychological and Sensory Processing Theories in Autism' for more details). Additionally, children with autism need to be exposed to a variety of strategies and approaches as much as possible to encourage their flexibility of thinking and behaviour, which is one of the main difficulties for most of them (APA, 2013).

- Nathan and his teacher are in the sensory room playing with the bubble tube. The teacher realises that Nathan had enough of this activity and chants '*What shall we do with Nathan now?*' (in the tune of 'What shall we do with the drunken sailor?') to get his attention before offering him some options.
- It is almost bedtime for Mike. Mum has to first get him to put the TV off in order to secure his attention before sharing with him the timetable he has to follow before going to bed.

4.2.2 Establishing appropriate proximity or touch

Establishing appropriate proximity or touch is a crucial element to enable successful communication. Nind and Hewett (1994) in their Intensive Interaction approach lay great emphasis on physical contact when interacting with people who are non-verbal or have got limited expressive and receptive language. Longhorn (1993) is on the exact same page, arguing that touch is a fundamental form of communication for what she calls the very special children (i.e. children with a range of SEN). Getting down to the child's level to have face-to-face interaction and physical proximity is advised by SCERTS (Prizant et al., 2006). Nind and Hewett (2001) advise adults to position themselves below the child's level as this increases the latter's confidence and sense of security. Kaufman's (1994) Option approach is in agreement with both. Sonders (2003) in her Giggle Time intervention maintains that the ideal distance to enable communication between the child and adults is 60 cm and Kaufman (1994) suggests sitting a metre away from the child. However, there are some people with autism who might feel uncomfortable when being touched due to sensory sensitivities (Bogdashina, 2003) and persons working or living with them should be aware of these and avoid touch. Blackburn (1999, cited in Bogdashina, 2005) draws NT's attention to the rate of approaching a person with autism stating that it is not a good idea to do this too quickly or from behind.

- The TA notices that there is nobody sitting next to Sarah when she is finishing her biscuit and she is about to ask for another one. It is very unlikely that Sarah will extend her arm over the long table to hand the biscuit symbol to the TA. Therefore, the TA moves next to her making sure that there is no more than a metre distance between them.
- Nick's sister wants to interact with him while he is playing his favourite video game. She slowly moves in front of Nick and sits close to him being at the same eye level.

4.2.3 Showing availability

Availability is a fairly subtle behaviour and as a result it is not easy to demonstrate. When interacting with a child with autism it goes without saying that availability has to be more prominent and possibly exaggerated, especially when this child has additional learning difficulties. Briefly, an easy way to show that adults are available for interaction is to extend their hands towards the child, with wide, questioning eyes (adapted from Prizant et al., 2006). Nind and Hewett (1994) give some more detailed advice on how to achieve availability, which can be used beyond Intensive Interaction. They claim that the adults' body should be slightly turned towards the child, their shoulders and legs should be down and relaxed, their head should be slightly turned to one side or back, the eyes have to be wide but mild and they should also adapt a questioning face.

Some interpersonal rules of the low arousal approach of Studio III, an organisation which trains in strategies to prevent and manage CB, can be conducive to a communication enabling style. Woodcock and Page (2010) in their book about managing family meltdown suggest that adults should avoid tensing muscles such as folding arms or clenching fists, keep their hands relaxed, open, and visible, and avoid staring at the child as this could be perceived as aggressive behaviour. Adults are also advised to maintain regular intermittent eye contact, breathe slowly and regularly, and move slowly and predictably. In my experience as a practitioner the most efficient way of showing availability to a child with autism is to extend the arms towards them with palms facing up and look at them in an expectant way.

- It is 1:1 work time and it becomes obvious to the TA that Oliver cannot figure out how the newly added to his workbox posting pegs activity works. The TA does not offer any help but holds out her hand so that Oliver can ask for help.
- Richard's parents decide to work on his communication by increasing the opportunities to ask for what he wants. As part of his plan, they move his favourite biscuits to a different cupboard. Richard enters the kitchen and goes to the cupboard to get his biscuits. Dad says nothing but keeps a relaxed body posture and looks expectantly at Richard waiting for him to ask for his biscuits.

4.2.4 Waiting for initiations

Waiting is not a straightforward concept, as it is a process people do in their minds and it cannot be observed. Adults may need to wait longer than feels comfortable when interacting with children with autism. However, they should try not to intervene too soon unless it becomes obvious that the child is not going to initiate. Ware (2003) considers waiting for the child to respond an integral element of a responsive environment. She acknowledges the fact that because children with communication difficulties tend to respond slowly and in unexpected ways, adults are very likely to behave as if they are not expecting a response. Ware (2003) also points to the awkwardness of having to wait for long time especially at first. The difficulty adults often have with waiting is evident in research too. Gillett and LeBlanc (2007) trained the mothers of three children with autism and little or no speech in a naturalistic approach and the results revealed that the component of the intervention mothers found most difficult to apply was waiting for initiations. Waiting can be even more difficult to achieve in a school environment where staff are expected to do things with the child, and quiet moments of waiting can be perceived by other colleagues as professional incompetence or laziness.

- The TA waits for Heath to hand in the biscuit photo before prompting him to do so. She only prompts him with a gesture 3 minutes later when it is highly unlikely that he will initiate.
- Helen received a new wind-up toy from her grandma. She does not know how to make it work by herself. Her grandma will not show her how the new toy works until Helen asks for it. If it becomes apparent that she will not ask for help and she is about to lose interest, her grandma will model how to wind it up.

4.2.5 Responding to the child's communicative attempts

It is of significant importance to show children with autism that their communication gets results. The adults should give the object the child asks for, take away the object they protest against, allow them to start and terminate activities. In cases that the child cannot finish their activity in time or have the object they want, the adults should acknowledge the communicative attempt and indicate steps for completion of the present task (Prizant et al., 2006). Nind and Hewett (2001) highlight the importance of celebrating all child's attempts to communicate, not only speech. The main reason that adults should respond to all the child's communicative attempts, even the ones which may be considered 'inappropriate' (e.g. running away, tantrums and self-injurious behaviour) is to ensure consistency and make it clear to the child that all communicative attempts receive a response. The need to respond to children's communication is further highlighted by Dale (1990, cited in Longhorn, 1993) who claims,

> No matter how much internal forces may prompt, if the effort [to communicate] goes unnoticed, the power and desire to communicate will lessen.
>
> (p. 155)

Conducive to the aforementioned point is Grove et al.'s (2000) argument that communication involves a certain degree of interpretation and guesswork. Sometimes the partner might get the message wrong, especially when they have to deal with people with autism and SPMLD. However, responding to a person's attempt to communicate even if the respondent gets it wrong still shows that the attempt entails a result and it is recommended.

- Alex wants to stop his work and go to play outside. Although it is not time for break yet, he tries to escape. His teacher shows him the timetable saying '*work first, then play outside*' acknowledging his message.
- Miranda wants to have a shower when it is not time for it and keeps handing in the shower photo to her mum. Her mum puts a photo of the clock showing 7pm in her timetable next to the shower photo and points to it every time Miranda asks for shower when it is not time yet.

4.2.6 Assigning meaning to random actions or sounds

The foundations of this principle lie within early mother-infant interactions; during these, mothers respond to their toddlers' random sounds and actions as if these conveyed some communicative meaning in order to teach them intentionality (Trevarthen et al., 1996; Nind and Hewett, 2001). Therefore, they react as if the child's behaviour is communicative long before this is the case. This is of exceptional importance when interacting with children with autism who more often than not need to be taught explicitly that their behaviour can affect the behaviour of others. Assigning meaning to random actions and sounds can be done in a number of ways. Greenspan and Wieder (1998) suggest, for example, that if the child rocks, the adult should sit face-to-face with them and rock along turning rocking into a two person '*row, row your boat*' game. However, Milton (2012), an academic with autism, has drawn my attention to the fact that responding to all child's behaviour as this being a communicative attempt might be very intrusive and put the child off. More precisely, during a personal communication I had with him, he said,

> Assigning meaning to unintentional communications and always reacting to them, can be internalised as invasive and overbearing.

On a similar vein, Ware (2003) claims that it is more important for people with PMLD to receive consistent responses to certain behaviours than to receive a response to everything they do. At this point, I feel the need to draw the reader's attention once again to the fact that idiosyncratic behaviours should not be given communicative meaning, as these are difficult to be understood by other communicative partners. I recall a child in a school I used to work in who coughed to request the continuation of an interactive game. This request of course could not be understood by anybody apart from the person who was present when this association was made.

- In the soft play area, the TA sits in front of George facing him and holding his hands. George pulls her towards him and the TA turns this into an interactive game while chanting '*see saw, see saw*' as if George had asked her to initiate this.
- Hannah plays alone with her toys while humming the tune of the 'roly-poly' song. Her mum who is sitting next to her sings the 'roly-poly' song as if Hannah had asked her to do so.

4.2.7 Imitating the child

When interacting with children with autism adults are advised to imitate the child's verbal (e.g. vocalisations, words) or non-verbal (e.g. actions) behaviour and pause waiting for further response from them. By imitating the child, adults create a turn-taking pattern and make the former understand that their behaviour can have an influence on somebody's else behaviour. Caldwell (2006) considers imitation a '*getaway to communication*' (p. 275) as it is the only thing which the child can

52 *Adult interactive style*

make sense of and understand in a sensory overloaded world. Christie et al. (2009) maintain that many children become more aware of themselves when they have their own behaviour reflected. Adults' turn in imitation games must be of the same length as the child's turn otherwise the child's interest might be lost (Sonders, 2003). Additionally, imitation should not be 'wooden', exact copying but a 'flowing dance' containing elements of surprise and fun. Christie et al. (2009) provide some ideas on what to do when the adults imitate the child but the latter does not notice them; they ask adults to vocalise through a cardboard tube or use an echo mike, a drum or another sound-maker to copy the child's actions and sounds. Adults can also add variations to the pitch and the pace of the verbal behaviours they imitate (e.g. whisper the words or articulate them at a slow pace).

- The teacher is in the sensory room with Molly. Molly is making some unintelligible vocalisations and the teacher imitates them and pauses in anticipation for more. Molly does not pay attention to the teacher who then imitates Molly's following vocalisations first using an echo mike and second whispering.
- Elliot is very excited with his new music toy flapping his hands while jumping up and down. His mum shares his excitement by tuning in his actions.

4.2.8 Following the child's lead or focus of attention

Following what the child does, or commenting on it, is essential when trying to foster their spontaneous communication (Prizant et al., 2006). Nind and Hewett (1994) encourage adults to provide a commentary on what the child is doing. If the child walks away and plays with another toy, adults are expected to follow them and say in simple language what they are doing. Christie et al. (2009) highlight the importance of having this commentary sung or chanted. The rationale behind using commentaries or action songs is that the child hears language which is meaningful and relevant to them at the time. As a result, they may be more likely to make connections between actions, objects and words they hear. Corke (2002) sees this as a celebration of the child's actions and underscores the importance of the child taking control over the interaction this way. Ware (2003) acknowledges that sharing control might be difficult for practitioners at school but this can be easier at home.

- In soft play area, the TA follows David on the mirror once he had enough on the trampoline and starts a new game there related to the mirror.
- Dad follows Olivia's little wander from one room to the other singing what Olivia is doing or looking at using the tune of 'this is the way . . .' nursery rhyme (e.g. *this is the way Olivia opens the door, this is Olivia's favourite train*).

4.2.9 Using exaggerated pitch, facial expressions, gestures and body language

The use of animated pitch, lively facial expressions, gestures and body language as a way to get the child's attention and promote their spontaneous communication is extensively explored in SEN and autism literature (e.g. Kaufman, 1994; Greenspan and Wieder, 1998). Longhorn (1993) gives some ideas on how to achieve effective exaggeration; she proposes acting the fool, blowing raspberries, whistling, an enthusiastic head nod, an exaggerated grin or a big shrug of the shoulders, playing rough and tumble and 'all fall down' games. An important relevant note is made by Sonders (2003), who suggests that the shorter the child's attention is, the more vestibular movements adults should use (i.e. they should move more). The list of exaggerations is endless and the child's likes and dislikes should be the starting point. It is then up to practitioners' and parents' creativity to add more examples to the list. Words such as 'Aaaaaaaand', 'uh-uh' and 'wheeee', enthusiastic singing, loud laughs are some examples of exaggerated pitch; wiggly fingers before tickling and reaching out in the form of '*I am coming to get you*' game are some forms of exaggerated gestures; stamping feet, clapping hands and tapping the floor can be ways of exaggerated body language. This is a principle which might apply more easily at home, as for some practitioners acting this way at their work setting might go against their personality and their professional role.

- The TA is very animated while jumping on the trampoline with Sue. Her tone of voice is gradually rising in pitch before the end of each turn and she laughs loudly once the turn is over.
- Every time mum sings with Greg at home, they are having a lot of shared fun. His mum sings very enthusiastically while smiling the whole time and using her whole body to emphasise key words and actions (e.g. she acts out the move of the wheels while singing '*the wheels on the bus go round and round*').

4.2.10 Using minimal speech

It is exceptionally important to use minimal speech when interacting with children with autism because of a number of cognitive, psychological and sensory processing characteristics they possess (see 2.6 'Cognitive, Psychological and Sensory Processing Theories in Autism' for more details). Adults are highly encouraged to use a few relevant concrete words and map them exactly onto aspects of the situation in hand (Potter and Whittaker, 2001). Christie et al. (2009) highlight the importance for adults to repeat their words a couple of times if necessary but this would better be the exact same way because of the perceptual profile of people with autism who tend to process information as a chunk or whole (Frith, 2003). This means that if adults slightly change the structure of a sentence the child has to process the sentence as a new whole.

- Nathan works 1:1 with his TA on a sorting activity. The TA speaks at a slow pace and stresses the key words '*Find same*'.
- It is time for Liz to go to the park. Her mum points to the relevant photo on her timetable and tells Liz in a clear voice '*bring coat, time for park*'.

4.2.11 Providing time for the child to process the given information

Adults need to slow down when interacting with children with autism as many of them might have different perceptual profiles (e.g. gestalt perception- process information as a whole, monoprocessing- use one sensory channel at a time) or cognitive styles (e.g. tunnel attention- intense but narrow, switching attention difficulties, gestalt memory- remember information only as chunks) (see 2.6 'Cognitive, Psychological and Sensory Processing Theories in Autism' for more details). Therefore, adults should always provide the child with some time to process the given information. Woodcock and Page (2010) estimate that there is an average 10-second delay in the processing skills of individuals with autism. However, from personal experience, and when there are additional learning difficulties, I have witnessed that this process might take a few minutes.

- Before moving from PE back to the classroom, the teacher shows Jonathan his timetable and gives him enough time to process the information that PE has finished and it is now time to walk back to the classroom. An indication that he has processed the information is that he starts moving towards the PE hall door or he tries to run away (meaning that he got the message but he would like to do something else).
- Emma keeps handing the orange juice symbol to her mum and her mum shows her back the finished symbol while saying 'finished'. Emma then goes to the fridge and cupboards looking for some juice. Her mum follows her pointing to the orange juice and finished symbols until she makes sure that Emma understood that there is no orange juice left (an indication for this might be that Emma stops looking for it or she throws a tantrum).

4.2.12 Expanding on the child's communicative attempts

Rogers and Dawson (2010) in their ESDM advise adults to use utterances which are the length of the child's utterance plus one. Therefore, if the child does not yet use words to initiate communication (e.g. gives the jar with chips to the adult to open it), adults should use single words (e.g. say 'open', 'more'). If the child uses some words to initiate communication (e.g. say 'more' or 'car'), adults should use two word sentences (e.g. say 'more juice', 'Tom's car'). Latham and Miles (1997) call this principle 'modelling the next stage of the child's communication development' whereas the SCERTS framework (Prizant et al., 2006) describe this as 'adjust complexity of language one stage above the child's level of language'.

> - The TA says '*biscuit*' when Rachel (verbal communication level = vocalisations) gives her the biscuit symbol but says '*more blackcurrant*' when David (verbal communication level = occasional words) gives her the blackcurrant symbol saying an approximation of the word 'blackcurrant'.
> - Tom's mum (Tom's verbal communication level = vocalisations) says '*train*' while watching her son playing with his train whereas Lidia's mum (Lidia's verbal communication level = two word sentences) says '*Lidia playing dolls*' while watching her daughter play with her dolls.

4.2.13 Using non-verbal cues

While interacting with children with autism, adults are expected to use a range of non-verbal cues such as gestures, physical prompts, body language, objects of reference, photos, symbols and signs to support understanding (Prizant et al., 2006). Christie et al. (2009) propose the use of some gestures purposefully and clearly; these can be '*come here*', mime drinking as saying '*Do you want a drink?*' or physically guide the child through the action which is expected from them. Body language, the silent language, refers to non-verbal communication which according to Borg (2008) represent at least 90% of total communication.

Objects of reference are concrete and can be one of the simplest ways to get a message across, as they are very similar to what they represent. Goodwin et al. (2015) suggest using objects of reference, which are tactile and visual, or adding smell, taste and sounds to make them more powerful for people with complex needs. Photos are also fairly easy to understand, as they are close to what they represent. However, some people with autism might get lost in detail due to Central Coherence difficulties (processing the details as opposed to the whole picture) (Frith, 2003) and might prefer to use symbols. There is a wide range of symbols which can be used by adults to support the child's understanding; Makaton, Boardmaker, Clicker, Widgit and Picture Communication Symbols are some of them. Overall, symbols are harder to get as they require a level of symbolic understanding which might be missing from children with autism and SPMLD. In terms of signing systems, there are two main ones in the UK: British Sign Language (BSL) and Makaton. BSL is a language in its own right. Makaton (Walker, 1976) is a language programme using symbols and signs with around 450 words of core vocabulary. All signs should be used alongside speech and not instead of it. Signing should also be in time with words which help adults to slow down their speech and emphasise key words (Christie et al., 2009). Additionally, signing gives the child more time to take in the given information.

There is some debate regarding the amount of information conveyed by non-verbal cues a child with autism is likely to absorb. Christie et al. (2009), for example, claim that children with autism do not seem to take in the clues from adults' body language, but that being introduced to gestures and signs often helps them. In my opinion, adults should use all non-verbal means they have at their disposal in order to get their message across; this will not do any harm to the child.

- When Louise stands up during work time and tries to escape the teacher shows her the timetable, taps on her chair and physically guides her to sit down.
- When it is bedtime mum gives Ben his little blanket (object of reference standing for bedtime). Then he goes and picks his timetable which has a number of symbols indicating his bedtime routine (e.g. have shower, put the pyjamas on, brush teeth). If he gets stuck, his mum reminds him what is next by pointing to the relevant symbol or using the Makaton sign for the next action.

4.3 Communicative AISI opportunities

4.3.1 *Offering choices*

Adults should always offer children choice of activity, equipment or food without presuming their preferences (Potter and Whittaker, 2001; Prizant et al., 2006). It is also important that they consider the number of choices they offer and the order they present these. For example, children with autism and SPMLD might find it very hard to select between more than two choices, and they also tend to go for the last option which was offered to them. Therefore, adults should not offer more than two options which are supported by clear visual cues and present these options every now and then in a different order to check the validity of the choice. Some children with autism and complex needs might have to be supported to show preference than make a choice as such (Ware, 2004). These children need to be exposed to a range of experiences in order to be able to express preference and eventually make choices. Special reference should be made to the importance of developing confidence through making choices as the specific population is very likely to have negative experiences of making choices in the past (Goodwin et al., 2015). For example, they might have experienced objects appearing and disappearing without them having any say whatsoever. This is why

> offering opportunities to make choices [. . .] is an important part of treating people in a respectful and inclusive way.
> (Goodwin and Edwards, 2009, p. 11)

- During work time, the teacher holds out two of the activities from the workbox for Lorna to choose the one she prefers. She has to do all the activities which are placed in her workbox, but she can decide on the order she is going to do them.
- When it is snack time, dad gives Stuart the option of having blackcurrant or water regardless of the fact that he always goes for blackcurrant. Dad often replaces the water option with another drink so as to show Stuart that he has got more options if he wants to.

4.3.2 Stopping part way

Stopping part way through an interaction or a child's favourite activity is an effective way to elicit their request to continue (Potter and Whittaker, 2001). Experience has taught me that it is more likely for the child to request an activity to continue when this activity stops in its peak (e.g. a rough and tumble game stops when the child shows great levels of engagement). Sonders (2003) recommends a variation of this principle by asking adults to start singing one of the child's favourite songs and drop the ending word or phrase (depending on the child's language abilities) and pause for the child to join in. With this idea, special attention should be paid to the fact that adults should add variety by keeping changing the words or phrases they drop so that they also work on the child's flexibility of thinking.

- During soft play, the TA sings John's favourite song. At some point, she drops the ending word of a phrase and pauses so that John joins in.
- Dad and Marie play a tickling game. Every now and then when Marie gets very excited, dad freezes the interaction and expects a sign from Marie in order to continue the game.

4.3.3 Giving small portions

Adults are highly encouraged to give the child small portions of food and drink and equipment 'bit by bit', so that the child can ask for more (Potter and Whittaker, 2001). This is a fairly easy way to give multiple communicative opportunities and make the child practise their requesting skills. However, adults need to make sure that only parts of the requested object appear in the photo or symbol (if the child functions at this level of symbolic communication) as some children might find it hard to understand why since they asked for a whole banana they only got three pieces of it. This difficulty can be explained by these people's rigidity of thinking and by some cognitive, psychological and sensory processing theories (see 2.6 'Cognitive, Psychological and Sensory Processing Theories in Autism' for more details). It is also important to bear in mind that the child needs to have the appropriate means (i.e. language, signs, symbols, photos) to ask for more portions of food, drink or parts of the equipment they want.

- The TA gives just one piece of chocolate to Katie every time Katie gives her the chocolate photo to make her ask for more.
- Ewan has to ask a few times for different bits of his train track in order to be able to complete the track before he puts his train on and starts playing.

4.3.4 Making items inaccessible

Another principle likely to increase a child's requests is to make items inaccessible. Adults are therefore encouraged to put items in sight but out of reach so that the child needs to ask for them (Potter and Whittaker, 2001). Experience has taught me that this principle can be more effective when adults make inaccessible items the child is currently engaged with. If the child has autism and SLD/PMLD, they are very likely to have poor Executive Functioning skills (Ozonoff et al., 1991; Hill, 2004) and as a result they may choose another item if their favourite one is unavailable.

- In the sensory room, the teacher puts the light curtain out of reach but in sight after having a few turns on it with Edward so that he can ask her to take it down again.
- Dad always places Angie's favourite DVDs on a high shelf so that she needs to ask for help in order to get them and watch them.

4.3.5 Giving the child materials they will need help with

Children with autism are likely to initiate communication more often if they are given materials they cannot make work themselves, and for which they need adults' help (Potter and Whittaker, 2001). The danger with this principle is that it may encourage behaviours which are seen commonly in autism such as prompt dependence (Blackburn, 2011) or rigidity of thinking (APA, 2013). For these reasons, adults should only offer help when this is needed and not when this is part of a learnt routine (e.g. a child might want the adult to wind up a toy despite the fact that they can do it themselves because this is the routine they are used to).

- Lucy likes playing with her Jack in the box. However, she cannot make it work by herself and she needs to ask her TA to make it work.
- Brandon likes eating grapes. Mum always put his grapes in the fridge in a container with a firm lid on and Brandon has to ask somebody to open the lid.

4.3.6 Contradicting expectations

When adults contradict the child's expectations, perhaps by doing something unexpected and out of routine, it is very likely that the latter will make a request or comment (Potter and Whittaker, 2001; Griffin and Sandler, 2010). Greenspan and Wieder (1998) give some examples of how this can be achieved in their DIR-Floortime approach. They suggest that adults should do the following: i) turn a toy animal over and see whether the child will restore it to the original position, ii) read a book upside down and turn the pages backwards, iii) get the car the child plays with caught under their leg so that in order to get it the child has to deal with them and iv) turn the child's staring into the space into a two person game by getting in front of them. A danger with this principle which can be of particular concern at school is to offer the child unhelpful work models (e.g. drive toy cars upside down, reading book backwards).

- Emily asks her TA's help to put her socks back on after PE. The TA attempts to put Emily's socks on her hands instead of her feet.
- Mum asks James's TD brother to go to bed with his clothes on. This gives James the opportunity to comment on the need to put pyjamas on before going to bed.

4.3.7 Giving non-preferred items

Adults can give the child items they are not interested in to elicit protest or comment (Potter and Whittaker, 2001). For example, adults can put in the child's plate snacks they do not like, or give them a toy they do not want. It has to be noted here that adults should give the child these items only if the latter had not asked for something else. Otherwise, this principle would confuse and/or upset the child. Many practitioners and some parents might avoid using this principle for fear of making children upset. However, Ware (2004) highlights the importance of offering children with communication difficulties choices that they do not like and teach them how to say 'no'. Blackburn (2011) admits that she so much prefers to be exposed to negative experiences by people she knows and trusts. She often narrates the story of her mum having taken her to bowling knowing that the bowling centre was closed. It was hard for her to deal with it but reflecting on the event some years later makes her think that this was a great learning experience.

- The TAs puts some vegetables in Oliver's plate knowing that he does not like them to elicit reject/protest.
- Dad asks Richard whether he wants to watch a DVD that he does not like.

60 *Adult interactive style*

4.3.8 *'Forgetting' something vital*

This last AISI principle concerns asking adults to set up a situation where they 'forget' to do something of vital importance, which will very likely elicit request or comment from the child (Christie et al., 2009). Giving the child paper without crayons or yogurt without a spoon are two examples of this principle. However, it is of crucial importance that the child has the means (e.g. language, signs, symbols or photos) to ask for the missing part otherwise it is very likely that this principle will cause confusion and upset.

- During changing clothes after PE, the TA gives Melanie only one shoe to put on. Melanie has to ask for the other one.
- Chris asks his dad to bring him his click clack track. Dad brings the track but not the cars. Chris has to ask for them.

4.4 AISI in drawings*

The illustrations in Figures 4.1–4.8 show some examples of AISI principles from school practice.

Figure 4.1 a) Establish appropriate proximity, b) show availability and c) wait for initiations

*All drawings have been created by Nikos Papadopoulos based on stills from video recordings in the school AISI was developed. Permission to use them has been granted.

Figure 4.2 a) 'Forget' something vital and b) offer choices

Figure 4.3 a) Assign meaning to the child's random actions or sounds, b) imitate the child and c) follow the child's focus of attention

Figure 4.4 a) Make items inaccessible and b) offer choices

Figure 4.5 a) Gain child's attention, b) show availability, c) wait for initiations and d) give the child materials he or she will need help with

Figure 4.6 a) Expand on child's communicative attempts and b) give small portions

Figure 4.7 a) Establish appropriate proximity/touch, b) use exaggerated pitch (e.g. singing) and c) stop part way

64 *Adult interactive style*

Figure 4.8 a) Respond to all of the child's communicative attempts, b) use minimal speech, c) use non-verbal cues (i.e. symbols, gestures) and d) give the child time to process the information

4.5 Reflection activities

- Go through the 13 general AISI principles. Knowing the child with autism you want to apply them on, the setting you would like to apply them in (e.g. home or school) and your personality, can you select five of them that you can start using very soon? Which ones did you select and why? Are there any principles which you think will not work with your child or in your setting and why?
- Go through the 8 communicative AISI opportunities. Knowing the child with autism you want to apply them on, the setting you would like to apply them in (e.g. home or school) and your personality, can you select three of them that you can start using very soon? Which ones did you select and why? Are there any principles which you think will not work with your child or in your setting and why?

5 The research project

5.1 Introduction

Although literature has highlighted the importance of a communication-enabling interactive style while working with children with autism, studies often fail to establish links between adult interactive style and children's spontaneous communication. They are often descriptive in nature or do not have ecological validity, and their findings cannot be easily implemented into real-world settings. Therefore, the call is now for more evidence-based research in naturalistic settings following robust research designs and involving end-users into the development of the intervention from the outset (Weisz, 2000; Kasari and Smith, 2013). This chapter presents the research design of a study which aimed to address the need for rigorous evidence-based participatory research designs conducted in real-world settings.

The study used a Participatory Action Research (PAR) methodology, involving practitioners in the research process from the outset. Three members of staff and 6 children with autism and SLD/PMLD from an Early Years class in an autism specialist school participated. Pre-intervention, each member of staff was video recorded while naturally interacting with the pupils across four different activities. The researcher edited the pre-intervention videos focusing on good staff practice. Then the videos were shown to the staff, who were encouraged to comment on them. As a result of this, an initial set of principles was put together and practised for four weeks. At the end of this period, the researcher decided on a final set of principles with the staff; these were called AISI. Post-intervention, staff were video recorded while implementing AISI during the same four activities as pre-intervention. Apart from the video recordings, focus group interviews were employed to measure the extent of the post-intervention change and to obtain staff views. This chapter outlines the research methodology i.e. the research aims and questions, philosophical underpinnings, samples, settings, and the advantages and challenges of using PAR methodology. It also describes the data collection process in detail and reports on the main ethical considerations of the study.

5.2 Research aims and research questions

The research aims are concerned with the overall purpose of the study: they are the general intentions of the research (Barney et al., n.d.). This study's overarching research aims were to develop an intervention which focused on adult style (AISI) and then measured its effects on children's spontaneous communication.

In order to achieve the aims of a research study the researcher must pose some research questions. Effective research questions should be clear, specific, answerable, interconnected and substantively relevant (Punch, 1998, cited in Robson, 2002). Research questions should inform the literature search (Bryman, 2008) but also influence the choice of research methodology and methods to be employed. The five main research questions of the current study were:

1 To what extent did the intervention (AISI) affect the frequency with which children initiated communication?
2 To what extent did the type of activity affect the frequency of the children's spontaneous communication?
3 Was there any difference in the reasons for which children initiated communication when adults changed their interactive style?
4 Was there any difference in the methods children used to initiate communication when adults changed their interactive style?
5 To what extent were adults able to change their interactive style?

5.3 Philosophical underpinnings of the study

This section briefly discusses the most common philosophical theories influencing social and educational research. It defines terms such as ontology, epistemology and methodology and concludes by presenting the philosophical foundation of the current study.

The philosophical underpinnings of a study are often unrecognised or taken for granted in educational research (Scott and Usher, 1999). However, research is not just a technical exercise but is closely related to the way the researcher understands the world (Cohen et al., 2007). This means that a researcher's beliefs and values play a critical role in the way they conduct research. This set of beliefs and values is what Kuhn (1962) coined as 'paradigm' and Johnson et al. (2007) call 'research culture'. There is a debate with regard to the number and the content of research paradigms (Mertens, 1998; Burrell and Morgan, 2005; Johnson et al., 2007). This book embraces the opinion that there are three main research paradigms in social sciences and educational research; these are the positivist, the interpretivist and the pragmatic or mixed-methods paradigm (Johnson et al., 2007). Each one of these encompasses different ontological, epistemological and methodological positions.

For a paradigm to be understood, its ontology, epistemology and methodology should be defined. Questions of an ontological nature investigate whether the reality is external to the individual or a product of one's cognition (Burrell and Morgan, 2005). For Guba and Lincoln (1994), ontology answers the question '*What is the nature of reality?*' Assumptions of an epistemological type are connected to the nature of knowledge and whether it is hard, real and objective or soft, subjective and dependent on context (Burrell and Morgan, 2005). For

Scott and Usher (1999), epistemology is concerned with '*How do we know what we think we know?*' With regard to the methodology, Burrell and Morgan (2005) offer two potential approaches. The first, nomothetic, are strictly based on systematic protocols, while the second, ideographic, imply the researcher's involvement in the participants' flow of life. To sum up, ontology represents the way a researcher interprets reality, and epistemology, the way they approach knowledge. Based on their ontological and epistemological standpoints, the researcher has to decide on the methodology: the stance they will adopt with regard to sample selection, data collection methods, analysis and finally, interpretation of the findings.

Positivists advocate the existence of an objective reality (ontology), which the researcher should approach by being neutral to the subject of the research (epistemology) and using mainly quantitative data for this purpose (methodology) (Mertens, 1998; Cohen et al., 2007). Interpretivists, on the other hand, believe in the existence of multiple and socially constructed realities (ontology), which influence to a great extent what is being researched (epistemology) and ask for primarily qualitative data (methodology) (Mertens, 1998; Cohen et al., 2007). The researchers who believe in the idea of mutually exclusive paradigms (i.e. positivism or interpretivism) are often called purists (Onwuegbuzie and Leech, 2005). However, there is a tendency recently to question this strict paradigm discrimination and to challenge paradigm-bound research (Cohen et al., 2007). These researchers belong to the pragmatic or mixed-methods paradigm and believe that they should use the philosophical assumptions and methods which work best for each piece of research (Robson, 2002).

This study operates within the pragmatic paradigm in the sense that I have selected data collection methods which best suit the purpose of the specific research. However, its ontology and epistemology lie within the interpretivist paradigm. My position is that social reality was depicted as experienced by the participants (ontology) who were influenced by my (i.e. the researcher's) presence (epistemology). This means that if I had conducted the study with different participants or if another researcher had taken my role, the results might have been different. In terms of methodology, equal emphasis is put on both quantitative and qualitative data to answer the specific research questions. Quantitative data were needed to compare differences in the frequency of initiations, the communicative functions and methods and AISI principles pre- and post-intervention. These data were supplemented by gaining qualitative data from staff on the intervention and its impact on the children.

5.4 Research design

Yin (2003a) defines research design as

> the logical sequence that connects the empirical data to a study's initial research questions and, ultimately, to its conclusions.
>
> (p. 19)

68 *The research project*

It includes defining the research problem, formulating the research questions, collecting and analysing data and writing the final report. This section illustrates how the research has been designed to explore the five main research questions.

There are many different research designs. Tesch (1990, cited in Creswell, 2003) identified 28 of them. A common classification of designs follows the typology of research paradigms. So there are quantitative (fixed) and qualitative (flexible) designs. The distinctive hallmark is that in quantitative designs there is a great deal of pre-specification before the fieldwork, whereas in flexible qualitative studies, the design evolves and develops during the research process (Robson, 2002). The most common quantitative designs are experiments, quasi-experiments, relational designs, comparative studies and longitudinal designs. The most widely used qualitative designs are case studies, ethnographies, grounded theory studies, evaluation studies and action research. There is a third, mixed-methods design, which shares features of both quantitative and qualitative research designs (Creswell, 2003; Teddlie and Tashakkori, 2003; Creswell and Plano Clark, 2007; Leech and Onwuegbuzie, 2009). To answer the research questions in this study a mixed-methods research design was selected.

5.5 Research methodology

Action research has been used for over 70 years. Kurt Lewin coined the term in the 1940s (Lewin, 1946). It was broadly used in education in the 1950s in the US and it was introduced to the UK in the 1970s. Currently, action research is a growing field in special education addressing the need for more evidence-based practice (Odom et al., 2005; Parsons et al., 2011). It is a practice-driven approach in which researchers and practitioners work in close partnership to produce viable improvements to real-world problems. Reason and Bradbury (2001) give the following definition:

> Action research is about working towards practical outcomes, and also about creating new forms of understanding, since action without understanding is blind, just as theory without action is meaningless.
>
> (p. 2)

The aim of educational action research is to improve practice by making changes and learning from the consequences of these changes (Kemmis and McTaggart, 1992). However, serious concerns have been raised about the quality of many of these studies (Adelman, 1989). Zeichner (2001) maintains that the great variation in both the conceptualisation and interpretation of educational action research accounts for its poor quality.

Good action research involves four key features: it is a cyclical process, it involves change, it is practical, and it requires participants' contribution in the research process (Denscombe, 2010). Its main aim is '*to improve practice rather than to produce knowledge*' (Elliot, 1991, p. 49) and one of its principal contributions is that it helps practitioners to better understand their practice (Zuber-Skerritt,

1996). Change and reflexivity are also integral parts of action research and they determine its spiral format. Reflection on the initial findings generates ideas for change which then shape the next stages of the study. In the beginning, the researcher plans a change, implements a solution agreed with the people involved and then observes what happens. The researcher and the participants reflect on the effects of the change and plan the next stage of the research process together. They then implement the amended plan and observe the consequences. This process is repeated several times until a final solution is established.

The researcher and the research participants work in close collaboration through all the stages of action research. Participants have to take an active role. For this reason, action research is often described as participatory research (Kemmis and McTaggart, 2000) or PAR (Nind, 2014). Action research is described as a 'bottom up' approach in which the 'researched' are involved in some or all stages of the research process (e.g. planning, research design, data collection and analysis, distribution of the research findings) with their key premise being that '*action and research are simultaneous and inseparable*' (Nind, 2014, p. 9). Because of the participants' active role, the ownership of action research is a recurring debate (Reed, 2005).

Action research can be conducted in two ways: either a researcher observes practitioners doing research and speaks on their behalf (i.e. interpretive approach) or the practitioners themselves are the researchers. Although some scholars such as Elliot (1991) are in favour of the interpretive approach, the concern is that practitioners might participate to a great extent in the data gathering but it is eventually the researcher who generates the new theories and disseminates the findings (Whitehead and McNiff, 2006). On the other hand, Whitehead (1989) supports a more equal contribution not only to the process but also to the end product between researchers and research participants maintaining that teachers and researchers should work in '*democratic partnership*' so that both can learn and grow together. Likewise, Hall and Hall (1996) wrote about this partnership between the researcher and the research participants:

> The research relationship is between equals and is not exploitative. [. . .] There is a genuine exchange. The research is negotiated.
>
> (p. 12)

5.5.1 Advantages of action research

There are a number of advantages in using action research. Most importantly, it bridges the gap between academic research and practice (Somekh, 1995). It is true that schools, practitioners (and even more, parents) often feel excluded from what is happening in academia. Most findings are published in specialised journals with high subscription fees or presented at scientific conferences which are primarily attended by academics. Additionally, it is argued that teachers tend to have '*a consumer approach to read research*' (Zeuli, 1994, p. 53). This means that they are more interested in having information about the end product but are less interested in the process and the rationale behind it. This might be happening as although many teachers are very keen to get ideas on how to improve their skills in the classroom, they have difficulties in identifying those principles in academic publications (Zeuli, 1994). Parents are even more disadvantaged as more often than not, they have very limited access to and understanding of research. Action research can address this issue by making teaching staff and parents a part of the research process.

Professional and personal development is another important strength of action research (Denscombe, 2010). Research participants have the chance to be trained free of charge in up-to-date interventions without having to leave their setting. This can be much appreciated, especially by TAs who rarely might obtain extra training apart from the few official school training days (offered as whole day events or afternoon sessions), and by parents who are often lost in a plethora of contradicting information given to them by the professionals working with their child and the internet.

The researcher benefits too, from working closely with practitioners and parents. S/he learns how to better plan research and to understand the constraints of using interventions in real-world environments. This contrasts with confined laboratory-based studies, in which the researcher is in more control of the variables under investigation but the findings cannot be directly transferable to real-world settings.

The notion of empowerment is of equal importance (McNiff and Whitehead, 2006), especially for TAs who do not often have the chance to voice their opinion, and for parents of children with autism who are more likely to develop mental health issues (Giallo et al., 2013) and have lower quality of life (Vasilopoulou and Nisbet, 2016).

Teamwork is another significant advantage of action research (Koshy, 2005), often neglected in schools due to the quick pace that staff have to follow. It can also be helpful for parents who often feel they are fighting a 'constant battle' (Sloper, 1999) to find out what is available for their child and understand the multitude of different professionals working with them. The importance of teamwork should be seen in the light of the findings that teaching staff working with pupils with special needs are reported to experience high rates of stress and burnout (Male and May, 1997) and especially staff working with autism '*can sometimes find themselves feeling deskilled, over-responsible, isolated or overwhelmed*' (Pittman, 2007, p. 31). As far as parents are concerned, teamwork seems of crucial importance, especially at the very early stages after they receive their child's diagnosis. Indicative is the example of a mother who lost her ability to teach her son as soon as he got the diagnosis of autism and professionals started behaving according to the deficit model (e.g. emphasising what he could not do rather than what he could do) (Hodge, 2006, cited in Hodge and Chantler, 2010). She said, '*I felt that someone had taken my son away*' (p. 12). Action research can remind the participants of the importance of sharing knowledge and difficulties with other people having similar interests but complementary expertise.

5.5.2 Challenges of action research

There are several criticisms of action research worth mentioning. The two most widely known are related to its rigour and generalisability (Koshy, 2005). Action research cannot certainly claim the rigour and validity of laboratory-based studies. In real-world environments, the researcher cannot isolate the variables they are interested in, which means that changes due to other factors cannot be excluded (Denscombe, 2010). However, using a variety of data collection methods can enhance the standards of rigour and validity of such studies. Data generalisability is another issue that should be handled with caution. Action research does not set out to seek data which can be generalised to the wider population. Data can only be generalised within the situation in which the study took place. The aim of action research is to provide data which informs future practice in that setting and to form the basis of future more rigorous research.

The issue of ethics is another challenge when conducting action research (Koshy, 2005; McNiff and Whitehead, 2006). The presence of the researcher and an audio or video recorder in a classroom or home setting can be anxiety-provoking for professionals and parents, and may also be a challenge for pupils. Finding time to discuss the research with busy people can be another concern. Both professionals working with children with special needs and their parents have a very demanding and time-consuming job to meet the children's individual needs. Their time is more limited when at their home or school settings (as opposed to when they visit a laboratory) since they have to contribute to the study on top of all their other ongoing responsibilities.

One cannot either ignore the challenges posed to the researcher's objectivity (Burns, 2000; Denscombe, 2010) primarily because of their long stay at the setting, and their level of involvement in the participants' everyday activities. Burns (2000) suggests that after a long stay in a setting, the researcher might feel so familiar with the participants and the environment that they lose their personal perspective of reality and objectivity and 'go native'. More ideas on how to improve practice at school and at home as well as the way ahead for future research resulting from reviewing relevant literature and my experience of conducting PAR in real-world settings can be found in Chapters 7 and 8 of this book.

Below, several key research terms playing a crucial role in planning and conducting action research are explored, including validity, reliability and reflexivity. The following sections discuss the background of each one of them.

5.6 Validity

Validity refers to the degree to which '*a method, a test or a research tool actually measures what it is supposed to measure*' (Wellington, 2000, p. 201). Cohen et al. (2007) and Robson (2002) highly suggest piloting the research tools to enhance their validity. Moreover, employing standardised measures or instruments (which are known to have good validity) can add to a study's validity. A strategy that Yin (2003a) proposes to improve validity particularly for qualitative data is triangulation. This can be achieved by using three or more different types of respondents (e.g. teacher, parent, pupil) or three or more different types of data collection instruments (e.g. interview, questionnaire, observation).

External, internal and ecological validity are of crucial importance when designing a research study. Both external and internal validity are two validity types which can be problematic in naturalistic studies (Yin, 2003a). External validity relates to the extent to which the findings of a study can be generalised (Cohen et al., 2007), whilst internal validity refers to the potential of a causal relationship between two or more variables (Bryman, 2008). A solution to the threat of external validity is to follow Burns' (2000) advice and provide a full description of the unit of analysis leaving the readers to decide whether the findings apply to their case or no. Internal validity is extremely difficult to achieve in studies being conducted in real-world settings. Advocates of the interpretivist paradigm often use the terms credibility instead of internal validity (Riege, 2003) and transferability (Riege, 2003) or generalisability (Robson, 2002) instead of external validity. Ecological validity considers whether *'social scientific findings are applicable to people's every day, natural social settings'* (Bryman, 2008, p. 33). Therefore, if a study is conducted in a school setting without changes to the curriculum and the daily timetable of the class, its ecological validity is high.

5.7 Reliability

Reliability is a concept closely linked to validity which is also often difficult to achieve in real-world research (Wellington, 2000). The term can have different meanings in quantitative and qualitative research (Cohen et al., 2007). In quantitative studies, reliability is used to ascertain whether if the same methods were used with a similar sample, the results would be the same. In qualitative research, reliability refers to the accuracy between what the researcher records and what is actually happening. The term dependability instead of reliability is often used in qualitative studies (Mertens, 1998; Robson, 2002).

5.7.1 Inter-rater reliability

Inter-rater reliability is a test of the degree to which two or more raters agree that a phenomenon has occurred. Coolican (2006) highlights the great importance of conducting inter-rater reliability checks in naturalistic settings where the likelihood of rater bias is high due to the unpredictability of the observed behaviours. A study is considered to have inter-rater reliability when two or more raters with the same theoretical background interpret the research phenomena in the same way with agreement ratings over a certain percentage (Cohen et al., 2007). Reichow et al. (2008) suggest that this percentage should be of a minimum of 80%. One of the most common ways of calculating inter-rater reliability is the percentage agreement (Watkins and Pacheco, 2000). Percentage agreement is defined as the number of agreements between two or more observers divided by the sum of both agreements and disagreements and then multiplied by 100:

$$\frac{Agreements}{Agreements + Disagreements} \times 100$$

5.8 Reflexivity

Since researchers are part of the social world that they are researching, they bring their own biases, values, interests and experiences to the research and participants are likely to behave in certain ways in their presence. This is a reality which needs to be acknowledged and the term used to describe this process in research methodology is reflexivity. A number of scholars (Creswell, 2003; Cohen et al., 2007; Denscombe, 2010) highlight the importance for a researcher to bring their background to light as this is very likely to shape to a great extent the research design, the findings of a study and their interpretation. This is why Cohen et al. (2007) state that instead of the researchers trying to eliminate their effect on the study (which is unlikely), they should openly disclose values, biases, beliefs, experiences, decisions and their mere presence in the situations they explore, as all of these are an integral and influential part of it. The notion of reflexivity is inextricably linked to action research, as reflexivity should always be part of the cyclical process action research entails. However, reflexivity is not easy to achieve and researchers should be aware of and acknowledge this difficulty. To this end, Denscombe (2010) asks,

> How far can my description of [. . .] (an) event depict things from the point of view of those involved when I can only use my own way of seeing things, my own conceptual tools, to make sense of what is happening?
>
> (p. 86)

5.9 Research design of the adult interactive style intervention study

The AISI study used action research as defined by Whitehead (1989) and Hall and Hall (1996) (i.e. a democratic partnership between researcher and participants) to explore the differences in children's spontaneous communication when classroom staff changed the way they interacted with them and to examine the extent to which staff managed to change their interactive style. The ultimate goal was to conduct research which would give an end product which was transferable to real-world settings after the end of the study. An equal contribution by the researcher and the research participants was more likely to produce findings directly transferable to the school setting. The researcher may have better knowledge of the literature but the school-based participants know the setting and the children, and can predict practical difficulties before they occur.

This study used a mixed-methods approach to answer the research questions as it is proposed by the literature for similar studies (Creswell, 2003; Creswell and Plano Clark, 2007; Ollerton, 2008). Quantitative and qualitative data were collected using video recordings and focus group interviews. Quantitative data (obtained from the video recordings) were necessary to show changes in children's spontaneous communication and adults' interactive style while qualitative data (obtained from the focus group interviews) were needed to explore the impact of each principle of the intervention and to get a more in-depth view of the reasons for the changes in both children and staff. The combination of quantitative and qualitative data coming from different sources enhanced the rigour of this small-scale study. Details on the setting and the sample selected are now given whilst the data collection methods are discussed later in the chapter.

5.10 The sample: the school, the children and the teaching staff

There are two kinds of sampling techniques: probability sampling in which the participants are a representative cross-section of the whole population, and non-probability sampling in which the sample has not been chosen using random selection (Bryman, 2008; Denscombe, 2010). Denscombe (2010) maintains that small-scale research tends to have non-probability samples. Purposive sampling is a type of non-probability sample. In this, the researcher selects a small number of cases based on their known features. Denscombe (2010) maintains,

> Purposive sample can [. . .] be used as a way of getting the best information by selecting items or people most likely to have the experience or expertise to provide quality information and valuable insights on the research topic.
> (p. 35)

He continues that such a sample can work as an exploratory sample. This was the case for the current study in which a purposive sample was used. The following sections give information first on the school and then on the children and the staff who comprised the sample.

5.10.1 The school

An all-age autism specialist school was selected to be the exemplary case (Yin, 2003b) for this study. Three consecutive outstanding Ofsted inspection reports (2007, 2010, 2014) describe the school's high standards in educating autistic children and adolescents. At the time the study was conducted the school accepted pupils with an autism diagnosis and communication and social difficulties. It had 16 classes which on average had 10 students. Some of them followed the National Curriculum, whilst others followed an Extended National Curriculum which was tailored to the children's specific needs. The staff:pupil ratio varied depending on the children's needs, and may have been as high as 1:1. The school used an eclectic approach taking elements from different interventions to meet each pupil's needs. These included ABA (Cooper et al., 2007), Daily Life Therapy (Kitahara, 1984), Intensive Interaction (Nind and Hewett, 1994, 2001; Caldwell, 2008),

SCERTS (Prizant et al., 2006), Sensory Integration Therapy (Ayres, 1998), Structure Positive Empathy Low arousal Links (SPELL) (National Autistic Society-NAS, n.d.), Son-Rise (Kaufman, 1994; Kaufman, 2002), TEACCH (Lord and Schopler, 1994) and Team Teach (Allen and Matthews, 2008). Over time, the school also developed their own programmes for assessing and teaching communication, early literacy and numeracy and toilet training as well as pre-empting and dealing with behaviours of concern. A class of young children following the Extended National Curriculum was selected to be the sample of the current study as the children within it were at an early stage of communication and language development. More specifically, the sample consisted of six children and three members of staff (one teacher and two TAs).

5.10.2 The children

Six children who met the inclusion criteria and were aged between 4 and 5 years old formed the sample (see Table 5.1 for their details). The inclusion criteria for the children were to

- have a diagnosis of autism and learning difficulties, already confirmed by a health care practitioner;
- regularly use up to 20 words (spoken, signed, pictures, symbols, objects), both referentially and with communicative intent; and
- initiate communication infrequently.

Children with other syndromes or conditions which might have affected the study (e.g. Down syndrome, cerebral palsy, epilepsy) were not included.

5.10.2.1 Data on the children

A number of checklists, tests and assessment tools were administered by school staff to ensure that the selected children met the inclusion criteria. Additionally, the researcher reviewed several reports (e.g. statements of special educational needs (SEN) and other school documents). The assessments included:

- the Childhood Autism Rating Scale (CARS) (Schopler et al., 1988);
- the Development in Areas Related to Learning (DARL) (unpublished);
- the Symbolic Play Test (SPT) (Lowe and Costello, 1988);
- the children's level of verbal communication (informal assessment by the school SLT); and
- the Questionnaire for Determining Spontaneous Communication in Children (QDSCC; developed for this study).

The remaining of this section gives a brief description of these assessments and the children's scores on these. A summary of their details can also be found in Table 5.1.

Table 5.1 Details of the children in the study (n = 6)

Children*	Molly	Alex	Robert	Nathan	David	Oliver
Sex	Female	Male	Male	Male	Male	Male
Age at pre-intervention assessment	53 months	61 months	49 months	48 months	62 months	45 months
Diagnosis	autism	autism	autism	autism	autism	autism
CARS score (January 2010)	51.5	51.5	54	46	40.5	51.5
Level of learning ability (DARL) (January 2010) 1 = profound, 5 = mild or no impairment	2	3	1	2	3	2
SPT (January 2010) Score Age equivalent in months	0 <12	2 <12	0 <12	3 <12	12 22	1 <12
Level of verbal communication (January 2010)	Vocalisations	Vocalisations	Vocalisations	Vocalisations	Occasional words (10–20 words)	Very little vocalisation
English as first language	No	Yes	Yes	Yes	No	Yes

| Comments on communication QDSCC (January 2010) | Rarely initiates communication with adults and peers. *Means*: looking at other people, touching, pushing, pulling and manipulating their hands. *Reasons*: requests and rejects objects and activities. | Often initiates contact with adults and less often with peers. *Means*: approaching/touching other people, pushing, pulling or manipulating their hands, using pictures/symbols. *Reasons*: requests objects and activities and sometimes rejects and starts social games. | Does not initiate communication often. Only to adults. *Means*: looking at other people, approaching/touching them, pushing, pulling and manipulating their hands. *Reason*: rejects objects and activities. | Does not often initiate contact with adults and peers. *Means*: looking at the other person, approaching/touching them, crying, screaming. *Reasons*: requests and rejects and sometimes initiates social games. | Often initiates communication with both adults and peers but in an 'inappropriate' way. *Means*: crying, hitting, throwing objects, word-like sounds and one or two clear spoken words, looking at another person, approaching/touching others and pointing to objects or people. *Reasons*: requests, draws another's attention to himself, performs simple social routines and initiates social games. | Rarely initiates communication and only with adults. *Means*: approaching/touching other people, pushing, pulling and manipulating their hands. *Reasons*: requests and rejects objects and activities. |

*All names are pseudonyms.

Statements of SEN (which are now being replaced by Education, Health and Care Plans- EHCP) present children's diagnoses, identify their educational difficulties and describe the provision (e.g. equipment, staff arrangements) which should be in place for them at school. The children's statements of SEN were examined and all had autism stated as a diagnostic category. The SEN statements were also used to get the children's date of birth. The teacher completed the CARS (Schopler et al., 1988). CARS is a diagnostic rating scale in which children are rated from 1 (typical behaviour) to 4 (atypical behaviour) against 15 items-behaviours. It then gives an overall score ranging from non-autistic (from 15 to 30) to severely autistic (from 38 to 60). Children with scores between 30 and 38 are rated as mildly to moderately autistic. All six children of the sample scored between 40 and 54, which classified them as severely autistic. The children's level of learning ability was obtained using a school assessment tool called the DARL (unpublished). DARL rates learning ability on a five-point scale from 1 (profound impairment) to 5 (mild or no impairment). Ratings for the children of the sample ranged from 1 to 3. The teacher and the Speech and Language Therapist (SLT) administered the SPT (Lowe and Costello, 1988) to get data on children's cognitive development. SPT assesses the children's early concept formation and symbolisation, abilities which precede and develop alongside receptive and expressive language. The children were asked to play with miniature toys in a variety of situations and they were assessed on handling and relating the toys to each other. The test gives a score ranging from 0 to 24 and an age equivalent of score ranging from < 12 to 36 + months. The SPT raw scores for the children in the sample ranged from 0 to 12 and the age equivalent from < 12 months to 22 months.

The children's level of verbal communication was assessed by the SLT and ranged from very limited vocalisations to occasional words (10–20 words) (see Table 5.1 for each child's verbal communication level). To assess the frequency with which children initiated communication, the methods they used and the reasons for their communication, the class teacher completed the QDSCC which the researcher developed based on the Pragmatics Profile of Early Communication (Dewart and Summers, 1988). A blank copy of the QDSCC can be found in Appendix 1.

5.10.3 *The staff*

Three members of staff (1 Teacher and 2 Teaching Assistants-TAs) formed the sample (see Table 5.2 for their details). 'Lorna' was the pseudonym for the teacher, with 'Amber' and 'Emma' being the pseudonyms for the two TAs. The only inclusion criterion for staff was to be employed by the school (full-time or part-time). I debriefed the classroom teacher on the project focusing on the general aims of the study, the importance of staff participation and the methods to be employed. The teacher then presented the study to the other class staff in my absence to give them the chance to raise concerns and ask questions. After that, I approached each member of staff to ensure that all potential participants understood the process and get their consent.

Table 5.2 Details of the staff in the study ($n = 3$)

Teaching staff*	Lorna	Amber	Emma
Level of education	BEd in teaching children with severe learning difficulties	Level 3 BTEC** for TA	Level 3 BTEC** for TA BSc in human psychology
Length of time at the school (years)	15	7	4
Type of employment	Part time	Full time	Part time

* All names are pseudonyms.
** The BTEC (Business and Technology Education Council) Level 3 extended diploma is a secondary school leaving qualification and vocational qualification taken in England, Wales and Northern Ireland.

5.11 The data collection methods and sequence of implementation

The main data collection methods were: (i) video recordings of the 6 children and the three staff across 4 activities and (ii) focus group interviews with 3 staff to get their views on their interactive style and the progress of the children. Table 5.3 shows in summary the sequence of actions taken from the beginning to the end of the study.

5.11.1 Video recordings of staff and children across four activities

It is often difficult to determine whether a child intends to communicate. Having a permanent video record allowing repeated viewings by the researcher and for other raters to check the reliability of the data makes the process easier. In this study, data

Table 5.3 Action research sequence

Research phase	Action taken	
Pre-intervention (8 weeks)	• Videos taken of the 6 children and 3 staff in four activities.	
Development of the intervention (8 weeks)	Cycle 1	• Researcher presented key intervention principles to staff from the videos taken at pre-intervention and got their views.
	Cycle 2	• Staff practised these principles with the six children over a four-week period.
	Cycle 3	• Staff took part in focus groups to finalise AISI.
Post-intervention (8 weeks)	• Videos taken of the 6 children and 3 staff in the same four activities. • Staff took part in a focus group to discuss AISI and the progress of the children.	

were needed on different aspects of communication (e.g. functions and methods) and it is extremely difficult for an observer to capture and record all of these by purely taking notes. In addition, data on the adult style were required and it was impossible to observe the actions of both staff and children simultaneously. Having the video allowed the researchers to analyse and code these separately.

Video recording has a number of strengths and limitations. The openness of the data to multiple scrutiny (Heath et al., 2010) is one of the most significant advantages of this method. Different researchers can code the same video multiple times, increasing the reliability of the data. Additionally, video data have 'longer shelf life' than other types of data (Stigler et al., 2000). Researchers can re-code and re-analyse past videos in the light of new theories and then compare the findings to that of the initial analysis. Video data is also likely to promote inter-disciplinary research (Stigler et al., 2000), as it can be available to a wider range of researchers who might not have the chance or the knowledge to conduct studies with certain groups (e.g. ICT engineers can develop software for children with autism while the fieldwork is conducted exclusively by experienced psychologists and educators). However, the use of videos has some disadvantages. Like observations, video data are limited to whatever the observer can record (Stigler et al., 2000). This might be unrepresentative of what usually occurs and the researcher should bear this in mind when analysing the data. The camera effect is another important limitation which should be considered (Stigler et al., 2000). Teaching staff might show their best when the camera is in the classroom and children might feel excited or embarrassed and behave in a different way from usual. Additionally, video poses a number of practical and ethical problems. Practical concerns might be related to where the camera is placed as well as lighting and sound issues. Gaining consent from parents and staff can be an issue as video is likely to put the participants off (Heath et al., 2010). Parents might feel exposed to criticism for their child's behaviour and their parenting skills and class staff can be worried about the possibility of senior staff watching the videos and assessing their skills.

In this study, videos were taken at the school as opposed to asking children and staff to come to a university setting, where video recording may have been easier. In such an environment the researcher could have more control over variables such as noise level, duration of the sessions, staff's full attention. However, naturalistic observations are reported to be the most valid form of assessing social communication skills in children with autism (Clifford et al., 2010) and it was my utmost objective to develop an intervention which could be applied straight away in real-world settings. Using video provided first-hand information on what was happening in practice, instead of getting this indirectly from staff (Robson, 2002; Cohen et al., 2007). This is a significant point as there might often be discrepancies between what teaching staff think they do and what they actually do.

5.11.1.1 Effects of video on behaviour of staff and children

In order for the researcher's presence to have the minimum effect on the children, Denscombe's (2010) advice was followed and I tried to become part of the furniture. During video recordings, interactions with the staff and the children were kept to a minimum. Children appeared to be oblivious to being videoed. Staff might have tried to give their best performance. For example, they might have used more strategies advised by the school such as visual supports and limited speech than they would if the researcher and the camera were not there. However, this could only be beneficial as building on their existing good practice was one of the aims of the study.

5.11.1.2 *The researcher's role*

Gold (1958, cited in Bryman, 2008) identifies the following participant observer roles: (i) the complete participant (i.e. the researcher is fully part of the setting and often observes covertly), (ii) the participant as observer (i.e. the researcher observes while being part of the studied group), (iii) the observer as participant (i.e. the researcher has minimal involvement in the studied group) and (iv) the complete observer (i.e. the researcher does not take part in the studied group at all). I assumed the role of the participant as observer researcher as this fits the best with the PAR methodology of the study. This type of observation differs from previous studies in the field (Stone and Caro-Martinez, 1990; Stone et al., 1997; Keen et al., 2002; Chiang et al., 2008; Agius, 2009; Chiang, 2009), in which the researchers were not participating in the change but they were just describing what was happening (i.e. observer as participant). As I occasionally worked with the children to model the AISI principles, it is possible that I was a factor in the outcomes and I could have biased the findings. To minimise the likelihood of this happening, some measures were put in place. The use of video recording to allow inter-observer reliability checks and focus group interviews to validate the observation data diminished this possibility. To reduce observer effect, minimal interaction with the staff was also established during the video recordings and the focus group interviews.

5.11.1.3 *Type of activities to video record*

Children experience a variety of activities during the course of a school day. Some are more conducive to elicit spontaneous communication than others. Evidence on which activities are likely to elicit the most spontaneous communication is inconclusive. Some studies (e.g. O' Reilly et al., 2005; Chiang, 2008b; Chiang, 2009) argue that academic activities elicit more spontaneous communication while other studies (e.g. Stone et al., 1997; Potter and Whittaker, 2001) claim that unstructured activities are more likely to promote spontaneous communication (see 2.7.4 'Activities and Their Effect on Spontaneous Social Communication' for more details). Four activities were chosen to be video recorded based on SCERTS guidance (Prizant et al., 2006) which suggests that to get representative data on the social communication of autistic children with limited language and communication, observations should include at least four activities which should vary across at least four of the pairs of the ten variables presented in Table 5.4. These variables are likely to influence children's behaviour in different activities.

82 *The research project*

Table 5.4 Ten pairs of variables across which activities should vary in order to gather representative information about the abilities and needs of children with autism within natural environments

Structured		Unstructured
Must do		Fun
Adult-directed		Child-directed
Motor-based		Sedentary
Familiar	vs	Unfamiliar
Preferred		Non-preferred
Easy		Difficult
Language-based		Non-language-based
Social		Solitary
Busy		Calm

The four activities which were selected on the basis of the aforementioned pairs of variables were as follows:

1 sensory room;
2 soft play;
3 snack time; and
4 1:1 work.

Sensory and soft play activities are often fairly unstructured, motor-based and child led. The focus is on developing children's social communication and interaction skills (e.g. eye contact, turn-taking, anticipation and initiations). These activities take place in separate, calm rooms designed for these purposes. Snack time and 1:1 work are carried out in the classroom. These tend to be highly structured, sedentary, adult-led activities conducted in a busy environment.

5.11.1.4 Adult: child ratio and size of group

In special and specialist schools, the class size is often between five and ten children with two to five adults. Some work occurs on a 1:1 basis, some as a small group and some with the whole class group. However, children's behaviour varies according to the adult:child ratio and the number of other children in the group. The SCERTS team (Prizant et al., 2006) suggest that autistic children with limited communication and language should be observed in at least two of the following group sizes: (i) 1:1, (ii) small group and (iii) large group. Taking into consideration some research which evidences that most spontaneous communication occurs in 1:1 or small group activities (Potter and Whittaker, 2001), it was decided to select activities performed in these two size groups. Work and snack time operated on a 1:1 basis whilst sensory room and soft play activities were set up on a small group basis. Although the adult:child ratio in the sensory room and the soft play activities was 1:2, staff were asked to focus on the target child while being filmed.

5.11.1.5 Length of video recordings

Studies, which have explored communication, have taken data on the children for various lengths of time. In an early study with TD children, Sylva et al. (1980) observed each participant for 20 minutes. Before concluding on the 20 minutes, the researchers experimented with longer and shorter periods but they finally decided that 20 minutes were long enough to capture the data they wanted but not so long as to exhaust the observer. It is noteworthy that studies involving autistic children spent more time on observations. This might have happened because these children tend to have limited spontaneous communication and more observation time is needed. Stone and Caro-Martinez (1990) observed the children of their sample for a minimum of 2 hours each. Hauck et al. (1995) observed children for 4 fifteen-minute periods, most of them conducted on 4 different days. Potter and Whittaker (2001) video recorded the spontaneous communication of each child who participated in their study for one whole school day. Chiang and Lin (2008) videoed their participants for 2 hours. The SCERTS team (Prizant et al., 2006) suggest that to get representative data for autistic children with limited communication, it is important to observe each child for at least 2 hours. They also advise that these videos should be taken on at least 2 different days. SCERTS (Prizant et al., 2006) recommends that autistic children with less severe language and communication difficulties (i.e. can use < 100 words or phases referentially, regularly and with communicative intent) should be observed for 3 to 4 hours. In the current study, each child was videoed for 30 minutes (3 sessions of 10 minutes) in each of the four activities amounting to 2 hours per child per research phase (i.e. pre- and post-intervention).

Studies, which have explored child-adult interactions, have used the same video segments to code adults' and children's behaviour (Hwang and Hughes, 2000; Doussard-Roosevelt et al., 2003; Ruble et al., 2008). Following this example in this current study, extracts from the children's videos were used to code staff's interactive style. Each member of staff was coded for 40 minutes per research phase. The specific videos to be coded were selected randomly and they were 10 minutes of each of the 4 activities in which the children were filmed (i.e. sensory room, snack time, soft play and 1:1 work).

5.11.1.6 The use of the camera

Lonergan (1990) maintains that the quality of the sound, the level of lighting and the use of the zoom are key factors to consider. He highlights the drawback of using a built-in microphone and proposes the use of an extension microphone to get clearer sound. A decision needs to be taken as to whether to use a fixed position for the camera or not (Heath et al., 2010). I decided to hold the camera instead of using a tripod, which might have caused accidents. In the latter case,

84 *The research project*

the continuous movement of children and staff might have ended up in important data being lost. The use of an extension microphone was ruled out, as it would add extra weight and sound zoom was used instead. This is an extra setting which works alongside the optical zoom. Microphones attached on children and staff were not used due to funding restrictions and ethical concerns (e.g. people being recorded outside the indicated video recording times). Filming was conducted at the highest possible resolution to ensure the best video quality. Optical zoom was adjusted before starting recording and it was kept steady to avoid degrading the quality.

5.11.1.7 Video data coding

Broadly speaking there are different types of observational recording in which the degree of structure may considerably vary. Hopkins (2002) states that there are two types of observation coding: open observations in which the observer keeps notes on a blank sheet and focused observations in which the observer ticks every time a particular event or behaviour occurs. Cohen et al. (2007) add a third category in between the highly structured (i.e. pre-determined categorised recording sheets) and the unstructured (i.e. uncategorised note taking) observational recording; this is the semi-structured coding (i.e. there is a degree of predetermination).

This section considers how the data captured from the video camera was coded and analysed. At this point, there were a number of different decisions to be made. These include the amount of video to be coded; how the spontaneous communication of the children is categorised in terms of frequency, functions and methods; and how staff behaviour is classified in terms of their interactive style. Regarding the amount of video observations to be coded it was decided to use all children's data and 40 minutes per research phase (i.e. pre- and post-intervention) for the adults' data. The amount of children's data to be coded is in line with previous studies in the field. The amount of adults' video data was considered adequate given the use of another method to explore adults' style (i.e. focus group interviews) and the great extent of children's video data which needed to be analysed. To categorise and code children's spontaneous communication and adults' style, two highly structured checklists were developed; these are the Checklist for the Initiation of Communication in Children with Autism (CICCA) and the Adult Interactive Style Coding Checklist (AISCC).

CHECKLIST FOR THE INITIATION OF COMMUNICATION IN
CHILDREN WITH AUTISM

CICCA was developed for this study and it was based on previous studies (Stone and Caro-Martinez, 1990; Keen et al., 2002; Roos et al., 2008) and mainly that of Agius (2009). It includes 16 methods (e.g. eye contact and vocalisations) and 9 functions (e.g. request and reject) of communication. The communicative methods were further classified into 2 groups (i.e. pre-symbolic and symbolic) and the functions were grouped into 3 categories (i.e. behaviour regulation, joint attention and social interaction). The method(s) and function(s) of each behaviour, which meet the criteria of spontaneous communication (as defined by Potter and Whittaker, 2001 and Bogdashina, 2005), were coded using numbers to indicate the order in which the child used these. For example, if a child used eye contact and simple motor actions to request, a *1* was recorded in both boxes in the request column and if then the child used CB to protest, a *2* was recorded in the relevant row and column (see Table 5.5 for an example on how to code using CICCA).

Defining what should be coded was a very significant issue which needed to be considered when developing the coding schedule. Chapter 2 has shown that there is a great variation in the way spontaneous communication is defined. Given the young age and the communication difficulties of the children who participated in this study, a fairly liberal definition of spontaneous communication was used. Potter and Whittaker's (2001) definition was chosen as they coded as spontaneous, every child's intentional act which occurs *'without verbal prompting from adults'* (p. 25). Bogdashina's (2005) definition of what constituted a communicative act was also considered in this study. She thinks that the pre-conditions for an act to be communicative are the following: (i) something to communicate about, (ii) a sender, (iii) a receiver, (iv) a medium of transmission and (v) communicative intent. A definition was given for each communicative function and method (see Appendix 2 for the list of definitions) based on previous studies and the definitions provided by the school's SLT.

Two postgraduate students who were qualified teachers of children with special needs checked inter-rater reliability. The raters were blind to the aims of the study and to the order the videos were taken. I trained the two observers in CICCA on separate samples of videos until an 80% agreement was achieved. Then the two observers independently coded 22% of the total video samples (i.e. 5 of the total 23 hours) which were randomly selected. An 85% inter-observer reliability agreement was reached for the total number of initiations. A 70% inter-observer reliability agreement was reached for the communicative functions and 82% was reached for the communicative methods. These percentages approach or exceed the minimum 80% Reichow et al. (2008) recommend.

ADULT INTERACTIVE STYLE CODING CHECKLIST

To measure the extent to which staff implemented AISI principles pre- and post-intervention, a checklist was developed and was used to code adult behaviours seen in the videos. This was named the AISCC and it is based on event sampling. Every time an AISI principle was observed, a tally was put in the relevant box. When each video was coded, frequencies were calculated (see Table 5.6 for an example on how to code AISCC).

A qualified teacher of children with special needs who was 'blind' to the aims of the study was asked to code some of the sessions to check inter-observer reliability for AISCC. I trained her on separate samples of videos until an 80% agreement was achieved. She then independently coded 21% from the total adult videos

Table 5.5 Checklist for the initiation of communication in children with autism*

Functions/ means of communication	Behaviour regulation		Joint attention		Social interaction				Unclear
	Request	Reject/ protest	Comment/give information	Seek information	Express feelings	Seek attention	Seek approval	Social routines	Social games

Pre-symbolic means
- CB   2
- Eye contact   1
- Eye pointing
- Laugh
- Point
- Proximity/touch
- Re-enactments
- Simple motor actions   1
- Smile
- Vocalizations/babbling
- Other:

Symbolic means
- Delayed echolalia
- Immediate echolalia
- Object of reference
- Single words
- Signs/gestures
- Symbols/pictures
- Word combinations
- Other:

*Developed for the current study based on other studies.

Table 5.6 Adult interactive style coding checklist

General principles	Tallies	Frequencies
1. Gain attention	IIII	4
2. Establish appropriate proximity		
3. Show availability		
4. Wait for initiations		
5. Responds to communicative attempts		
6. Assign meaning to random actions or sounds		
7. Imitate the children		
8. Follow children's lead/ focus of attention	II	2
9. Use exaggerated pitch, facial expression, gestures and body language		
10. Use minimal speech	IIII	5
11. Provide time		
12. Expand on communicative attempts		
13. Use non-verbal cues	IIII IIII	9

Communicative opportunities	Tallies	Frequency
14. Offer choices		
15. Stop part way		
16. Give small portions	II	2
17. Make items inaccessible		
18. Give material they will need help with		
19. Contradict expectations		
20. Give non-preferred items		
21. 'Forget' something vital		

sample (i.e. 1 of the total 4 hours) which were randomly selected. This exceeds the 20% minimum of sessions across conditions recommended by Reichow et al. (2008). A 90% inter-observer reliability agreement was reached which is above the minimum 80% Reichow et al. (2008) recommend.

To sum up, CICCA and AISCC gave quantitative data which needed to be checked against the qualitative data from the focus group interviews with the staff to keep the balance a mixed-methods approach requires (Creswell, 2003; Teddlie and Tashakkori, 2003; Creswell and Plano Clark, 2007).

THEORETICAL MODELS OF SPONTANEITY TO DEVELOP CICCA AND AISCC

Two highly structured checklists were employed to code data on children's spontaneous communication and adults' interactive style. Apart from their similarity in the degree of structure, the two checklists have a significant difference. CICCA was developed based on the binary model of spontaneity, whereas AISCC has its roots in the continuum conceptualisation of spontaneity. The binary model considers spontaneity as an all-or-none act where the terms *communicative initiation* and *spontaneous* communication are used interchangeably (Carter and Hotchkis, 2002). In the continuum model, instead of *spontaneous* and *non-spontaneous* communicative acts, there is a degree of spontaneity for each communicative attempt based on the intrusiveness of the antecedent stimuli (Kaczmarek, 1990; Carter and Hotchkis, 2002). The less intrusive the stimulus, the more spontaneous the communicative attempt.

The binary model of spontaneity on which CICCA was based is the most commonly used in describing spontaneous communication in research (Potter and Whittaker, 2001; Chiang and Lin, 2008; Agius, 2009; Chiang, 2009), but it has several limitations. Within the binary perspective there is neither consensus regarding the antecedents which lead to communicative spontaneity nor convincing justification as to why some antecedents are indicative of spontaneous acts (Carter and Hotchkis, 2002). For instance, it is not clear why a child's request in response to an adult's extended palm is more spontaneous than a response to an adult's verbal instruction. Acknowledging these limitations, AISI was developed having the continuum conceptualisation of spontaneity in mind. The rationale behind AISI was to maximise the number of unintrusive antecedent stimuli provided by staff in order to increase the frequency of communicative attempts elicited by the children. Therefore, AISCC, which was developed to measure the extent to which AISI principles were implemented, was based on the same model too.

5.11.2 Focus group interviews with staff

Focus group interviews are a form of group interview in which reliance is placed on the interactions within the group rather than the participants' individual views (Morgan, 1988). Some of the main advantages of this data collection method are that they are time-economical, producing great amount of data in short time and their great fit for gathering data on attitudes and opinions (Morgan, 1988). The fact that only limited topics can be explored because of privacy issues (Morgan, 1988), the inability to provide quantitative and generalisable data (Cohen et al., 2007) and the long time needed for transcriptions (Litoseliti, 2003) are some of the challenges. Focus group interviews were conducted in the current study to get staff's views on developing and evaluating AISI as well as on changes in children's communication. This is in accordance with Morgan's (1988) point that focus groups '*excel at uncovering why participants think as they do*' (p. 25). I conducted two focus groups with the three members of staff. In all of them, I assumed the role of facilitator/moderator and I met with them in the classroom after the end of the school day for about an hour, following Bloor et al.'s (2001) and Litoseliti's (2003) advice on the place and the duration of focus groups (i.e. focus groups for a workgroup would better take place at the worksite for 1 to 1.5 hour). My involvement was minimal as advised by Morgan (1988) when conducting exploratory research.

Having focus groups instead of separate 1:1 interviews was very significant for this study. The interactions among the group were the basis for developing and evaluating AISI as each participant built on the ideas of the others. Although some researchers may believe that focus groups can be a very artificial set-up where the researcher may influence participants to express or act unnaturally resulting in findings that are not completely true (Institute of Consumer Rights, 2012), Wilkinson (2008) believes that focus groups are well suited to exploring topics and suggests that it is a common misconception that people will be inhibited in disclosing information. This did not seem to be a problem for the current study, as conducting focus group interviews strengthened the team and made the process potentially less stressful for them. This was very important given that I was an outsider, not having worked with them before.

For both of the focus group interviews, I followed a semi-structured interview schedule which was structured around staff views on AISI principles and potential changes in children's spontaneous communication. This is in accordance with Smith and Osborn (2008) who believe that semi-structured interviews are probably the best way to collect data as the researcher's questions can be modified depending on the response, compared to a structured interview where the researcher needs to stick very closely to the planned questions.

On a practical note, an external multi-directional microphone was used to ensure better sound quality and to capture the voice of people who spoke softly. This made transcription easier and faster. However, despite constant reminders to the interviewees about the importance of not speaking one above the other, this was not completely avoided.

It is interesting to note here how two of the main limitations of using focus group interviews – the lack of data generalisability and the possibility of *false consensus* (i.e. when some participants dominate the discussion at the expense of others' different views) – were addressed in this study. There was no intent for generalisation as focus groups were primarily used to reflect on the AISI principles and to validate video data. In addition, the PAR methodology of the study would not allow any generalisable conclusions to be drawn anyway regardless of the use of focus groups. Being aware of the possibility of *false consensus* (Litosseliti, 2003), on top of potential group and power dynamics due to the participants' different roles (e.g. teachers vs. TAs, parents vs professionals/academics), I encouraged the two TAs to speak more, by asking them to elaborate on short answers, giving them eye contact and using supportive body language (e.g. smiles, nodding).

The next section outlines how the intervention was developed using the action research cyclical process and the VIG principles of attuned interaction (Kennedy, 2011).

5.12 The development of the adult interactive style intervention

After having collected the pre-intervention video data for the children, the researcher analysed these to explore adult style and identify principles facilitating

90 *The research project*

children's spontaneous communication. These videos were then presented to the staff and I talked with them about how we could build together on these ideas. As a result of this presentation, an initial set of general principles was decided (Cycle 1). Then staff were asked to practise the decided principles for 4 weeks and think of further potential implications. During this period, I had been visiting the school three times a week and had short sessions with the staff to discuss any difficulties experienced and to explain the principles again if necessary (Cycle 2). When the practice period ended, a final set of principles was agreed and given the name AISI (Cycle 3). AISI consists of 13 general principles and 8 communicative opportunities thought to be effective in fostering spontaneous communication. The process of developing AISI is illustrated in Table 5.3. More details on the intervention itself but also its links to other interventions in the field of autism and special needs can be found in Chapters 3 and 4.

Video Interaction Guidance (VIG) (Kennedy, 2011) was adapted to train staff in using AISI principles. VIG is an intervention aiming to improve communication between parents and children, building on their existing skills. Parents are shown by the VIG guide edited video clips of interactions with their children during which the best aspects of the interaction and the key principles that work are highlighted. The aim of VIG is to improve interactions within a coaching relationship. Parents are encouraged to '*become as active as possible in experiencing and thinking about their own change*' (p. 31). More details on VIG can be found in 7.3 VIG. So VIG seemed very appropriate to this study and fitted very well with the PAR methodology. The researcher had to be clear not to deskill staff but to build on what they were doing already. By showing them positive video clips of what they were doing, while naming the principles as in AISI, it was hoped that they would be enabled to implement more of the principles.

The next section discusses some of the most significant ethical issues arising when conducting research with vulnerable children and young people. Additionally, ethics should be very carefully considered when the researcher is using a video camera in a real-world setting such as school or home (Heath et al., 2010).

5.13 Ethical considerations

Ethical issues are defined as '*rules of conduct*' (Robson, 2002, p. 65) which distinguish socially acceptable behaviours from socially unacceptable acts. In other words, ethics are concerned with protecting the well-being and interests of people taking part in the research and preventing them from harm (Lankshear and Knobel, 2004). Prior to the study onset, ethical approval was given by the University of Birmingham's Ethical Review Committee (Application for Ethical Review ERN_09-353). According to the University of Birmingham Code of Practice for Research, all data collected will be preserved and accessible for ten years after the completion of the study. Electronic and paper copy data are stored in my office and I will be the only person having access to these. After ten years, all electronic documents and videos will be deleted and all paper copy documents will be shredded. This study also complies with the ethical guidelines and requirements specified by the British Education Research Association (BERA) (2011).

Informed consent from the participants was sought. Two types of consent form were developed, one for the parents and one for the staff. These forms provided the participants with information about the researcher and the research focus and made it clear that they had the right to withdraw at any point if they wished (BERA, 2011). It would have been ideal to obtain the children's assent too as there is currently some debate as to who should be in charge of giving consent and often the issue of consent is opaque in projects which involve children with disabilities (Moore et al., 1998). However, due to the children's young age and their severe communication difficulties, it was not possible for them to give or deny assent. This meant that a parent or carer allowed or denied their participation. If a child showed frustration as a result of taking part in the study, they would be automatically withdrawn.

Ensuring participants' confidentiality is another very important ethical issue (Robson, 2002; Lankshear and Knobel, 2004; BERA, 2011). Special attention should be paid to confidentiality in small-scale studies like this one, in which the cases can be easily identified. For this reason, pseudonyms instead of participants' real names were used throughout the research (collecting and presenting data). An issue arose with how to protect participants' confidentiality when presenting videos at conferences and workshops. So an extra consent form was given to ask permission for using the videos for data dissemination and training purposes. Moreover, only video segments in which participants' names are not mentioned and the school's logo on the children's uniforms is not clear were used. The three raters who carried out the checks for inter-observer reliability on the videos were also asked to keep confidentiality. At this point, the difference between confidentiality and anonymity should be clarified. Confidentiality can be ensured when the researcher knows the participants' personal information but they do not disclose them whereas anonymity can only be claimed when the researcher is completely oblivious to the identity of the participants. Therefore, there are only few types of research in which participants' anonymity can be ensured (e.g. data collection via online questionnaires) but this was not the case in the current study.

In an attempt to comply with Moore's et al. (1998) point that disabled people should be placed at the centre of research which concerns them and this should be done at every stage of the project (e.g. from the conceptualisation to the dissemination of the findings), I consulted with two individuals with autism regarding the current study and the intervention. More precisely, I had the chance to present my work in progress at two student conferences at the University of Birmingham (Kossyvaki, 2010; Kossyvaki 2011) which were attended by two colleagues of mine (former PhD students) who are autistic. They both offered me the required support to ensure that what I was doing was in accordance with their aspirations and ethics.

Finally, it had to be demonstrated that children and staff would benefit from their participation. The research focus and methods were directly relevant to their work in the classroom. It was expected that developing a set of principles on adult style could have a use beyond the research in the school which would benefit both the staff and the pupils involved in the study. BERA (2011) requires researchers to act in the participants' best interests without adding extra work or stress on them. This was achieved by extending my presence at the school where I often had informal discussions with the staff to share their concerns. We often discussed concerns related to children who were not part of the study or topics beyond the scope of the study (e.g. sensory issues, eating difficulties, toileting). I always listened to what staff had to say and I advised them based on my personal experience and knowledge. When no recordings were being conducted, I took part in activities with the children to give them the chance to know me better and decrease staff's workload.

5.14 Reflection activities

- Think of a research topic within your setting which you can explore using a PAR methodology. Which are the main challenges you are going to face while conducting your study and reporting your findings?
- If video recordings seem to be the ideal data collection method in your setting, how are you going to address the practicalities and ethical issues (e.g. minimise the video effect, your role, type of activities to be recorded, size groups, length of the recordings, coding schedule)?
- What are the main difficulties you would anticipate if you decided to use focus group interviews to collect data in your setting?
- Ethics form a very important issue when working or doing research with young and vulnerable people. After having read the section on ethics, can you name a few things you would do to ensure that your work/research is ethical?

6 Analysing and discussing the findings

6.1 Introduction

This chapter presents the most significant findings of the AISI study described in the previous chapter. Quantitative data obtained from the video recordings are presented in tables and figures and qualitative data from the focus group interviews are presented as transcript extracts. The two strands of findings are linked and discussed in themes related to the research questions. This is the expectation of mixed-methods research: the provision of a fuller understanding of the phenomenon under study (Creswell and Tashakkori, 2007). Not all collected data for the study are presented in this chapter for a number of reasons: (i) cleaning the data and grouping some of them in meaningful sets is an integral part of the data analysis process, (ii) it is the researcher's job to protect the reader from 'information overload' and (iii) it is never feasible in a study to present all collected data. It should be noted here that for communicative functions and methods, only video data were considered in this chapter as it proved very difficult for staff to remember and comment on changes of these aspects of children's communication pre- and post-intervention during the focus group interviews.

The first section of this chapter presents the findings related to the frequency of children's spontaneous communication pre- and post-intervention. The second and third sections describe the effect of type of activity on children's spontaneous communication, and the children's communicative functions and methods respectively. The chapter closes with the findings on the implementation of AISI by the staff. The current study's findings are compared with those of similar studies, acknowledging the similarities and differences between them.

6.2 General notes on the analysis of the data

The six children of the sample were quite different in terms of their abilities. This heterogeneity is common among people with autism (Georgiades et al., 2013) as well as people with SPMLD (Male, 2015). Apart from the severity of autism and the level of learning difficulties, communication and language skills, children's personality, strengths, interests and challenges differentiate one child from another. There can also be differences in what staff do with children, even within the same session of an activity, which can potentially affect the degree to which the latter communicate. To address the two aforementioned points, children's data are presented for both the whole group and each individual. This is also the case for staff data as their personality, their role in the school and years of experience may have played a role in the extent staff used AISI and the principles they preferred.

Effect size (Cohen, 1988; Dancey and Reidy, 2002) and Excel spreadsheets were used to analyse the quantitative data coming from the videos. Effect size was used to calculate the clinical or practical significance of the data whereas Office Excel spreadsheets were used to find averages, ranges, standard deviations (SDs) and percentages as well as to create figures to present the data. NVivo (QSR International Pty Ltd, 2012) was used to analyse the qualitative data from the focus group interviews.

6.2.1 Effect size

No hypothesis test (e.g. t-tests, ANOVA) was used as the sample size was very small and this would not convey anything reliable about the population. Therefore, effect size calculations and, more precisely, Cohen's d was used instead. Effect Size (ES) was calculated to measure the size of the difference between pre- and post-intervention data. Cohen's d is the index used to show the size of the difference between group means in terms of SDs (Cohen, 1988). The exact formula used was as follows (Table 6.1):

Table 6.1 Formula to determine effect size

$$d = \frac{m_A - m_B}{\sigma}$$

d = ES index for t-tests of means in standard unit,

m_A, m_B = population means expressed in raw unit (original measurement), and

σ^* = the standard deviation of either population-since in this study they are assumed equal.

*The variance was assumed to be equal, as there was no reason to believe that the variance of the sample was different to the variance of the population. However, if one claims that the variance of the population is different to the variance of the sample and this is taken into consideration, the ES would be even higher.

Cohen's d gives the clinical or practical significance of the difference (Dancey and Reidy, 2002), rather than the statistical significance, which is used with larger samples (usually for $n \geq 30$). Sometimes researchers know the size of the effect they are looking for based on previous studies, and carry out research to prove or challenge it. However, if there is no previous research in the area, the researcher can fall back on the values Cohen (1988) proposes; Cohen's $d \geq 0.2$ shows a small ES, ≥ 0.5 shows a medium ES and ≥ 0.8 shows a large ES. The American Psychiatric Association (APA) recommends the use of ES calculations for every published work (Field, 2005). More and more international journals have either added ES to the statistical significance calculations or replaced them with ES (Cohen et al., 2007). If the ES is 0.8 or more, researchers can be confident that they have detected a real effect. If it is less than this, they may need to replicate the study, with more participants to increase the power (Field, 2005).

6.2.2 NVivo

For the analysis of the focus group interviews, NVivo (QSR International Pty Ltd, 2012), qualitative data analysis software, was used. The interviews were transcribed and then the researcher assigned codes to different thematic categories. These categories took the experiences and views of staff as a starting point rather than attempting to fit staff's experiences and views into fixed pre-determined categories.

6.3 Frequency of spontaneous communication

6.3.1 Video data

Children were filmed in 4 activities (i.e. sensory room, snack time, soft play and 1:1 work). Two hours of video recordings (i.e. 30 minutes per activity) were coded for each child pre- and post-intervention using CICCA. Video data are presented first for the whole group of the six children (see Table 6.2) and then for each child individually (see Figure 6.2).

Table 6.2 Total number of initiations, average (per 2 hours and per minute), SD and range across the four activities pre- and post-intervention for the six children and Cohen's d ES

Spontaneous initiations with adults	*Pre-intervention 0 month*	*Post-intervention 6 months*
Total initiations across four activities	631	1097
Average initiations for 2 hours	105	183
SD	53	40
Range	63–184	128–232
Average per minute initiation	0.9	1.5
Cohen's d		1.6 (large ES)

Total initiations for the six children increased from 631 pre-intervention to 1097 post-intervention and the mean numbers of initiations from 105 to 183. The SD decreased post-intervention (i.e. from 53 to 40) suggesting less variation among the children's spontaneous communication. To show the size of the difference between group means (i.e. pre- and post-intervention) Cohen's d was used. Cohen's d was 1.6 exceeding by far the 0.8 cut-off for a large ES. This suggests that the total initiations for the whole group significantly increased following the introduction of AISI (Figure 6.1).

96 *Analysing and discussing the findings*

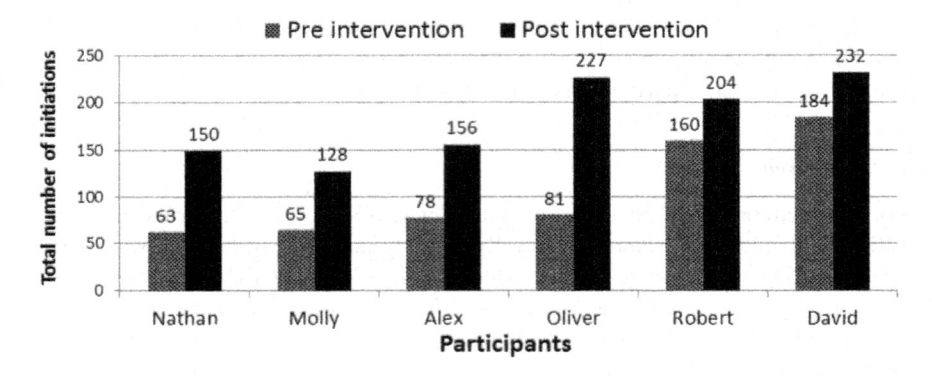

Figure 6.1 Total initiations pre- and post-intervention for each child across all four activities

All children significantly increased the frequency of their individual initiations. Nathan initiated the least communication pre-intervention and David the most, with three times as many as Nathan. Oliver showed the greatest increase post-intervention going from 81 to 227 initiations. Robert and David showed the smallest increase.

6.3.2 Focus group interview data

A focus group interview was conducted with the three members of staff post-intervention to get their views on children's progress and AISI. This section presents staff's views on the children's frequency of spontaneous communication.

Lorna and Emma both felt that David, and then Robert, were the children who increased their initiations the most, post-intervention. Lorna remarked that David

> . . . is using his communication much more effectively because we are more open to him initiating it. He is still difficult and it [AISI] hasn't taken away all the challenges but I do feel that there have been some really nice positive chatty bits with him where he has been relaxed with you and talked to you in a very functional way.

Emma added to this:

> His anxiety seems less [. . .] because he feels comfortable with you if you communicate with him. And he knows that he will make himself understood.

They all agreed that Robert changed a lot post-intervention and Emma mentioned that he became '*much more sociable and willing to initiate*'. The three staff considered Molly and Oliver the most difficult children to reach, arguing that they wanted to do things only on their own terms. Lorna remarked that Molly was definitely '*much more people orientated*' post-intervention and for Oliver that '*we are still tools in his environment but we are more useful to him now than we were before*'. She continued by saying that it was still unlikely for Molly and Oliver to engage in interactions purely for interactions' sake or enjoyment, and that their communication was still mainly instrumental, a medium to a particular end (e.g. requesting a toy or help). The three staff found it difficult to say whether Alex had changed, and argued that Nathan had not greatly changed, as he had always been '*reasonably sociable*'.

6.3.3 Discussion

It is hard to compare these findings with other studies, as to my knowledge there is no other study which followed a PAR methodology to measure the number of children's spontaneous communication before and after the implementation of an intervention focusing on adult interactive style. Moreover, in no other study were all children observed in a school setting over a six-month period across such a range of activities. Therefore, these findings will be compared to those of similar studies, whilst acknowledging their differences.

There are a number of reasons why findings from this study might not be similar to the findings of other studies with different sample characteristics and definitions of spontaneous communication being two of them. The present study found that the six children initiated communication on average 0.9 times per minute pre-intervention and 1.5 times per minute post-intervention. Both these figures are well above the 0.06 mean initiations per minute Stone and Caro-Martinez (1990) found and the 0.2 mean initiations per minute Chiang (2009) found. This discrepancy may be because the present study used a more liberal definition of spontaneity (i.e. all the child's attempts to communicate, which were not verbally prompted, were counted). Additionally, in Stone and Caro-Martinez's study, observations were not filmed, so some communicative acts might have been missed. Clifford et al. (2010) reported two initiations per minute for their sample, which is higher than the post-intervention initiations in the current study. However, their sample included children from the wider autism spectrum who were also slightly older than the sample in the current study (i.e. 48–73 months as opposed to 45–62 months).

The children in whom staff saw the greatest difference post-intervention were, interestingly, the two children who increased their initiations the least according to the video data (i.e. David and Robert). However, when their communicative functions and methods were analysed both these children decreased the times they initiated reject or used behaviours of concern (e.g. self-injurious behaviours, throwing tantrums) to communicate. This might be one reason why they were perceived as being more communicative, post-intervention. According to the video data, Oliver increased his initiations the most post-intervention (from 81 to 227) followed by Nathan (from 63 to 150). None of this was reiterated in the

98 *Analysing and discussing the findings*

focus group data in which Oliver's change was given little credit. This might have happened as Oliver's communication post-intervention was perceived as lower level initiation (e.g. using adults as tools). From staff discussions, it became clear that while they tended to give communicative intent to joint attention (e.g. comment, seek information) and social interaction acts (e.g. social games, express feelings), they did not often attribute communicative intent to behaviour regulation acts (e.g. request, reject). With regard to Nathan's spontaneous communication, staff did not notice the difference depicted in the video data, possibly because he was a passive child whose behaviour did not disrupt the classroom; often his subtle communicative initiations went unnoticed.

6.4 Effect of type of activity on spontaneous communication

6.4.1 Video data

Only five children were video recorded in the sensory room. David showed some intense CB (e.g. lashing out at people, damaging equipment) during his last pre-intervention session in the sensory room, perhaps due to hypersensitivity to visual and hearing stimuli. Staff did not feel that he would benefit from continuing the sensory room sessions and it was, therefore, decided that he would stop taking part in this activity.

Interestingly, the activities which showed greater clinical significance (i.e. large ES) post-intervention are not the same with the activity which increased the most when the total number of children's initiations is considered. When ES was calculated, the largest increase was found in snack time and 1:1 work (Cohen's d: snack =1.5 and 1:1 work = 0.97). However, when the total number of children's initiations was considered, the greatest increase was found during soft play. Table 6.3 presents data for the whole group.

Figure 6.2 shows the number of initiations per child in each activity. Oliver significantly increased his attempts to communicate in all four activities. Molly also increased her initiations in all four activities and David in all three activities he participated. Alex and Nathan increased their initiations in three out of the four activities and Robert increased his initiations in only two of the four activities.

6.4.2 Focus group interview data

During the post-intervention focus group interview staff were asked about the activities they had seen greater differences with regard to children's spontaneous communication. The three members of staff agreed that children's initiations increased the most in sensory room and soft play. This agrees with the findings when the total number of children's initiations was considered but goes against the Cohen's d findings. Staff beliefs that most initiations occurred in sensory room and soft play post-intervention might have also been related to some preconceptions they had for the other two activities. For example, the three members

Table 6.3 Total number of initiations, average initiations per 2 hours across the four activities pre- and post-intervention for the six children and Cohen's d effect size

Activities	Spontaneous initiations	Pre-intervention	Post-intervention
Sensory room*	Total initiations	137	225
	Average initiations for 2 hours	38	45
	Cohen's d		0.91 (large ES)
Snack time	Total initiations	100	199
	Average initiations for 2 hours	17	33
	Cohen's d		1.5 (large ES)
Soft play	Total initiations	209	376
	Average initiations for 2 hours	35	63
	Cohen's d		0.76 (medium ES)
1:1 work	Total initiations	186	297
	Average initiations for 2 hours	31	50
	Cohen's d		0.97 (large ES)

*Only five children were coded for sensory room.

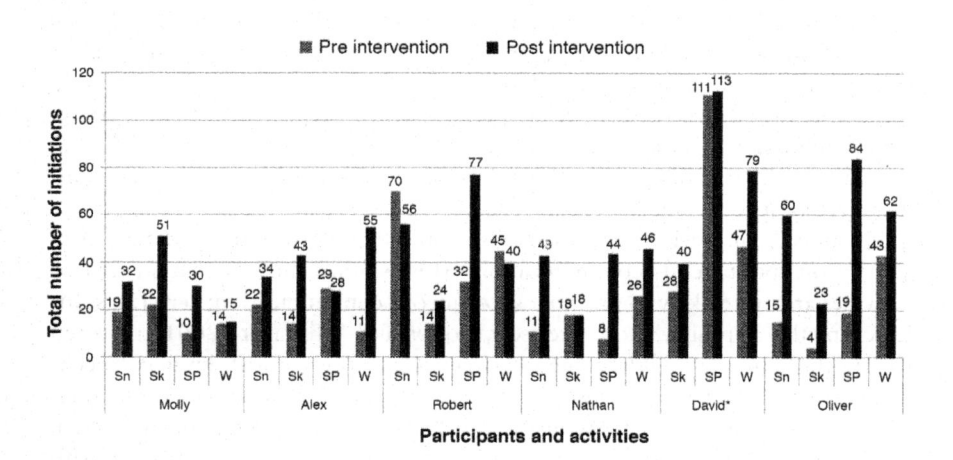

Figure 6.2 Number of initiations for each of the six children in each of the four activities pre- and post-intervention

* David did not participate in sensory room.

** Sn = sensory room, Sk = snack time, SP = soft play and W = 1:1 work.

of staff acknowledged that in work sessions, initiations were not easy. Lorna explained that by saying:

> [In 1:1 work] there is an element of adult direction that we can't get away from. So there is less opportunity for child initiations.

Regarding snack time, none of the staff thought that children significantly increased their initiations. Interestingly enough, snack time was the activity with the largest ES, post-intervention.

6.4.3 Discussion

The findings with regard to activity effect were contradictory. According to the video data, the activities which had the largest ES post-intervention (i.e. snack time and 1:1 work) were not the same with the activity which increased the most in terms of the total number of children's initiations (i.e. soft play). This finding suggests that the majority of the children increased their initiations in snack time and 1:1 work but that there were a few children who greatly increased their initiations in soft play. The fact that only five children were video recorded in the sensory room should account for the fact that the total number of initiations in the sensory room was so much lower than the initiations in the soft play despite their similar nature and structure. One explanation for the larger ESs for snack time and 1:1 work might relate to the fact that the children enjoyed the structure and predictability of these activities. These two elements are likely to make activities highly motivating for children with autism (Mesibov et al., 1997; Prizant et al., 2006). In the current study, almost all children enjoyed snack time and most of them also liked doing their work. On the other hand, in the sensory room and soft play, children often needed skills such as anticipation, turn-taking, physical proximity, reading other people's minds to keep the interaction going, which children with autism often find difficult (Baron-Cohen, 1995; Frith, 2003; Bogdashina, 2003). Therefore, this might have affected the spontaneous communication of some children.

Findings from previous studies are also contradictory in terms of the effect of activity on spontaneous communication. Most studies showed that structured activities are more likely to promote spontaneous communication; very few studies claim the opposite. More precisely, Potter and Whittaker (2001) reported that in their sample (children aged between 2 and 6 years with limited speech) unstructured activities such burst and pause, rough and tumble games and imitation of the children were more likely to promote spontaneous communication. On the other hand, O' Reilly et al. (2005) found that a 12-year-old student with autism, learning difficulties and no speech initiated the most communication during academic activities. Similarly, Chiang (2008a) reported that autistic children and pre-adolescents (age range from 3.4 to 16.2 years, with limited or no speech) were likely to initiate the highest level of communication (i.e. caused by the least intrusive prompts such as natural cues) during lunchtime without giving very precise information on the level of structure the activity involved. In a later study, Chiang (2009) reported that participants in her sample (aged between 2.2 and 16.2 years, with limited or no speech) were more likely to initiate communication in academic activities. Overall, a recurring issue which should be addressed in future studies regarding the activity effect on children's spontaneous communication is the need for clearer definitions of what exactly each activity entails; the same activity may greatly vary from one setting or research project to another.

6.5 Communicative functions and methods

6.5.1 A note on the analysis of the video data on functions and methods using communication in children with autism

CICCA was used to code the frequency of children's initiations alongside the functions their initiations served and the methods they used. Three issues arose when coding communicative functions and methods, and a decision had to be made for each one of them.

- When a child used the same method repetitively for the same function (e.g. constantly pushing away the adult's hand to protest), the method was coded as one occurrence. A five-second-rule was put in place and if the child continued to use the same method for the same purpose after 5 seconds, a second occurrence was recorded.
- When a child used more than one method at the same time to serve the same function (e.g. using eye contact, manipulating the adult's hand and uttering a single word to request an object), all the different methods were coded under the relevant function.
- When a child's behaviour could be coded as serving more than one function (e.g. touching the adult to request a social game or express feelings), only the dominant function had to be coded. This decision can be argued against but it simplified the calculations concerned with the frequency of the communicative acts.

6.5.2 Communicative functions

6.5.2.1 Video data

The communicative functions were split into the three broad categories of behaviour regulation (i.e. requesting and rejecting or protesting), joint attention (i.e. commenting or giving information and seeking information) and social interaction (i.e. expressing feelings, seeking attention, seeking approval, social routines and social games). Cohen's d was calculated to measure the size of the difference between group means in terms of standard deviation. Requesting was the function which showed the largest ES (Cohen's d = 1.67), post-intervention followed by initiating social games (Cohen's d = 1.48), seeking attention (Cohen's d = 0.95) and expressing feelings (Cohen's d = 0.88). This means that the frequency of the aforementioned functions increased for the majority of the children in the sample. It is interesting to note here that Cohen's d showed large ES only for behaviour regulation and social interaction functions. Cohen's d as well as the total number of times each function appeared was coded. Average, range and percentages are presented in Table 6.4.

The function that showed the most increase when the total number of children's initiations was considered was also requesting (i.e. from a total of 286 to 460). Protests considerably increased for two of the children, Alex and Oliver, while Robert decreased his protests, which were very frequent pre-intervention. The frequency, with which children expressed feelings, considerably increased post-intervention (from a total of 133 to 264). The increase in expressing feelings for Oliver was great (i.e. from 13 times pre-intervention to 84 post-intervention). Four children increased their initiation of social games while the occurrence of social routine acts dropped post-intervention (the vast majority of which were initiated by David). Commenting also showed an increase post-intervention. This was largely down to one child, David, who initiated 31 of the total 32 comments pre-intervention and 72 of the total 74 comments post-intervention. None of the children sought information pre-intervention but David did so, post-intervention; he initiated 15 of the total 16 seeking information acts. It should also be noted here that the children initiated fewer social routines post-intervention.

6.5.2.2 Discussion

Requesting was found to be the most commonly used communicative function reflecting the results of previous studies. Chiang and Lin (2008) and Chiang (2009), in their studies of 34 autistic children and young adults with limited speech (aged between 2.2 and 16.2 years), reported that request was the most frequent function. Stone and Caro-Martinez (1990) in their study of 30 children with autism (aged between 4 and 13 years) found that requesting was the third most common communicative function accounting for 22% of total communication in their sample. The fact that the children in Stone and Caro-Martinez's study (1990) were considerably older than the children of the current study may account for fewer occurrences of requesting and more occurrences of functions pertaining to social interaction (i.e. seeking attention and initiating social routines).

In the current study, protests did increase post-intervention but the increase was not significant as this was not evident across all participants. Several studies found that both requesting and rejecting were equally frequent. For example, Potter and Whittaker (2001) found that the children in their sample mainly communicated to request and reject or protest. Their sample was very similar to the sample of the present study (e.g. young children with autism – aged between 2 and 6 years – with minimal or no speech) but larger (n = 18). Similarly, Agius's (2009) found that requests and protests were the most common functions in her

Table 6.4 Total number of times the six children showed each of the communicative functions, average per two hrs, range, percentage pre- and post-intervention and Cohen's d effect size

Communicative functions	Pre-intervention				Post-intervention				Cohen's d
	Total numbers	Average per 2 hrs	Range	Percentage	Total numbers	Average per 2 hrs	Range	Percentage	
Behaviour regulation									
Request	286	48	21–81	45	460	77	62–99	42	**1.67***
Reject	155	26	11–59	25	200	33	12–65	18	0.38
Joint attention									
Comment	32	5	0–31	5	74	12	0–72	7	0.31
Seek information	0	0	N/A	0	16	3	0–15	2	0.62
Social interaction									
Express feelings	133	22	6–48	21	264	44	11–84	24	**0.88***
Seek attention	9	2	0–4	2	26	4	0–11	2	**0.95***
Seek approval	2	0	0–1	0	5	1	0–2	0	0.64
Social routines	7	1	0–7	1	2	0	0–1	0	–0.32
Social games	7	1	0–2	1	50	8	0–15	5	**1.48***

* Cohen's d ≥ 0.8 = large ES.

sample of 11 non-verbal children with autism (aged between 3 and 5:06 years) whom she observed during meal times at school and at home.

Most children increased their expression of feelings. This finding suggests that the introduction of AISI might have made them more aware of the adults. Few naturalistic studies have included the function of expressing feelings. In Stone and Caro-Martinez's (1990) study this function was coded only four times. This might have happened for two reasons. Firstly, the fact that the observations were not video recorded may have led to missed occurrences of feelings being expressed in unconventional ways. This is common in people with autism (Mesibov et al., 1997; Freeman et al., 2002). Secondly, the widespread belief at this time (i.e. 1990s) that children with autism rarely express feelings (Dawson et al., 1990; Ozonoff et al., 1990) may have biased the observers. A more recent study by Freeman et al. (2002) challenges this finding, reporting that the most frequent function 36 students with autism (aged from 6 to 24 years) showed while interacting with adults was expressing feelings. It should be noted here that these students were filmed during unstructured social interactions with familiar adults, which possibly gave them more opportunities to express their feelings.

Initiating social games was increased for four of the six children post-intervention. The two children who did not increase this function were Molly and Oliver, who were described by their teacher in the focus group interview as '*object- rather than people-orientated*'. Possibly children with these characteristics prefer to initiate communication to get an object rather than an interactive game. It should be also noted here that in some studies (e.g. Chiang and Lin, 2008; Chiang, 2009), social games were not explored as a separate function but they were included in the category of requesting.

Initiating social routines was coded few times in the present study; the frequency dropped post-intervention. David was almost the only child who initiated social routines and the drop post-intervention might be explained by the fact that he possibly replaced these learnt behaviours (mainly say '*hello*') by more meaningful comments (e.g. pointing to and naming objects in his environment/peers).

Both commenting and seeking information were coded few times in this study, mainly for David. This is more or less depicted in Stone and Caro-Martinez's (1990) study in which commenting was coded 41 times accounting for 15% of the total initiations whereas seeking information was coded only 7 times accounting for 3% of the total initiations. However, these functions are not often measured in relevant studies. For example, neither Agius (2009) nor Chiang (2009) coded the seeking information function.

It is useful to consider these findings within the theory of social communication development. Bruner (1981) describes three communicative functions that emerge prior to the onset of speech in infants with TD, namely behaviour regulation, joint attention and social interaction. Although TD children acquire the three functions synchronously, children with autism often develop one function at a time (Wetherby, 1986). Behaviour regulation is the first communicative function that autistic children acquire, followed by social interaction and then joint attention (Wetherby, 1986). In the present study, requests, within the behaviour regulation category, increased the most. Initiating social games, seeking attention and expressing feelings (within the social interaction category) had a large ES, whereas joint attention behaviours were observed only a few times and mainly in David, the verbal child of the sample.

6.5.3 Communicative methods

6.5.3.1 Video data

The communicative methods coded from the video data were split into two broad categories, pre-symbolic and symbolic. From the pre-symbolic methods, the following 5 had a large ES (i.e. their frequency increased for the majority of the sample post-intervention): proximity/touch (Cohen's d = 2.35), re-enactments (Cohen's d = 1.47) simple motor actions (Cohen's d = 1.01), smile (Cohen's d = 0.98) and vocalisations (Cohen's d = 0.97). From the symbolic methods, two had a large ES. These are objects of reference (Cohen's d = 1.22) and symbols/pictures (Cohen's d = 0.96). Cohen's d for each method are presented in Table 6.5.

Simple motor actions were coded the greatest number of times both pre- and post-intervention, with vocalisations/babbling being the second most frequently coded method post-intervention. Additionally, proximity/touch, re-enactments and use of pictures and symbols increased for all six children post-intervention, whereas smiles, laughter and eye contact increased for five of the six children of the sample. CB was the only communicative method which decreased post-intervention (i.e. from 70 times pre-intervention to 51 times post-intervention). The total number of times each method was coded, average, range and percentages are presented in Table 6.5.

6.5.3.2 Discussion

Very few studies explored in detail the communicative methods that children with autism use (e.g. Agius, 2009). Most of them classified the methods in broader categories (e.g. unaided AAC, aided AAC and speech for Chiang and Lin, 2008; Chiang, 2009 and motoric acts, speech, vocalisations and gestures for Stone and Caro-Martinez, 1990) and gave results for these. Alternatively, others (Potter and Whittaker, 2001) did not provide a list with all the communicative methods which were researched but only presented the methods which were more frequently observed.

The fact that proximity/touch, re-enactments, simple motor actions, smile and vocalisations had a large ES suggests that the six children were more aware of the adults' presence post-intervention. More specifically, the increase in smiles may further mean that children enjoyed more being with adults post-intervention.

When the total number of children's initiations was considered, simple motor actions were the method which increased the most. This reflects to a certain extent the findings of previous studies. Stone and Caro-Martinez (1990) found that motoric acts were the most frequently used communicative method in their

Table 6.5 Total number of times the six children used each of the communicative methods, average per two hrs, range, percentage pre- and post-intervention and Cohen's d effect size

Communicative methods	Pre-intervention				Post-intervention				Cohen's d
	Total number	Average per 2 hrs	Range	Percentage	Total number	Average per 2 hrs	Range	Percentage	
Pre-symbolic methods									
Challenging behaviour	70	12	2-35	7	51	9	3-18	3	-0.33
Eye contact	74	12	0-33	8	134	22	3-48	8	0.64
Laugh	61	10	0-31	6	135	23	0-63	8	0.66
Point	18	3	0-16	2	24	4	0-24	1	0.12
Proximity/touch	49	8	1-20	5	136	23	13-29	8	**2.35***
Re-enactments	20	3	0-7	2	66	11	2-21	4	**1.47***
Simple motor actions	303	51	32-66	32	488	81	48-161	29	**1.01***
Smile	47	8	0-20	5	87	15	9-25	5	**0.98***
Vocalisations/babbling	159	27	15-45	17	267	45	13-72	16	**0.97***
Symbolic methods									
Echolalia (IM+DE)	4	1	0-4	0	18	2	0-10	1	0.65
Object of reference	2	0	0-1	0	8	1	0-3	0	**1.22***
Single words	97	16	0-89	10	159	27	0-128	9	0.24
Symbols/pictures	37	6	3-13	4	92	15	4-34	6	**0.96***
Word combinations	12	2	0-11	1	16	3	0-14	1	0.13

* Cohen's d ≥ 0.8 = large ES.

study accounting for 52% of the total children's spontaneous communication. Vocalisations were the second method to increase in terms of total initiations. The frequency with which vocalisations were coded in this study (16% of total initiations) concurs with Stone and Caro-Martinez's (1990) study in which the occurrence of vocalisations was 16% of the total spontaneous communication and it is also comparable to the 22% figure Agius (2009) found in her study, in which vocalisations was the most frequent communicative method.

Proximity/touch accounted, in the current study, for 8% of the total communication post-intervention. Agius (2009) investigated touch alone, and this was coded for only 0.6% of the total communication. However, the method of reaching out in her study was very similar to how proximity was defined in the current study (i.e. the child either approaches a person by extending arms, touching or hugging them or bringing an object towards the direction of another person). Reaching out was coded for 7% of the communication acts in the Agius's study which when added to the percentage coded for touch, gives a total of around 8%.

In the current study, the average smile per child was 15 post-intervention and the average number of laughs was 23. The findings are similar to Agius's (2009) study in terms of smiles but not for laughs. In her sample, the average number of smiles was 10, but the average times of laughs was 6. A possible explanation as to why children in the present study tended to laugh more than in Agius's sample might be the different activities in which the children were observed. In the present study, children were video recorded in places such as sensory room and soft play, which are more likely to promote laughter as a result of interactive games such as burst and pause and peek-a-boo. On the contrary, meal times, in which the children in Agius's study were video recorded, are not as likely to promote laughter.

With regard to eye contact, the findings of the current study are not very similar to that of previous studies. In Agius's (2009) study, the average use of eye contact was 31 times accounting for 16% of the total children's communication. This is above the average 22 times eye contact was coded for the present study accounting for 8% of total communication. This difference could be attributed to the stricter definition of eye contact used in this study (i.e. the child had to look directly into another's person's eyes or face for at least 2 consecutive seconds).

The decrease in CB, found in this study, concurs with many researchers arguing that as communication improves, the incidence of CB reduces (Sigafoos, 2000; Whitaker et al., 2001; Clements, 2005). However, CB is coded more frequently in the current study than in other studies. Occurrences of CB account for 3% of the total children's communication even post-intervention. This figure is above the 1% coded in Agius's (2009) study. It should be noted here though that Agius used a stricter definition of CB excluding behaviours such as crying, kicking, hitting, shouting and screaming, which were coded as CB in the present study.

All children, with the exception of David, increased their use of symbols or pictures post-intervention. The average number of times they used these was 15 (as opposed to 6 pre-intervention). Both these figures are well above the once per 120 minutes on average found by Chiang (2009). This might have happened as the present study was conducted in an autism specialist school in which symbols and pictures were the main communicative method used. Chiang's (2009) study included children and young adults from a variety of naturalistic settings (e.g. autism specialist schools, generic special schools, mainstream schools and children's homes) and the preferred communicative method in each one of these is not known. Other methods (e.g. sign language, Makaton, speech) could have been used instead.

6.6 Implementation of AISI

6.6.1 Video data

To code staff videos, AISCC was used. Every time an AISI principle was observed, an occurrence was coded. A five-second-rule was put in place meaning that if staff continued to use the same AISI principle for more than five seconds, a second occurrence was recorded. The number of times staff used the AISI principles pre- and post-intervention was measured using the video recordings to show the extent to which staff implemented the intervention as a whole (see Figure 6.3). ES Cohen's d was also calculated to give the clinical significance of the difference between pre- and post-intervention use of AISI. Then the 4 principles each staff used the most, post-intervention are presented in Figure 6.4. Last but not least, Table 6.6 shows the times each principle was used, in an effort to see which of the principles were more useful and applicable for the children and the staff of the study. Cohen's d was also calculated to show the clinical significance of the pre- and post-intervention difference for each principle.

All three staff significantly increased their use of AISI principles post-intervention. Emma increased the use of AISI principles the most, followed by Lorna and Amber. Emma used AISI the least pre-intervention and the most

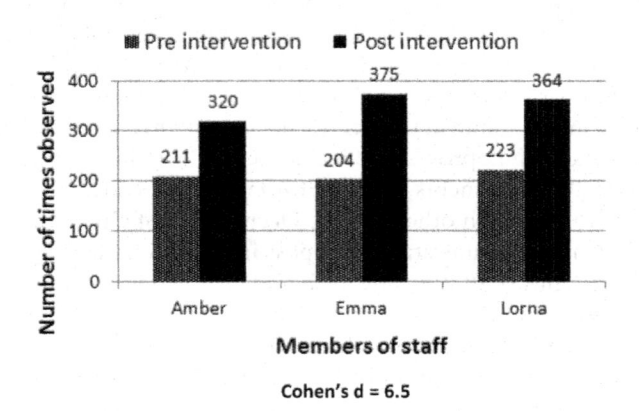

Figure 6.3 Total number of times each member of staff used AISI principles pre- and post-intervention

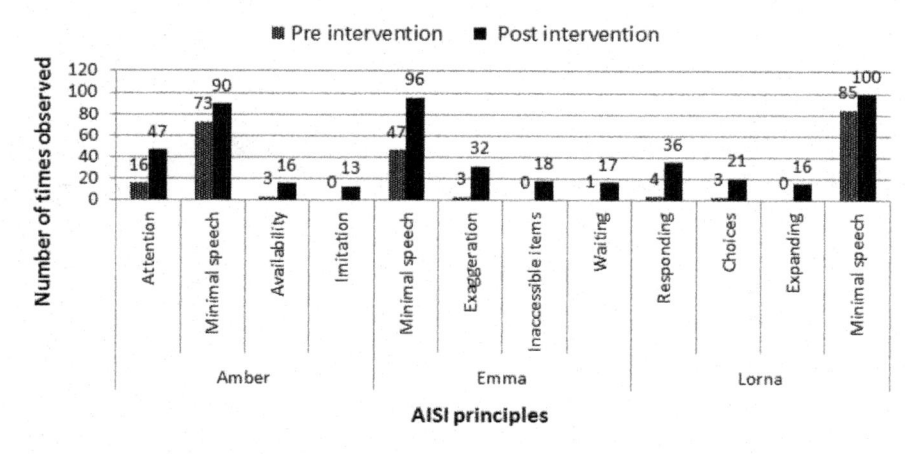

Figure 6.4 The four AISI principles each member of staff increased the most

post-intervention. The high starting point for the three members of staff which was the result of building on their existing good practice in order to develop AISI should also be noted here.

According to the video data, the use of minimal speech is the only common principle among the four which the three members of staff increased the most.

Fourteen of the 21 AISI principles (10 general principles and 4 communicative opportunities) had a large ES post-intervention meaning that their use significantly increased for the three members of staff. Imitation was the principle which had by far the greatest clinical significance, post-intervention (Cohen's d = 9.88) followed by using minimal speech (Cohen's d = 1.90), responding to all the child's communicative attempts (Cohen's d = 1.83) and establishing proximity (Cohen's d = 1.43). With regard to communicative opportunities, offering choices (Cohen's d = 1.53), stopping part way (Cohen's d = 1.3), giving small portions (Cohen's d = 1.05) and making items inaccessible (Cohen's d = 0.87) had a large ES post-intervention.

When considering the total number of times each AISI principle was used, using minimal speech is coded the most post-intervention (286 times) followed by using non-verbal cues (212 times). Gaining the child's attention and responding to all their communicative attempts were also widely coded post-intervention (66 times each).

6.6.2 Focus group data

Two focus group interviews were conducted with the three staff regarding developing and evaluating AISI (Cycle 3: development of the intervention and post-intervention). The aim of the first focus group interview was to decide on the final

Table 6.6 Total number of times the three staff implemented each of the AISI principles, average, range, percentage pre- and post-intervention and Cohen's d effect size

AISI principles	Pre-intervention				Post-intervention				Cohen's d
	Total number	Average	Range	Percentage	Total number	Average	Range	Percentage	
General principles									
Gain child's attention	39	13	1–22	6	66	22	4–47	6	0.51
Establish proximity	21	7	2–14	3	41	14	12–16	4	1.43*
Show availability	39	13	3–25	6	75	25	16–41	7	0.95*
Wait for initiations	6	2	0–5	1	23	8	1–17	2	0.92*
Respond to communicative attempts	15	5	1–10	2	66	22	13–36	6	1.83*
Assign meaning to random actions or sounds	34	11	9–13	5	55	18	12–27	5	1.23*
Imitate the child	4	1	0–2	0.6	36	12	11–13	3	9.88*
Follow child's focus of attention	27	9	3–20	4	26	9	8–10	2	-0.05
Use exaggerated pitch, facial expression, gestures and body language	19	6	3–8	3	49	16	5–32	5	0.99*
Use minimal speech	205	68	47–73	32	286	95	90–100	27	1.90*
Provide time	0	0	N/A	0	10	3	0–8	1	1.13*
Expand on child's communicative attempts	1	0	0–1	0.2	21	7	1–16	2	1.18*
Use non-verbal cues	208	69	60–85	33	212	71	54–84	20	0.09

Communicative opportunities

Offer choices	11	4	3–5	2	39	13	4–21	4	**1.53***
Stop part way	2	1	0–1	0	15	5	0–9	1	**1.3***
Give small portions	1	0	0–1	0	15	5	0–12	1	**1.05***
Make items inaccessible	6	2	0–6	1	24	8	0–8	2	**0.87***
Give materials they will need help with	0	0	N/A	0	0	0	N/A	0	0
Contradict expectations	0	0	N/A	0	0	0	N/A	0	0
Give non-preferred items	0	0	N/A	0	0	0	N/A	0	0
'Forget' something vital	0	0	N/A	0	0	0	N/A	0	0

* Cohen's d ≥ 0.8 = large ES.

112 *Analysing and discussing the findings*

set of the AISI principles after a month of practising them (e.g. explore potential difficulties in understanding and implementing AISI, discuss first changes seen in children) whereas the second focus group interview attempted to get the staff's views on the effectiveness of each principle and their impact on the children. This section aim to explore staff's views on AISI principles.

6.6.2.1 General principles

All three staff reported that using non-verbal cues and minimal speech were the two most effective and easily implemented AISI general principles. However, Amber stated that using minimal speech does not come without effort, as it goes against the personality of some people:

> I am finding it easier than I used to. Because I made a real effort not to say too much hopefully and I think I've improved with that.

Both Emma and Lorna agreed that minimal speech is a subjective issue and it needs to be explained in detail to the staff, with specific examples provided.

The principles of showing availability and waiting for initiations also arose during the focus group interviews. Specifically, Lorna reported that showing availability can be '*a good way of reducing children's prompt dependence*'. She also went on to describe how this can be done effectively:

> You take your hand away but you leave it in sight [. . .] and you just wait for them [the children] to take it.

As far as waiting for initiations is concerned, the two TAs were concerned that this might be perceived by other staff as laziness or lack of creativity. However, Amber admitted that she felt more confident about using it post-intervention:

> I was probably too eager to anticipate what the children wanted and I feel I benefitted from that principle.

Responding to all the child's communicative attempts was another AISI principle further explored during the focus group interviews. Emma said that responding to all the child's communicative attempts was an effective and important principle which was becoming easier with time and practice. She mentioned the example of Alex who

> sometimes does not know that we've understood him and so he still tries to communicate what it is he wants to do. But the answer is no.

Despite having used most AISI principles to a great extent as the video data show and staff admits during the focus group interviews, staff also highlighted some issues which should be taken into consideration before using AISI principles with children of similar abilities to the children of the sample. For example, imitation was widely used by the staff but this was not always done with great confidence. They reported that Robert and Molly responded best to being imitated, with Robert significantly increasing his eye contact when being imitated. Amber recalled a session with him in which imitation worked very well:

> When he was in the sensory room he was lying on his back and he had his legs up and I just copied him and he started looking at me. Then he got one of the cushions and he put his head on it and then I got a cushion and I put my head on it. We were facing each other and I felt we had some moments of communication.

Lorna found using exaggerated pitch, facial expressions, gestures and body language difficult to implement in practice due to embarrassment. She admitted:

> That's easy [. . .] as long as nobody is watching you.

Amber mentioned that gaining the child's attention can be difficult to achieve for certain children or under certain circumstances, while Lorna mentioned the difficulty of establishing appropriate proximity or touch in a classroom environment:

> I think this is quite hard to implement because it's fine if you are in a situation where you can back off, wait for them and get the appropriate proximity. But when you are in the middle of doing things [. . .]. For David, for example, appropriate proximity would be him over there and us somewhere else, in another room probably. And Robert quite often gets upset when you are too close to him but you need to be close to him to stop him from hurting himself. So I think in some respects that's quite hard.

Amber voiced her concerns about respecting the sensory hypersensitivities some children experience when using this principle: '*There are times that I feel we are invading their space*'.

During focus group interviews, staff did not express any strong views on the effectiveness of following the child's lead, assigning meaning to their random actions or sounds, expanding on their communicative attempts and providing time for them to process the given information. These general AISI principles appeared to be more complicated for them. For example, staff mentioned being often confused about the difference between following the child's lead and imitating them as well as waiting for them to initiate and provide them time to process given information. Moreover, they were afraid of becoming overbearing by assigning meaning to many of the child's unintentional communicative attempts and Amber reported uncertainty on how to expand on the child's communication.

6.6.2.2 Communicative opportunities

Offering choices was used a lot post-intervention and was considered one of the easiest principles to understand and implement. Staff used this principle extensively during 1:1 work time. More precisely, children could choose the order of the activities which were placed in their workboxes. For children who needed more support in order to make choices, staff often physically picked up two activities at a time and showed them to the child until the latter intentionally chose one. If this did not happen, staff assumed that the child wanted to work first on the activity they looked at or touched by chance trying to teach them intentionally.

The three members of staff considered giving small portions of food or drink very effective with some children but they also thought that it was problematic with some other. The problem was mainly with children who have rigid thinking which is a common characteristic among individuals with autism (APA, 2013). Lorna mentioned the example of Robert and Oliver who wanted their whole biscuit. If the biscuit was cut into smaller pieces, they would not eat it. A possible explanation Lorna gave for this was that for their level of understanding a piece of biscuit on their plate does not look as the whole biscuit in the photo on their communication board. This was not an issue for other snacks such as fruits, crisps and chocolate or drinks, where quantities were less precise in the picture.

The three members of staff had difficulty in stopping part way through an activity. They mentioned that this was due to the children's limited concentration span which sometimes led to their walking off as soon as the adult paused. Amber expressed further concerns about using this principle in the classroom with children who are hard to engage or get easily frustrated. She argued:

> I need to be engaged with Alex especially or else he just walks off and then I've got to get him back to the table, which is not easy. I feel that this is not the right thing for Alex, at least in the classroom. But it does work in sensory room or soft play. I don't do it when I am too focused on the table because I feel I have such a job getting him at the place I want him to be. I just feel that doing this would wind him up.

Making items inaccessible was not broadly used by the staff as they were afraid that '*[. . .] children [. . .] would just get extremely angry or lose interest*'. This principle worked more effectively when the adult put away a toy the child was currently playing with instead of a child's favourite toy, which was out of their focus of attention at the specific moment. Staff had to be quick and give the toy back to the child as soon as they asked for it to prevent confusion and upset.

Additionally, there were some reservations about giving the child materials they would need help with. Lorna said:

> Some children become quite motoric in that. [. . .]. Although they know how to do it they systematically take your hand to do it because they see that being part of the activity. For example, Nathan has a tendency to do that. [. . .] It's

not asking for help, it's a learnt sequence of events. And you have to watch that because it's difficult to spot. It looks like they are asking for help but they are not. Because they don't need help, they can do it themselves.

The three staff also reported some issues while contradicting the child's expectation. More specifically, Lorna said:

[In previous years] with more able children I've put sometimes the days of the week up and I put one upside down or we looked at the book and put it upside down. We've done it when we've had a group of verbal children. [. . .] If I start now putting them upside down, many children will start putting them upside down. That's a tricky one. I can see the usefulness of it with certain children here. Maybe with David. David drives cars around; he knows which way they go so we can do something with this. We don't want to provide the others with an unhelpful work model, do we?

Staff were not always comfortable using the principle of giving children non-preferred items. However, Emma admitted having seen this principle working with David:

When you give him the snack board with only fruit pictures on it, which isn't a preferred item to him, he will ask for the preferred item [i.e. biscuits].

Lorna then commented that this principle is more effective for

children who are further down the line with their communication skills [. . .] and much more verbal. You could do stuff like that with them because they could cope with that and then ask you what they want.

An effective way of using the principle of 'forgetting' something vital was mentioned by Lorna:

Not pulling their coats' zip up. I've done this with David and he asked for the zip to be done up. That's actually a really positive communication from him rather than lying on the floor and laughing at you.

However, Lorna also highlighted potential problems arising from using this principle. She said:

You could trigger a problem with behaviour if you get them the car mat out forgetting to give them the cars. Because if you got them to ask for something, it is an achievement in itself. If you then forget parts of it, it seems a bit cruel. They've got to ask for parts of it again and most of our children do not have this understanding[. . .] We have to do it only with the children that they can cope with it such as David or Nathan, possibly, not the others.

Amber maintained that another difficulty with this principle is that some children

> [. . .] may get upset since by giving a picture which in the past was bringing them the whole set of toys now will bring them only the garage without the cars or only the train without the man to put on.

6.6.3 Discussion

The current study found that teaching staff were able to change their interactive style by reflecting and building on their existing good practice. Video data showed that all three members of staff changed their interactive style significantly. When use of AISI was considered, the three staff increased the number of times they used AISI by at least 100. The fact that the 4 principles each staff member increased their use of most were different (with the exception of the principle of minimal speech) suggests that they used a wide range of AISI principles post-intervention. The clinical significance of the difference between pre- and post-intervention data for the whole AISI was high (Cohen's d = 6.5) meaning that the three staff increased a lot the number of times they used most principles post-intervention. Overall, there were a number of principles which staff considered most effective, and could use fairly easily in their everyday practice. Certain other principles needed to be further considered and explored before being put in place. The children's characteristics (e.g. young, non-verbal or with limited speech, SLD/PMLD) as well as some features related to staff (e.g. personality, professional status, years of experience and self-confidence levels) played a role in the extent each principle was used post-intervention. During focus group interviews, staff tended to show more concerns about communicative opportunities than general principles. Using non-verbal cues, minimal speech, and offering choices were the three principles reported to be more widely applied. This might be accounted for by the fact that these three principles were already core elements of staff practice, with AISI reminding them of their importance and giving them further practically-orientated ideas.

Literature extensively supports the use of minimal speech and non-verbal cues when interacting with people with autism; too much speech is likely to confuse and possibly disengage them from their social environment (Klin, 1991). One common mistake that NT people make is to overestimate how much speech individuals with autism understand (Potter and Whittaker, 2001), as the latter tend to use situational cues to make sense of the environment and this can mask their difficulties with language. Even people with extensive expressive vocabularies may have limited ability to process other people's speech (Mesibov, 2007). Potter and Whittaker (2001) explored the connection between minimal speech and spontaneous communication and found that when staff adopted a minimal speech approach consisting of no more than two relevant concrete words, the children increased their spontaneous communication. Similarly, Ingersoll (2011) trained adults to use simplified language and this spurred more initiations and more precisely comments by the children. When using non-verbal cues, adults are likely to speak slowly emphasising key words and giving the child more time to take in the information. The importance of this principle is reflected in a study conducted by Doussard-Roosevelt et al. (2003) who examined the interactions of 9 mothers with their autistic children and noticed that the children were more engaged when non-verbal behaviours were employed.

Imitation was the principle which had the largest ES (i.e. its use significantly increased for the three members of staff post-intervention). However, focus group interviews revealed that staff were still somewhat uncomfortable using this principle. The reason behind staff's hesitancy imitating the children might lie in EIBI theories (Richman, 2001; James and Fletcher, 2011) which claim that mirroring a child's movements may encourage 'inappropriate' behaviours. However, this fear looks unrealistic and of secondary importance when compared to teaching a child to become a competent communicator. Another reason possibly explaining staff's reluctance to imitate children can be Caldwell's (2006) point that mere copying is inadequate and in some cases insulting if done in an inflexible and mechanic way.

The principle of responding to all the child's signals for communication also substantially increased for the three members of staff. This specific principle worked very well for David, the only verbal child, who decreased his behaviours of concern when staff started responding to all his communicative attempts. The importance of using this principle is highly promoted in the literature as it makes the child feel that their communication gets results (Greenspan and Wieder, 1998; Nind and Hewett, 2001; Rogers and Dawson, 2010). This is another point where AISI differs from some EIBI interventions in which adults should model more advanced methods of communication (Cooper et al., 2007).

Staff thought that waiting was an effective principle often overlooked pre-intervention, but the two TAs in particular showed some reluctance in using it. This difficulty with waiting is illustrated in Gillett and LeBlanc's (2007) study who trained the mothers of 3 children with autism and little or no speech in a naturalistic approach. The results revealed that the component of the intervention mothers found most difficult to apply was waiting for initiations.

The staff, and more precisely the teacher, expressed some reservations about being animated. This might have been viewed as a lack of professionalism or cause embarrassment contradicting her role as the classroom lead. During the focus group interviews, it became apparent that being animated could be easier for some people than some others depending on their mood and personality. Greenspan and Wieder (1998) advise people who might feel embarrassed to be animated to use puppets pretending that it is the puppets' voice which is animated. Using coaching strategies to build on staff's existing good practices such as VIG (Kennedy, 2011) is another way of persuading staff of the effectiveness of those principles they feel less confident with. However, staff confidence should come first; it is the cornerstone of every effective intervention and they should be allowed to abandon principles which for one reason or another do not work for them.

Expanding on the child's communicative attempts and assigning meaning to their random actions or sounds were also viewed with some diffidence by staff. Nonetheless, both these AISI general principles are routed in well-known theories of pedagogy and developmental psychology such as Vygotsky's (1978) zone of proximal development and Bruner's (1981) theory of language development. According to Vygotsky (1978) the adult who is defined as the '*more knowledgeable other*' should foster cognitive development by engaging the child in challenging and meaningful activities. The adult's input must be carefully matched to the current level of the child, especially when a child has got autism and SPMLD. When considering assigning meaning to random actions or sounds, Bruner (1981) maintains that this is exactly how mothers teach their toddlers language; they constantly assume intentionality in their children's utterances until they finally verbalise with intent. In the light of the aforementioned theories, it would be interesting to carry out further research exploring the reasons why these principles appear more difficult than others.

In terms of communicative opportunities, staff reported several difficulties in implementing some of them. There was some hesitation about stopping part way through an activity. This can be due to the children's limited concentration span, which resulted in them walking away as soon as the adult stopped. Making items inaccessible was considered effective but difficult to implement since staff were afraid of children's negative reactions such as anger or anxiety. This was mainly because the children of the sample did not have the level of understanding that if they asked for the toy which had just been removed they could have it back. This might be the reason staff did not use this principle as much as they wanted. Moreover, giving children small portions of food or drinks was not used a lot by the staff post-intervention. This was expected as it is a principle which could mainly be used during one of the four observed activities (i.e. snack).

Giving children materials they would need help with to elicit communication and forgetting something vital were not widely used either. The main argument against using these two principles was the difficulty of keeping the balance between encouraging spontaneous communication and independence. This is a very important point as many individuals with autism are prompt dependent (Blackburn, 2011) or show behaviours of learned helplessness (Seligman, 1975, cited in Imray and Hinchcliffe, 2014). Learned helplessness which is more common among individuals with autism and SLD/PMLD is a condition in which a person has learnt to behave helplessly even when they actually have the power to take action and change an unpleasant situation (Imray and Hinchcliffe, 2014). Therefore, NT adults should creatively use the two aforementioned principles in a range of different situations while avoiding rigidity and watching out for patterns. Otherwise, asking for help or the missing part might become part of a learnt process and further promote prompt dependency and helpless behaviours.

6.7 Reflection activities

- Assuming that you would like to collect some quantitative data for your research project (e.g. measure the frequency a certain behaviour appears in a given time), create some fictitious data, insert them on Excel spreadsheets and experiment with creating charts/figures and using formulas such as sum, average, max, min and percentages.
- Assuming that you would like to collect some qualitative data for your research project (e.g. interview your colleagues to get their views and beliefs on a certain phenomenon), get a few pages of any Word document and insert them in a qualitative software analysis programme such as NVivo to experiment with its functions. Alternatively, you can use the text highlight colour function of Word to code some categories as these emerge from the data you have got (i.e. quotes belonging to the same category should be highlighted with the same colour).
- Another function of Word or Excel spreadsheets which you might find useful for the presentation of your data is that of tables. Try out some of the given options to find the table which fits the purpose of your study (e.g. table styles, merge/split cells).

7 Participatory research designs
Implications for practitioners and parents

7.1 Introduction

This chapter explores in detail five themes resulting from the AISI study described in Part 2 (Chapters 5 and 6) and my overall experience of working as a frontline practitioner, not only in the field of autism and special needs but also as an active researcher and academic. The five themes are (i) the importance of being a reflective practitioner, (ii) the use of Video Interaction Guidance (VIG) as an effective way of facilitating reflection, (iii) the need for a team around the child involving practitioners from different disciplines, with an emphasis on teachers, TAs, parents and the child's family, (iv) the significance of involving the voices of individuals with autism in decision-making and (v) the impact of cultural differences on viewing autism and special needs in general, and on selecting educational approaches.

Adhering to the title of the book *Bridging the Gap between Academic Research and Practice*, the next two chapters are strongly intertwined. This chapter focuses on implications for practice for parents and practitioners, and the next concerns implications for future research. Both follow a similar theme outline to help readers to identify thematic overlaps. This is done intentionally since, as a practitioner and academic who has used action research extensively, it is my strong belief that practice should be evidence-based and research-informed, whilst research should aim to give hands-on solutions to real-world problems. Although the AISI study described in the previous chapters concerns working with practitioners in the field of autism, it is my intention to involve in this chapter implications for parents, as more often than not they can benefit from advice addressed to practitioners.

7.2 Being reflective

7.2.1 *The notion of reflection*

Being reflective is about questioning what one is told to do, whether they are a practitioner (e.g. by their manager, colleagues) or a parent (e.g. by practitioners working with their child). This questioning should not, however, happen for the sake of questioning. One should pose questions in order to think carefully about what one's own practice is all about, who is it for and what is the best way to carry it out. Being reflective is a never-ending endeavour. It involves a continuous process of collecting data, analysing them, evaluating them, reflecting on what they mean and where to go next, devising a plan for trying out ideas, carrying out the plan and evaluating what happened before beginning the whole process again. In a sense, being reflective is what good practice is about, and many practitioners and parents behave in this way, often unconsciously. The first aim of this section is to help the reader become conscious of the times they are being reflective. This should precede any learning about the theories of being reflective, the skills they need to develop and ways they can do it.

It is widely evidenced in the existing literature that one is more likely to improve practice by reflecting on the successes and failures of previous events. For Vincett et al. (2005), reflective practice means '*having ideas, planning, reviewing how plans worked out, and revising*' (p. 33). In a more educational context, reflexivity is an interactive process between the adult (e.g. practitioner/parent), the child and the learning context in which the former have to acknowledge underlying assumptions and priorities of the interaction in a given time, place and situation (adapted from Wilson, 2009). Literature has provided a number of models of reflection and ways of being reflective. Drawing on Ghaye and Ghaye's (1998) work, I focus on 4 which I have found relevant for practitioners and parents working and living with individuals with special needs. These are (i) reflection on practice, (ii) reflection in practice, (iii) reflection on values and (iv) reflection on improvement. Reflection on practice concerns thinking about an event after it has happened. This type of reflection fosters personal self-knowledge, an ability to 'see through' situations and an understanding, in retrospect, of the meaning of what has happened. Reflection in practice is a behaviour which often happens unconsciously in the midst of an action. It often calls for rapid interpretation of a situation and immediate solutions to be put in place. Reflection in practice usually takes priority over reflection on practice as the parents or professionals are expected to react instantly as a result of the here and now demands. However, deeper awareness and understanding develops when one reflects on practice, and parents and practitioners should aim to make use of both type of reflection. Reflection on values is also of crucial importance, as people's values are reflected in the actions they carry out. For example, a teacher who values pupils' input is very likely to create many opportunities for them to voice their opinion, while a parent who rates emotions highly will try to teach their child to be affectionate and caring. Reflection on improvement is another important type of reflection, as change of a person's behaviour does not necessarily mean improvement for everybody around this person. Systemic change can be a contentious issue in some organisations: not all staff would like to follow the pattern of being reflective, and then developing from this. I have talked so far about turning individuals into reflective practitioners, changing themselves, their ideas and their practice. However, being reflective usually means that one will be making changes in one's organisation, especially if they hold a position of influence. It is notoriously hard to change other people's practice, especially when they see no reason to change.

Improvement is a slippery and subjective term and improvement in one field might entail holding back improvements in another. For example, teaching children to communicate might impact on their independence skills; if adults have to provide them with the object they need so that their communication gets results, this can discourage them to get the object independently.

According to Pollard (2008) when it comes to teaching, reflective practice should consist of the following characteristics. It should:

- imply an active concern with aims and consequences, as well as means and technical efficiency
- apply to a cyclical or spiralling process in which practitioners monitor, evaluate and revise their own practice continuously
- require competence in methods of evidence-based enquiry to support the progressive development of higher standards of practice
- require attitudes of open-mindedness, responsibility and wholeheartedness
- be based on practitioner judgment which is informed by evidence-based enquiry and insights from other research
- be enhanced through collaboration and dialogue with colleagues
- enable practitioners to mediate externally developed frameworks for teaching and learning creatively

In a similar vein, reflective practice requires a wide range of skills including empirical, analytical, evaluative, strategic, practical and communication skills (Lacey, 2014). Empirical skills relate to gathering data about what is actually going on in a situation (i.e. what are pupils or practitioners/parents actually doing? What are they feeling and thinking?). Analytical skills are needed to interpret collected data and begin to make sense of them within one's own values and beliefs. Evaluative skills are used to make judgments about one's practice in the light of aims and values and help people see where to proceed next. Strategic skills are required in order for somebody to make plans for action after data are gathered and analysed. Practical skills are concerned with the action itself, which should follow the data analysis. Communication skills are needed to present ideas to others with the aim to enable refinement and further development.

7.2.2 Ways of being reflective

On a more practical note, in order to be reflective, Ashton et al. (1980) advise practitioners to ask themselves the following questions:

- What did the learners actually do?
- What did they learn?
- How worthwhile was it?
- What did I do?
- What did I learn?
- What do I intend to do next?

These questions are of great relevance to parents too as they can be posed beyond an educational setting.

The reminder of this section seeks to present some ideas on how to be reflective in a real word setting. The first step in this process should be to *select a 'critical other'*, the person one will share reflections with. For parents it might be a good idea to select a friend or an acquaintance whom they share similar experiences with (e.g. another parent from a support group) as they will be the most well placed to offer insightful advice. Practitioners might do better to select a colleague whose approach and work they trust and whom they also get on well with, as opposed to a manager who may make the process stressful. The next step is to *select the medium of recording* the practice or behaviour they feel most comfortable with and which works well in their setting. As an example, keeping brief notes about what happens in a given situation, which they then discuss with their 'critical other', can be one way. During this discussion, they might identify behaviours of theirs and environmental factors which influenced the person's with SEN behaviour and which they were not aware of while being in the situation. The colleague or friend can also offer new ideas of what to try next time. If there is more time, or writing is a viable option, keeping details in a reflective diary is a good idea. When it comes to reflection, only small parts of practice should be selected to share with colleagues or friends, depending on how the person 'doing the reflecting' feels about being exposed, and the other person's free time. Voice recording of thoughts or video recording of practice are two further ways to encourage reflection. Both of these media, especially video recording, can provide a helpful source of data for analysis and discussion and can be performed more easily than note-taking. However, video recording can be uncomfortable for some people. Access to adequate equipment can also sometimes be an issue. Last but not least, for people who feel braver and less vulnerable to criticism, asking the 'critical other' to observe 'live' what is happening can also reveal a good deal. This medium of recording might be difficult to achieve in an educational setting due to staff restrictions. In order to make the process less threatening, the person doing the reflecting can take control and discuss only aspects of practice they want to reflect on.

The third step before one starts the reflection process is to *pose the question, 'Where should I start?'* The best advice is to start from where they are now, by recording something they currently do. A session which tends to go better than usual, a time of the day a child finds challenging. First of all, what happens needs to be recorded, and the person has to ask themselves some questions about why they do things in a certain way, what goes well, and what needs to be changed. Then they are ready to meet with the 'critical other' to have an open and honest discussion. It should be noted here that there are some very strong links between being reflective and doing action research (see section 5.5 'Research Methodology for Characteristics, Advantages and Challenges of Action Research'). Although an action researcher should by definition be reflective of their own and their colleagues' practice, being a reflective practitioner does not necessarily mean, conversely to what is widely but falsely believed, that action research is performed.

No matter which model of reflection or characteristics of reflective practice one is in favour of, being reflective is not easy and does not come without effort. A teacher noted:

> Reflection made me realise the complexities of a teacher's life, because through reflection I started questioning what was previously taken for granted. As a result I soon realised that at times the more I write, the more confused I feel.
>
> (Attard, 2008, p. 311)

The significance of reflective practice is very prominent at most courses of the Department of Disability Inclusion and Special Needs (DISN) at the University of Birmingham where I currently work. It is our utmost aim to train reflective practitioners. Indicative of the emphasis the whole department and I personally place on the idea of reflexivity, is the fact that one of the modules in the programme on SPMLD I lead on is entitled 'Reflective Practice'. As part of the course, the students are expected to identify aspects of their practice upon which to reflect through examination of current relevant developments in theory and practice.

7.3 Video Interaction Guidance

7.3.1 Introduction to VIG

Video Interaction Guidance (VIG) is an intervention used to improve communication building on each individual's unique and effective style in which clients are supported to reflect on moments of successful interactions (Kennedy, 2011; Association for Video Interaction Guidance UK-AVIGUK, 2016). VIG is recommended by the National Institute for Health and Care Excellence (NICE, 2012) guidelines for social and emotional well-being in the early years. The intervention is based on a model developed in the Netherlands by Harrie Biemans and his colleagues in the 1980s, according to which principles which promote successful interactions between mothers and infants in their earliest months should be used as a general framework for identifying positive moments in communicative exchanges (Kennedy and Sked, 2008; AVIGUK, 2016). The way VIG works is the following. Clients (e.g. parents, teachers, TAs, other professionals) are first video recorded by the VIG guider while they naturally interact with people in their environment. Then the guider micro-edits the film and selects a few very short clips between a few seconds and a minute long of 'better than usual' patterns of interactions. The clients watch these micro moments together with the VIG guider, reflect on them and set goals for the next session. This joint viewing of the clips is called shared review and is unique to VIG (as opposed to other methods of reflective practice) (Landor, 2015). VIG usually consists of at least three cycles; each cycle involves a session during which the client is video recorded and a shared review with the guider (AVIGUK, 2016). VIG guiders vividly argue that change is more likely to occur within collaborative and empowering relationships. To this end, Kennedy and Sked (2008) maintain:

> The VIG approach takes the view that change can be achieved more effectively in the context of a 'coaching' relationship than 'teaching' relationship, because this is collaborative rather than prescriptive, empowering rather than de-skilling.
>
> (p. 2)

The moments of successful interaction are selected bearing in mind the principles of attuned interaction and guidance (formerly known as contact principles) (Kennedy, 2011). These six principles entail: (i) being attentive (e.g. giving time and space for the other, looking interested with friendly posture), (ii) encouraging initiatives (e.g. listening actively and waiting), (iii) receiving initiatives (e.g. receiving the other with body language and with words), (iv) developing attuned interactions (e.g. receiving and then responding, giving a second and further turn on the same topic), (v) guiding (e.g. scaffolding and building on the other's response) and (vi) deepening discussion (e.g. naming contradictions and reaching new shared understandings). These principles are considered to be the basic building blocks of communication. Overall, the overarching VIG element is that interaction is not only what a person does but also, and even more, what the person does in response to another person (Cross and Kennedy, 2011). Although clients are initially very self-conscious about being filmed, reviewing moments of successful interactions alongside the VIG guider is a very empowering and positive experience for them. VIG has traditionally been used in a family setting, but is increasingly being used to assist the communication of professionals and clients (Kennedy and Sked, 2008). In the last 15 years, VIG has been adapted for use as a staff training method in educational, medical and social work settings.

There is no prescribed number of VIG cycles in order for the intervention to be successful. Anecdotal evidence shows that the length of the intervention does not affect its effectiveness; shorter interventions are at least as effective as longer ones and the greatest progress is usually noticed in the first two shared reviews (Kennedy, 2011). As a rule of thumb, families are offered three or four filming sessions followed by three or four shared reviews as an initial stage (Kennedy, 2011). The intervention is then evaluated and more support is offered if needed.

7.3.2 VIG theoretical foundations, values and beliefs

There are a number of theories which support the use of VIG with Professor Colwyn Trevarthen's theory on primary and secondary intersubjectivity arguably being the theoretical cornerstone of VIG. Trevarthen studied the rhythm, the tone and the pauses which help communication work during moments of vitality between parents and their infants (Kennedy, 2011) and talked about primary intersubjectivity (i.e. when communication is a two-way 'dialogue' between two people) and secondary intersubjectivity (i.e. when a joint focus on something external can be added to the dyadic communication). The VIG guider uses the clips as the object of shared interest (secondary intersubjectivity) while building attuned interactions with parents or practitioners (primary intersubjectivity).

Theories of mediated learning, according to which the adult can be a mediator to the child's intentions, are also very relevant here (Vygotsky, 1978; Wood et al., 1976). More precisely, Vygotsky (1978) in his *zone of proximal development theory* argues that the level of support the adult provides should be carefully chosen to extend the child from their current level but not so advanced that it fails to connect with the child. This process has been described as *scaffolding* (Wood et al., 1976) in the context of mother-child interactions.

Two theoretical models for the use of video, those of self-modelling and self-confrontation, can also apply in the context of VIG. Self-modelling derives from Bandura's (1977) *theory of social learning* which purports that learning occurs through observing and imitating more experienced others. In Bandura's theory the closer the model to oneself, the more effective the learning. In a similar vein, the self-confrontation model (Wels, 2002) proposes that one by viewing themselves they gain greater insight into their behaviour and '*see yourself as others generally see you*' (p. 52).

Last but not least, I would like to draw some parallels between VIG and the theories of positive psychology and empowerment. Positive psychology proponents claim that optimal human functioning pushes individuals and communities to thrive (Seligman, 2002). Seligman and Pawelski (2003) state that the best way to help people who suffer is to focus on positive things and nurture strengths and virtues. The PERMA (Seligman, 2011) model which places great emphasis on positive emotions can be strongly linked to VIG. According to the PERMA model, there are five pillars to well-being: positive emotions, engagement, relationships, meaning, and accomplishment/achievement. Similarly, theories of change and empowerment (Cross and Kennedy, 2011) emphasise respect, building on strengths and collaboration between the consultant/guider and the consultee/guide to co-construct meaning of a situation.

Beyond its strong theoretical foundations, VIG has some very solid philosophical and ethical values and beliefs to draw upon and make it a success (Kennedy and Landor, 2015). First and foremost, VIG is respectful of the current situation and takes for granted that people are doing the best they can at the time, that they care about each other, and that they wish by nature to communicate. VIG also advocates that a crisis can be an opportunity for change and people in troubled situations do want to change; the power for this change resides within the individual or situation itself.

7.3.3 Video Enhanced Reflective Practice

Video Enhanced Reflective Practice (VERP) is a reflective practice method using video which grew out of VIG in order to develop professionals' interpersonal communication (Strathie et al., 2011). It is delivered by a VIG-trained guider who starts the process by providing a short introductory course to the trainees.

The introductory course can be offered as a one-day training session or it can be split in more than one shorter sessions to fit with the needs and the timetable of the organisation (e.g. afternoon sessions in a school). During the introductory course, the VIG guider presents the principles of attuned interaction, the theories underpinning VIG, its values and beliefs and demonstrates how the clips should be selected by showing specific examples. More technical support on how to edit videos can also be offered if needed. The course closes by the trainees identifying areas they would like to work on (i.e. forming their helping questions- deciding what they need help on) and the VIG guider explaining what they need to do before they meet again in small groups (i.e. shared reviews). More precisely, the trainees are asked to record a 10-minute video interacting with another person which they then watch while consulting with the principles of attuned interaction in order to select video segments of attuned interaction or segments where the interaction felt challenging. The trainees then bring these clips to the shared reviews where with the aide of the VIG guider, who takes on the role of the facilitator, are expected to take turns and reflect on their own practice, present clips of effective communication and 'working points' (Kennedy and Landor, 2015). Due to the format of VERP shared reviews the trainees learn from their own videos, the videos of their colleagues and the facilitator, who models the principles of attuned interaction with them (e.g. listens actively and waits, receives their initiatives and responds to them) during the shared reviews. The trainees are often from the same organisation or workplace, and form small groups of up to five people (Kennedy and Landor, 2015). They are expected to carry out at least three shared review sessions. However, the length of each shared review varies and follows the needs of the trainees and the organisation they belong to. In the final session, which is negotiated between the guider and the trainees as to when it should take place the trainees are asked to select a clip in which their helping question has turned into *pleased with* moment.

VERP has been proven an effective model of adult training for a number of reasons. First and foremost, the most significant strength of VERP is its *no blame* culture focusing on *what works* while acknowledging working points. Group learning is another important element of VERP; the facilitator/guider uses the diversity and different learning styles of the members of the group to reach new shared understandings. Additionally, autonomy and self-directed learning have proven to be an effective way of training. The findings of a phone survey of 750 workers by the Chartered Institute of Personnel and Development indicated that where workers are first shown how to do something, and then given the chance to practice what they have learnt, are trained most effectively (Sloman, 2003). Similarly, another study showed that the more active in the learning the participant is, the more knowledge they retain. Rogers (2007) found that only 5% of a didactic lecture is retained as opposed to 75% of a lecture containing practical elements; this percentage goes up to 90% when participants share their knowledge amongst them. For all of the reasons discussed earlier, VERP seems to resonate very well with the current need in workplaces for regular continuing professional development.

7.3.4 Studies on VIG and VERP effectiveness

Research on the use and effectiveness of VIG and VERP is still in its infancy with primarily small-scale studies having been conducted to date, many at masters' or doctoral level. Most of these studies were carried out with parents and very few were conducted in schools or other professional settings. I will present a few of them, which followed a rigorous research design and I think are relevant to the topic of this book, in the remainder of this section.

Gibson (2014) employed a single case design using VIG with a 5-year-old boy with autism and his mother. The video intervention involved 4 filming and shared review sessions within the family home. Each session included 10 minutes filming of parent – child interaction during shared activities (e.g. Duplo, drawing, sharing a book). The main data collection method was flexible semi-structured interviews which were completed with the mother before and following VIG sessions to get her hopes and goals for the intervention and to provide insights of her experience from VIG. Thematic analysis of the interview transcripts showed that VIG promoted greater awareness of the child's communication skills but also the mother's multiple roles (e.g. protector, translator and mind-reader for her son) and feelings of parental efficacy (e.g. techniques which work better with their son and the importance of belonging to a wider group of people with similar experiences, the autism community).

A study which involved both a teacher and a parent was conducted by Pilnick and James (2013), who explored how VIG can work with an 8-year-old boy with autism and hearing impairment. His teacher received several VIG sessions and the child's mother joined one shared review. Privileging some ways of seeing over others, the use of expert testimony (the VIG guider or the teacher in this case), moving from what to why were some of the themes that came up during the analysis.

Sked (2006) conducted a study to research communicative interactions among children with autism and educational staff. In this study, VIG was combined with an intervention of imitative responsiveness, similar to that described by Nadel (1993, cited in Sked, 2006). Six primary school-age boys with autism acted as the case studies. The sessions were filmed, and in each of the first four sessions, the adults also took part in VIG feedback sessions. One minute's worth of interaction from each of the five sessions was coded. Two more data collection methods were employed. In one, the staff completed questionnaires at the beginning and end of the study to gain insights into their experience of and attitudes toward the intervention. Secondly, the discussions that took place during VIG feedback sessions were video recorded, and the content of the discussion was then analysed. The results showed an increase in the adults' attunement to the child. Members of staff stated that following the child's lead helped the child 'feel their presence' and they could better support the child in making new initiatives. They also mentioned that they would consider using imitation as a communicative strategy in future. The films of their video feedback sessions demonstrated increase in their confidence and enthusiasm.

James et al. (2012) explored the impact of training staff members of a service for children and adults with autism in VIG. Four staff who received VIG participated in semi-structured interviews within six months after the end of the intervention. Thematic analysis was used to code the data and the results showed that the four participants had a positive experience of the intervention and raised their confidence and self-esteem levels. They also mentioned that they became more aware of the service users' needs and ways of communication as well as the subtleties of their in-between interactions.

There is even more limited research exploring the effectiveness and usefulness of VERP; these are small-scale studies employing self-report rather than objective measures. Jarvis and Lyon (2015) conducted a project to evaluate the effectiveness of VERP in a school setting in improving the quality of interaction between staff and children. Five members of staff took part in the VERP process, taking clips of themselves interacting with a child or group of children once a month for three months. After the end of the study, the five participants were shown edited clips of their shared reviews on a 1:1 basis and were interviewed. The main identified themes were the following: (i) initial concerns about videos and feeling self-conscious in front of their colleagues, (ii) initial difficulties in expressing their strengths *'helping you look for the good things is a massive turnaround'* (p. 39), (iii) impact on staff confidence who reported less reliance on colleagues and more self-reliance, (iv) benefits of group shared reviews as they mentioned that they learned from each other, emulating strengths from another's practice and comment on each other's practice in a supportive environment and (v) systemic change in that the relationships and trust between the team have strengthen. Hewitt et al. (2015) mentioned two small research projects. In the first one, 4 TAs working with children across the range of SEN in a mainstream primary school participated in five cycles of VERP. Each cycle involved video recordings of an activity between the child and the TA and a shared review between the TAs and the VERP guider. VERP seemed to have had a positive impact on the relationship between the child and the TA. The TAs also reported benefits in children's adaptive skills (e.g. independence) but also improvements in interactions with other children and colleagues who did not participate in the intervention. In the second project, 2 TAs from different schools worked with 2 boys with autism and attended three cycles of VERP. Research data were collected through semi-structured interviews with the TAs and analysis of the VERP video clips. The interviews showed that both TAs increased their professional confidence and competence stating that post-intervention they knew better how to interact with the boys. Video data showed an increase in the frequency and intensity of using the principles of attuned interaction.

It has to be noted here that some school studies which claim that they have used VIG, might have used VERP instead. Given that VERP is a very new approach with its core textbook having been published only in 2015 (Kennedy et al., 2015) and the fact that it is founded on VIG in terms of its theoretical background, values, beliefs and overall protocols, a number of people confuse the two interventions. I would like to highlight here that VIG and VERP are two very similar approaches. The only two points which distinguish them are that in VERP the trainees themselves, not the guider, select the videos to bring to the shared reviews and these are conducted in groups (as opposed to 1:1 shared reviews which are usually the case in VIG). VERP is more geared towards practitioners, while VIG is equally relevant for both parents and practitioners.

7.3.5 Training on VIG

As Kennedy (2011) argues, *'the delivery of VIG is an art and as such it requires skilled coaching and it cannot be easily taught'* (p. 39). The training programme consists of an initial two-day training followed by 3 stages of training. During these stages, supervision is essential in order to ensure and maintain high quality practice. These consist of 25 hours of individual supervision spread over a minimum period of 18 months. After the completion of each stage, the trainees have to go through accreditation before moving on to the next stage. After having successfully completed the three stages of training, the guider can pursue a fourth stage in order to train as a supervisor (AVIGUK, 2016).

7.4 Team Around the Child and the inter-disciplinary model

Effective liaison between professionals is vital to ensuring a coordinated approach when working with an individual with SEN. Especially in cases of individuals with autism and additional complex needs a number of therapists and medical professionals need to be involved in the team. Lacey and Oyvry (2013) call this model *'collaborative multidisciplinary teamwork'* and stress the importance of a strong commitment to it in order to ensure consistency and reduce overlaps. Terms such as Team Around the Child (TAC), inter-disciplinary or trans-disciplinary model have also been extensively used to denote this collaborative way of working. Limbrick (2001) is a fervent proponent of the TAC model which enables 'collaborative competence' among professionals in an effective way. The revised Special Educational Needs and Disability (SEND) Code of Practice (DfE and DoH, 2014) underlines the current prioritising of a joined-up approach. The aforementioned document and the gradual replacement of 'statements' (i.e. documents which will be used in schools in England until 2018 to describe a child's special needs and the support they should receive), which were primarily the responsibility of education (Local Authority), by EHCP, place far more emphasis on collaboration between education, health and social care departments.

The effectiveness of trans-disciplinary collaboration between teachers and other professionals such as SLTs, Occupational Therapists (OTs), physiotherapists, psychologists and social workers has been explored in the SEN literature (Lacey, 2012; Leko et al., 2015). For example, Lacey (1998) distributed questionnaires and conducted some interviews with students from the PMLD course at the University of Birmingham and found that collaborative working is likely to increase confidence levels. The collaborative element is still very prominent in the SPMLD programme at the University of Birmingham. As part of the course, students are asked to work in collaboration with colleagues from their setting in order to identify ways in which the quality of their provision can be enhanced.

Before moving on to talk about collaborative models and effective ways of professionals working together, the particular nature of practitioners working in the field of SEN and autism should be noted. Peeters and Jordan (1999) argue that these people are often '*qualitative*' different (p. 14) or '*bitten by the bug of autism*' (p. 15) as they should be able to give without getting 'ordinary' thank yous, have the courage to work alone in the desert and dare to engage in a never-ending detective work guessing and trying out new things. Additionally, they seem to face some extra difficulties as there are a number of studies reporting that practitioners working with people with special needs and more precisely learning difficulties are more likely to experience high stress levels and are more prone to burnout (Male and May, 1997; Robertson et al., 2005).

7.4.1 Teamwork models at schools

Having admitted that schools are not the most hospitable environment for effective teamwork, Vincett et al. (2005) present three effective models of organising teams in the classroom:

1   the room management model
2   the zoning model
3   the reflective teamwork model

In the room management model, each member of the teaching staff is given either the learning manager or the activity manager role. The learning manager works with individual students on intensive teaching, while the activity manager works with the rest of the students in the class mainly on areas of the curriculum, which have already been taught but not every student has mastered. In the zoning model, teaching staff take responsibility for specific zones or geographical areas in the classroom. Different activities take place in different parts of the room in which there is a responsible adult. This model reminds to a great extent the way nursery classes are organised offering corners for different activities. Both these models have been developed for mainstream schools whereas the reflective teamwork model has more potentials of adaptation in special settings. Its aim is to improve classroom teamwork by enhancing communication, planning and review and it entails teacher and TAs meeting shortly daily to plan and review their teaching session '*in full collaboration, as equal partners*' (p. 50). The TAs first identify two things of the session which went well, two things which need improvement and express their feelings about these. In the meantime, the teacher listens actively. When the TAs finish, the teacher summarises what has been said. Then the teacher goes through the exact same process. Once all have finished, TAs and the teacher brainstorm objectives and activities which are jointly agreed upon. The following two sections further focus on effective collaboration between teachers and TAs.

7.4.2 Collaboration among teachers

Although a form of collaboration is common practice in the UK for Newly Qualified Teachers (NQTs), who go through observations and meetings with more experienced teachers/mentors during their first year of teaching (Department for Education, 2015), this practice stops after teachers have qualified. In most cases they are left alone or with limited support to do their work. Although there is extensive literature on the inter-disciplinary collaboration between professionals, very little is written so far on the collaboration among teachers themselves. Lava et al. (2004) report that teachers consider collaboration with colleagues a vital support strategy within their career. In their review, Cordingley et al. (2005) found that collaborative working between teachers had a positive effect on their confidence and self-efficacy. In a similar vein, McCray (2012) found that a supportive peer network can reduce teacher vulnerability and minimise frustration and the potential for burnout. Lack of time appears to be another major theme when looking at collaborative working among teachers. Sharing ideas and joint problem solving are considered to be extremely time-consuming and can be a particular issue for teachers whose working days are strictly timetabled and who have considerable other pressures on their time (Lacey, 2012; Leonard and Leonard, 2003).

Filbey (2016) conducted a small case study to explore teachers' views on collaborative working at school. Six teachers working at a school for children with S/PMLD participated in semi-structured interviews. Among others, Filbey found that her participants placed high value on professional and personal relationships with their colleagues, and this greatly supported them to develop their knowledge and skills. More specifically, having a good knowledge of each other's strengths and interests was reported to ensure truly effective collaboration. Filbey found that collaboration needed to be facilitated by celebrating and focusing on the positives and success, not blame. More time to further discuss and develop ideas was perceived as extremely valuable to many of the teachers too.

7.4.3 The significant role of Teaching Assistants

The concept and role of Teaching Assistants (TAs) or Learning Support Assistants are not similar across the world. In countries where the concept of TAs is in existence, there is an ongoing discussion regarding the remit of their role, the effectiveness of the support they provide and the extent of their pedagogical formation (Webster et al., 2010). Currently, TAs in the UK are more involved into delivering academic activities than do auxiliary staff in other parts of the world. Their role consists of providing extra hands-on support to children who are in need of it (e.g. work in small groups to assist them with activities in literacy or numeracy). They are also expected to help teachers prepare lessons by getting resources ready or putting out equipment at the start of a lesson.

Research findings on the impact of TAs on pupils' performance are currently both limited and contradictory. Some studies have shown that pupils in classrooms where there are TAs tend to outperform pupils from classes where only the teacher is present while other studies reported that children with SEN tend to perform worse in classes with TAs (Education Endowment Foundation, 2016). Broadly speaking, it seems that TAs are likely to have a better impact on the students they work with when they receive personalised and bespoke training on interventions and approaches for the specific pupils they work with (National Foundation for Educational Research (NFER), 2014). Dean Beadle, an adult with autism who gives talks about his experience of being autistic, tends to always mention in his talks how important and helpful one of his TAs at school was and how much he owes her.

Although it is evident that collaboration between teachers and TAs is much more difficult to achieve than one might think, there are some rules in order to ensure effective teamwork. Elements such as communication, empowerment, autonomy, cooperative (as opposed to competitive) interactions, mutually agreed (as opposed to individual) team goals and positive interdependence (i.e. each member of the group is mutually dependent on the other members) as outlined by Vincett et al. (2005) can be the cornerstones of an effective collaboration between teachers and TAs. Potential difficulties sabotaging this collaboration might be the fact that teachers are not trained in the management and deployment of TAs (Farrell et al., 1999), some teachers' views that TAs lack the knowledge and the skills needed for their role (Lee and Mawson, 1998; Smith et al., 1998), the unsystematic knowledge sharing between the two with the expectation that teachers will provide 'on-the-job' training to the TAs (Martin and Alborz, 2014), and teacher-TA differences in status, pay, training, contract and role clarity (Vincett et al., 2005).

7.4.4 Parents', carers' and family members' involvement

Parents, carers and other family members (e.g. grandparents and siblings) are usually the prime people involved in the life and education of an individual. Parents of children with SEN have no choice but to enter the field without in most cases having any training on disability before they have to face and live with it. Sadly, parents are also left at the outside of the TAC, although in most cases they are the ones who have the knowledge and the persistence to co-ordinate all these professionals. For the aforementioned reasons, they should be given far more attention; as Peeters and Jordan (1999) claim:

> Parents are the experts about their own children and we need to take into account their wisdom and experience.
>
> (p. 16)

It is commonly perceived that parents of children with SEN are more likely to get divorced adding extra pressure and stress to an already demanding life. However, there is inconclusive evidence on this topic. A meta-analysis by Risdal and Singer (2004) found that between 3% and 7% more marriages of parents of children with SEN end in divorce, compared to parents of TD children. On the contrary, a Norwegian study (Lundeby and Tossebro, 2008) found that children with SEN were more likely to live with both their parents than TD children. What is interesting to mention here is an old literature review by Sabbeth and Leventhal (1984) which looked at 34 studies and found no increased risk of divorce rates in families of children with SEN, but did find higher rates of marital distress and lower marital satisfaction for parents with children with autism compared to parents of children with other SEN. In their literature review Saini et al. (2015) found that mothers of children with autism consistently reported working less outside the home and spending more time on children-related tasks than mothers of children without autism whereas the exact opposite was the case for some fathers of children with autism (i.e. they reported spending more time working outside the home and less time on child-related tasks than fathers of children without autism).

The parents' significant role in education of children with SEN is gradually more recognised. The *Rochford Review* (2016) clearly states that schools should officially establish a dialogue with parents to ensure accountability for assessing the low achiever pupils. Apart from consulting with their parents, carers and other family members, the involvement of people with SEN, despite the severity of their learning difficulties, in decisions made for them is also of crucial importance. The following section explores this issue in detail.

7.5 Listening to the voice of individuals with SEN

Listening to the voice of people with SEN is increasingly being acknowledged as an inalienable right (i.e. United Nations Convention on the Rights of the child-UN, 1989/ Articles 12 and 13; United Nations Convention on the Rights of Person with disabilities-UN, 2006/ Article 7) as well as an obligatory precondition for good practice. This widespread promotion has incurred new guidelines and legislation. It is interesting to note here that the new SEND code of practice (DfE and DoH, 2014) in England reinforces the importance of pupil voice and champions learners being given the opportunity to participate in decisions about their own life and education. The current legislation and practice is then in total agreement with Sfard's (1998, cited in Saddler, 2014) point that individuals, let alone children with SEN, should be viewed as people 'in action' rather than people 'as such' and they should, therefore, fully engage in family, school and wider community life.

7.5.1 Towards choice making

There is some debate, however, as to what participation and having somebody's voice listened to means. Brown et al. (1993) claim that every person, regardless of the severity of their SEN, can make significant choices and that the reason this does not happen is because many practitioners are not familiar with how to teach people with severe learning difficulties to make significant choices. To this end these authors developed a *model of choice diversity* which consists of seven categories of choices that are available in everyday routines (Brown et al., 1993). These are (i) within activities (e.g. colour of pen to draw with), (ii) between activities (e.g. stay indoors or go outside), (iii) refusal (e.g. reject participation in an activity), (iv) who (e.g. select who to work or not to work with), (v) where (e.g. choice of location), (vi) when (e.g. choice of time) and (vii) terminate (e.g. decide when an activity should end). These categories, which can be used by parents as well, give a number of ideas to reflect on in order to create as many opportunities as possible for persons with SEN to exercise a full range of choices within their daily routines. On the other hand, Ware (2004) questions whether expressing likes and dislikes equates to expressing a view or giving an opinion. To reinforce Ware's point the Mental Capacity Act (2005) stipulates that a person is unable to make decisions for themselves if they cannot: (i) understand the information relevant to the decision, (ii) retain that information, (iii) use or weigh that information as part of the process of making the decision or (iv) communicate their decision (by talking, using sign language or any other means). Therefore, it should be borne in mind that participation and expressing a view are defined in different ways, some more lenient and some stricter, by different people.

Hodges (2003) argues that establishing preferences is the first step to achieve meaningful choice. She advises professionals and parents to expose the person with SEN to a wide range of experiences, and give them time to build preferences as the initial reactions to these experiences will show just reactions (not yet preferences). She also suggests that choice making should start within activities as this places fewer cognitive and communication demands on the person who has difficulty with their memory and use of abstract symbols. Interestingly enough she thinks that to start establishing choices it is better when the choice is between one thing and nothing (e.g. one plate with a biscuit and a blank plate) as opposed to two things. When the child establishes the ability to make and communicate a single choice then two options can be introduced. Hodges is of the opinion that offering a blank choice works more effectively than offering an aversive option (e.g. a raw onion). Bondy and Frost (2002) in their PECS suggest the following two practices to teach people with communication difficulties to make choices, to offer: (i) preferred versus neutral items (e.g. something boring such as a piece of paper or tissue) and (ii) preferred versus disliked items (e.g. pickles, lemons). Establishing choices can be a very time-consuming process and if a child is rushed into making a choice because this is what s/he should do, this is very likely to be a false choice.

7.5.2 Some research on decision making

Having adopted a less strict definition of participation, research shows that this can be enabled with great benefits even for people with autism and SPMLD. In a relevant study, Cameron and Murphy (2002) showed that non-verbal autistic children were able to express coherent opinions. More precisely, they carried out a study into the effectiveness of using Talking Mats with 12 non-verbal young adults at a college for students with communication and learning difficulties.

The participants were asked to categorise different images into likes and dislikes and it emerged that they wanted new activities to be included into their routines which staff had not previously known they enjoyed. Another study by Wantanbe and Sturmey (2003) looked at changes in behaviour of three adults with autism living in a community vocational setting and found that when the participants were involved themselves in planning their daily activity schedules (instead of staff planning for them) the amount of time spent on task and their engagement levels increased significantly.

7.5.3 Enabling participation in autism

Despite its benefits, enabling participation is likely to be even more difficult in cases of individuals with autism for a number of reasons. Communication difficulties, often found among people with autism, can form a significant barrier. Practitioners and parents working and living with non-verbal people with autism need to be creative in order to gain an understanding of their experiences and preferences (e.g. Talking Mats, miniature toys, drama approaches). High stress levels associated with decision-making can be another barrier to including people with autism in the process. Grandin (2000, cited in Luke et al., 2012), an autistic professor at Colorado State University, describes a feeling of being '*locked up and overloaded with pictures*' (p. 17) when faced with making choices. Similar are the findings from a study conducted by Luke et al. (2012) who used an online questionnaire to compare attitudes towards decision-making in 38 autistic adults and a control group of 40 NT adults. The responses gave overwhelming evidence that autistic adults dislike making decisions. Additionally, it has to be borne in mind that people with autism might need extra time in order to process information (for more details on the issue see 2.6 'Cognitive, Psychological and Sensory Processing Theories in Autism') which is likely to have an impact on making decisions. Lawson (2003), an autistic psychologist with a PhD, describes the difficulty he has in responding quickly to questions or choices offered; claiming that more time is needed to answer questions. The idiosyncratic way people with autism might make choices should be also kept in mind. For example, it is common for young non-verbal children with autism to push or throw away the options they do not want instead of reaching out for the one they want. Therefore, extra time should be allowed, and caution used.

7.5.4 The role of advocates

Obtaining the views of individuals with SEN can often be challenging, and so involving advocates often seems necessary. Lawson et al. (2015) argue that the person who advocates for them should:

1. have built a relationship with them
2. have open-ended expectations about the extent of the person's participation
3. use a number of methods to get their views

4   provide opportunities for them to express their views
5   adopt an ethos and values to respect each individual

Goodwin (2013) adds that advocates should '*constantly check and revise*' (p. 26) how they interpret the intentions of people with SEN to make sure that they do not construct their own interpretations, but instead transfer what the person really wishes. In particular, advocates for people with PMLD should be extra conscious, as those in this group are likely to express a preference, like or dislike by very small changes in their behaviour such a change in breathing or stilling of the body (Manchester, 2012) which are not easy to detect.

Advocating for individuals with autism can have some extra challenges. Because of the struggles this population may have with eye contact, social situations and communication, there can be significant disparities between what children with autism and their advocates (usually parents) think and feel. A study carried out by Preece and Jordan (2010) looked into how 14 children (aged 7–18) with autism and their parents experience social care services, and reported a complete contrast between the child's perspective and the perspective of parents and professionals. Similarly, Coles (2014) carried out a study into families with children with autism who were making the transition from primary to secondary school. All participants (10 children with autism, 10 mothers and 3 fathers) were asked to complete questionnaires discussing their anxieties about the transition. The results showed that there were great differences between what caused anxiety for parents and their children. Therefore, since NT adults can easily misinterpret the children's or adult's with SEN behaviour and make mistakes regarding their wishes and likes, the latter need to be involved if possible rather than basing provision on advocating perspective or assumptions.

7.5.5 A small-scale study on practitioners' views

Although for people working and living with individuals with special needs, it is stating the obvious to claim that everybody regardless of their difficulties should be included in decision-making and have control over their lives, this does not often happen in practice. Students pursuing studies on SLD/PMLD at the University of Birmingham were asked to provide their views on how the participation of learners with SLD/PMLD is enabled in their educational setting. Fourteen part-time students who also work as frontline practitioners with learners with SLD/PMLD (including autism) from 2 to 25 years old offered a range of views, showing that listening to the pupils' voice is an issue of high concern for most settings. The majority of students ($n = 9$) reported overall positive experiences of involving individuals with S/PMLD in decision-making. More precisely, they focused on strategies used by the learners to express their preferences (e.g. switches, objects of references, photographs, symbols- to be exchanged, pointed to or touched) and initiatives their settings undertake to promote the learners' voice (e.g. forums, councils, mentor sessions, student-led assemblies, radio). The use of technology (e.g. photos and video recordings) plays an important role in

138 *Implications for practitioners and parents*

capturing the learners' engagement in preferred activities and sharing then these with classmates, broader school and parents. A strong relationship with parents who are often in a better position to interpret the pupil's voice has also been highlighted by the students as a tool of getting the learners' voice.

The students also talked about both the positive and negative effects staff might have on the learners and the additional impact of the environment. For example, one student highlighted the importance of staff knowing the child well in order to notice very subtle changes in their behaviour which can indicate choice. Another student mentioned cases of pupils' views being interrupted by an adult who knows them well. The need for adults to embrace a facilitative interactive style (Potter and Whittaker, 2001; McAteer and Wilkinson, 2009; Kossyvaki et al., 2012) and to create responsive environments for people with communication difficulties (Frost and Bondy, 2002; Ware, 2003; Ingersoll et al., 2005) has been widely explored in the literature. These two areas are very compatible with the social model of disability and the transactional model of child development (see 1.2 'Theoretical Frameworks' for more details).

Some well-founded criticism was offered by a number of students ($n = 5$) too. They claimed that listening to pupils' voice can be a tokenistic and ticking the box exercise at their setting as less able individuals are not represented in councils and forums and, as a result, they are not listened to. A significant number of them ($n = 6$) made a distinction between learners with SLD and PMLD, maintaining that when it comes to the latter some reliance on other people eliciting and interpreting their views is unavoidable. The need to be flexible and creative in order to maximise these people's participation is encapsulated in a student's quote. She said, '*If we are truly to give learners in our school a voice, then we must abandon the* '*one size fits all*'.

This chapter closes with a section on how special needs and autism in particular are viewed around the world and within different cultures in the same country. This section considers prevalence rates, characteristics and educational priorities and their implications for practice which is the connecting theme for all sections in this chapter.

7.6 Cultural differences

There is inconclusive evidence on prevalence rates, characteristics and educational priorities for people with autism around the world and from different cultures within the same country. Culture is defined in this section as the distinctive way of life of a group of people sharing similar attitudes and values (Kai et al., 2006). Variables such as participants' race, ethnicity and country of origin have been used in different studies as a proxy for culture (Brown and Rogers, 1997). Culture can also be attributed to parental place of birth (Dyches et al., 2004). Cultural differences in the way autism and SEN in general are viewed has been a great area of interest for me. Living in a foreign country (I am Greek) and in a multi-cultural city such as Birmingham made me, many times, challenge the Western European and North American way autism is diagnosed and the educational programmes and priorities this diagnosis induces, echoing Kim's (2012) fear that American or Eurocentric views of autism are likely to be imposed upon other countries.

Before moving on to talk about prevalence rates, symptoms and educational priorities it has to be noted that many countries and cultures around the world a) may still not recognise autism, b) might not have a word to describe the condition, and c) may group individuals with autism under a different diagnostic category or even perceive autism as something divine or spiritual (Grinker, 2009). The aforementioned reinforce Grinker's (2007) view that disability is socially constructed and is congruent with the social model of disability. More precisely, some Asian languages do not still have a word for autism (Dobson et al., 2001), whereas in native Hawaiian and native American autism is defined by longer descriptions rather than a single term (Connors and Donnellan, 1998). Additionally, for some people around the world, autism can be perceived as a synonym to the generic SEN term. In Nicaragua, for example, Kim (2012) asked a number of preschool teachers whether they had students with autism in their class and one responded: '*I have a child with visual impairment*', and another answered, '*I have a student with physical impairment*'. This is in agreement with my personal experience of how autism was (and is, still) viewed in some Latin American countries. A Chilean psychologist friend of mine was sponsored by her government 10 years ago to pursue a masters' degree in the UK; until we met she had never heard the word autism before. In 2015, I was funded by the British Council/FAPESP Early Career Researcher Link to visit Brazil to attend and present at a conference at the Federal University of São Carlos. There it became apparent that autism awareness among our Brazilian academic colleagues was nowhere near that of colleagues in the UK and in Europe. However, the fact that there is no widespread autism awareness in some countries does not necessarily mean that the provision and accommodation of autistic people's needs in these countries is of a poor standard.

7.6.1 Prevalence rates

Autism Society of America (2000) claims:

> Autism . . . knows no racial, ethnic, or social boundaries. Family income, lifestyle, and educational levels do not affect the chance of autism's occurrence.
> (p. 3)

However, there are studies which challenge the universality of autism reporting different prevalence rates and symptom description around the world and in different cultures. Norbury and Sparks (2012) conducted a review of autism prevalence and reported that some cultures appear to have higher autism prevalence rates than others. For example, they reported high prevalence rates for Anglo-technological advanced countries such as the UK (116 per 10,000) (Baird et al., 2006), the US (42–121 per 10,000) (Autism and Developmental Disabilities Monitoring Network Surveillance Year, 2006; Principal Investigators, 2009), Canada (60 per 10,000) (Fombonne et al., 2006), Western Australia

(51 per 10,000) (Parner et al., 2011) but also some East Asian countries such as Japan (181 per 10,000) (Kawamura et al., 2008) and South Korea (260 per 10,000) (Kim et al., 2011). Additionally, Norbury and Sparks (Kim et al., 2011) mentioned the examples of countries with very low prevalence rates such as Oman (1.4 per 10,000) (Al Farsi et al., 210) and Germany (1.9 per 10,000) (Steinhausen et al., 1986). In a similar vein, Sanua (1981a, 1981b, 1984) reported low incidence of autism in some Latin American (e.g. Peru, Argentina, Brazil and Venezuela) and some developing countries (e.g. Kenya, India, Hungary).

Many factors can be taken into account for the disparities in autism prevalence rates described earlier. Different sample sizes and characteristics of the participants (e.g. individuals with or without learning difficulties), different diagnostic manuals (e.g. DSM–III–R, DSM–IV, DSM–5 or ICD-9, ICD-10) and different data collection methods (e.g. reports or interviews with parents/teachers vs. direct observations) might only be some of them. It is beyond the scope of this section to explore in detail how each of these and other variables might affect autism prevalence rates around the world.

The picture is even less clear for autism prevalence rates in different cultures within the same country as in most epidemiological studies there is lack of research concerning the exact numbers of individuals with autism among immigrant populations. Fombonne (1998) conducted a meta-analysis of 19 epidemiological studies and reported that only 3 of them provided sufficient data on population classified as immigrants. This point is of great importance given that pluralistic societies where certain cultural groups appear to be a minority is a growing phenomenon nowadays especially in industrialised Western societies and most of current research presents higher prevalence of autism in immigrants when compared with the non-immigrant population (Dyches et al., 2004).

7.6.2 General views on autism

There is a great diversity in how autism and SEN in general are perceived around the world, with a totally different picture between Eastern and Western cultures. In China, for instance, many families feel ashamed about having a child with SEN, linking what they consider mental illness to a punishment for a parent's (more likely the mother's) behaviour (Tsang et al., 2003). Therefore, children with autism are often hidden away from relatives and neighbours (Grinker, 2009). The situation in Korea is similar, where women are fully responsible for raising their children and are the ones to blame for having a child with SEN (Kim, 2012). In many cases, they have to fight to raise their child by themselves, without support from her husband or other family members (Kim, 2012). In India, although extended family members can provide a huge amount of support, the existence of a child with special needs in the family is very likely to affect the marriage prospects of siblings and even cousins (Divan et al., 2012). This is also the case in other countries in South Asia where arranged marriages are the norm. The situation seems to be totally different in many Western societies where autism, especially when not accompanied by learning difficulties, is not anymore seen as a disability but as a different *'way of being and acting in the world'* (Milton, 2014a, p. 12). It is interesting to note here the distinctive approach to individuals with SEN that many Latin American countries adopt. For example, in Nicaragua, a purely collectivistic society, there is an embracing culture where the extended family accepts the child 'as is', and the society is willing to adapt the environment, as opposed to changing the child (Kim, 2012).

7.6.3 Symptom description

Symptom diversity when it comes to autism in different countries has been confirmed by a number of studies. Ametepee and Chitiyo (2009) note that the few studies on autism which have been conducted in African countries do not report certain stereotypical behaviours such as hand flapping, self-aggression and rocking which are observed in children with autism in Western countries. Similarly, Matson et al. (2011) conducted a study to report on cross-cultural differences in autism symptoms among Israel, South Korea, the UK and the US. Parents, guardians/carers and teachers of 145 children with autism completed a checklist listing autism symptoms and analysis of the findings showed significant differences in core autism symptoms such as verbal and non-verbal communication, socialisation, insistence upon sameness and restricted interests. More precisely, children from the UK were reported to have significantly more difficulties and children from Israel were the ones with significantly fewer difficulties. The authors attributed these differences to parents' views and cultural expectations of their children meeting certain developmental milestones. The frequency of CB among children with autism also shows some diversity across the globe. The prevalence of CB in people with autism has been reported as 36% in Norway (Holden and Gitlesen, 2006), 64% in Ireland (Murphy et al., 2009) and 30% in South Korea (Shin et al., submitted for publication) (all cited in Chung et al., 2012) suggesting that different cultures have different standards for judging CB.

7.6.4 Educational approaches and interventions

Although parenting style and cultural values and beliefs are not linked to autism, as opposed to common beliefs 50 or 60 years ago (e.g. the refrigerator mother theory formulated by Kanner (1943) and supported by Bettelheim (1967) and other psychoanalysts and the belief that individualistic societies or families of higher socio-educational level might present higher autism rates, Kanner, 1943), they can influence educational choices. For instance, in the Anglo-American culture high value is placed on individualism, whereas some other cultures have a more collectivist orientation prioritising the group over the individual. This is well depicted in a study showing that child-rearing practices of Mexican American mothers tend to focus more on teaching politeness and respecting authority figures, whereas Anglo-American mothers more often value self-directed learning and independent thinking (Rodriguez and Olswang, 2003). Fatalism (i.e. a doctrine according to which individuals are powerless to influence their future and should just accept their fate) is very prominent in some Latino countries and it can influence to a great extent parents' educational priorities (Flores et al., 1999).

A study by Perepa (2014) explored the importance that parents of children with autism give to various social skills and whether this varies on the basis of their cultural background. He interviewed parents of four different cultural backgrounds (i.e. White British, Somali, West African and South Asian) living in the UK and he found that Afro-Caribbean and Somali parents considered giving eye contact the most important skill for their children whereas the South Asian and White British parents considered following rules and respecting personal space the most important ones. Another cultural difference this study identified was the importance parent groups placed on teaching their children facial expressions; while White British parents felt that facial expressions had limited importance in communication, parents from the other three groups reported that by learning facial expressions their child would develop an understanding of others' emotions.

It is interesting to note here that even parents' priorities in terms of their own training in order to improve their parenting skills vary across different countries. Preece et al. (2016) distributed questionnaires to parents in three South Eastern European countries (i.e. Croatia, Cyprus and Former Yugoslav Republic of Macedonia-FYROM) to identify training priorities. The 148 returned questionnaires showed that although there were some common themes in priorities, there were equally a few differences. Communication and socialisation were clear priority areas for most respondents (83% of total number of respondents) whereas leisure and recreation issues were given a low priority overall. In terms of differences, significantly fewer parents in Cyprus were interested in being trained in specific approaches such as sensory integration therapy and ABA than in the two Balkan countries. Additionally, only 38% of Cypriot respondents felt that information concerning policy, legislation and rights should be included in parents' training, whereas this was considered important by 70% of Croatian respondents and 92% respondents from FYROM.

7.6.5 Implications for practice

The discrepancies in how autism is perceived, the symptoms and the educational priorities among different cultures and countries, have not been seriously considered when it comes to educational, health and care practice. For instance, although in the London borough of Hackney, only 65% of the residents are monolingual speakers of English, with approximately 100 different language communities in residence (Norbury and Sparks, 2012) approximately 97% of qualified SLTs in the UK are White, middle-class, English-speaking women (Royal College of Speech and Language Therapists, 2002). The demographics are very similar in the US (Norbury and Sparks, 2012). From my personal experience in schools in Birmingham although there are great numbers of pupils from ethic minority backgrounds (according to Birmingham City Council Census KS201 Ethnic Groups (2011) only 53% of the population living in Birmingham are British with the next more popular ethnic backgrounds being Pakistani/British or Pakistani

13.5% and Indian/British or Indian 6%), most senior staff in schools are still not representative of the city's population. It is also common practice for well-known primarily American and Western European academics, practitioners and individuals with autism to give lectures and provide training around the world without previous consultation with native stakeholders.

Although considering cultural differences in everyday practice for people with autism is often easier said than done, there are some points which can be adopted straight away. For example, speakers who provide training courses around the world can - and perhaps should - filter their perspectives through local contexts and norms. Indicative of this is an example that Rose and Doveston (2015) give about how teachers receive training in India. Teacher training there is didactic in nature, largely delivered through lectures with little opportunity to dispute the ideas presented by tutors. Therefore, finding the confidence to debate and disagree in class can be very daunting, a point tutors should bear in mind. Additionally, it is essential for practitioners who work with ethnic minority groups to be aware of the stigma that is associated with SEN in some cultures. Moreover, practitioners should consult with people from the child's ethic background (Rose and Doveston, 2015) and involve them in the intervention team (Norbury and Sparks, 2012). This point is largely congruent with *Rochford Review* (2016) which recommends that further guidance needs to be given to teachers in order to effectively assess a wide range of children with SEN with English as a Foreign Language. Since some behaviours which are perceived appropriate by practitioners may not be expected within the child's home setting, it is vital to come back to the point that parents are the expert of their child and they should be the first to be consulted alongside the child themselves if their views can be obtained.

7.7 Reflection activities

- Choose an aspect of your practice (for practitioners) or your child's life/behaviour (for parents) which you would like to reflect on. Aspects and behaviours of successful interactions or moments that you find challenging are recommended starting points. Once you have decided what you will reflect on, select a method of recording and a 'critical other' to share your reflections with. Then record the behaviour and after that try to answer the following questions with the assistance of your 'critical other'. What did you do? How did your behaviour impact on the individual with SEN (identify elements which had positive and negative impact)? What did you learn from the process? Was it a positive experience or did you feel under too much stress? If the latter was the case, what can be changed next time you try it (e.g. different behaviour to focus on-possibly a successful one-recording method or 'critical other')?
- As a parent or a practitioner can you think of a time when being part of an inter-disciplinary team for your/a child worked very effectively

and another time when the experience was not a very positive one? Can you now identify a couple of things which contributed to the success of the first experience and a couple of things which made collaboration difficult in the second case?
- Can you think a couple of ways to get a person's with autism and SPMLD views? What extent of interpretation is needed by you or an advocate? If this is quite considerable, what can be changed to increase the possibilities that the real views of the person are communicated?
- If you work with individuals with autism from different cultural backgrounds, what are the main 2–3 points that you got out of the section on cultural differences (e.g. striking points, facts that you were not aware of, ideas that you haven't thought of)? Reflecting on these, is there any action point that you can put in place or suggest to your colleagues?

8 Participatory research designs
Implications for research

8.1 Introduction

Autism has been attracting a lot of attention, and relevant research is fast growing in the last couple of decades with an average of 6.5 papers on the topic being published per day (Volkmar, 2016). In this chapter I undertake to identify trends and research gaps in the field of autism and then present different areas of participatory research I have explored. I am fortunate in that all the research projects I have been involved so far have included stakeholders as either active participants whose views informed further stages of the research (i.e. AISI: Kossyvaki et al., 2012; Kossyvaki et al., 2016; ECHOES: Avramides et al., 2012; Shape: Parsons et al., 2015; Share-it: Porayska-Pomsta et al., 2013; Monoma: Kossyvaki et al., in preparation) or as equal co-researchers (Transform Autism Education-TAE, Guldberg et al., 2016).

8.2 A general account of the current situation in autism research

8.2.1 Age

It is well known that the majority of the studies on autism include participants of younger age. Jang et al. (2014) reviewed autism studies which were published between 1994 and 2014 aiming to point out age trends and found that 94% of the 2857 studies which met their inclusion criteria included infants, toddlers, children and adolescents (> 19 years old) while only 21% of the studies included adults (< 20 year old) and 3% employed individuals over 60 years old. In a similar vein, Edwards et al. (2012) reviewed 146 intervention research studies published from 2009 to 2012 and found that most participants were between 2 and 8 years of age (mean age = 7 years) and only 2% of them were 20 years or older. Another literature review by Crosland et al. (2013) explored trends in autism intervention research between 1995 and 2009 and found that there was a very limited number of studies involving people between 18 and 21 years old (8 out of the 273 reviewed studies) whereas there was an increase in the number of studies including children from birth to 5 years old (from 21% to 36%) over the 15 years timeframe of the review. Congruent with the aforementioned review findings are the results of an empirical study by Pellicano et al. (2014) which explored stakeholders' (i.e. practitioners, researchers, individuals with autism and family members) views on current research priorities in the UK. The participants of this study reported that autism studies have primarily focused on young children.

The aforementioned findings suggest that research so far has largely overlooked the needs of older people with autism. However, it has to be noted that although early intervention is of crucial importance in order to minimise difficulties and maximise skills (Rogers, 1996), a great number of people with autism will continue facing difficulties throughout their lifespan and interventions beyond early years would be beneficial for them (Edwards et al., 2012) and therefore are much needed.

8.2.2 Intellectual functioning

There has been extensive debate as to whether existing IQ tests can convey important information about the intellectual capacity of people with autism. Social-emotional, attentional and Executive Functioning difficulties, very common in autism, may considerably affect a person's ability to take an IQ test (Scheuffgen et al., 2000). Additionally, a person's difficulty in understanding another person's intentions, thoughts and feelings is also very likely to affect the former's ability to do well in an IQ test (Happé, 1994; Frith and Happé, 1998, both cited in Scheuffgen et al., 2000). Therefore, a number of researchers, autism practitioners and individuals with autism have been claiming that IQ tests primarily assess a person's compliance and ability to sit through the test. Obtaining a clear view of a person's intellectual functioning obviously becomes even more difficult when they have additional learning difficulties, resulting in many of the aforementioned difficulties appearing to a greater extent.

The percentage of people with autism and additional learning difficulties and the extent to which this population is equally represented in research is another contentious issue. A review of ten empirical studies on the prevalence of learning difficulties among children with autism by Emerson and Baines (2010) gave a very wide range of prevalence rates from 15% (Williams, 2008) to 84% (Magnusson, 2001). However, it has to be noted that eight out of the ten reviewed studies had a prevalence of comorbidity of autism and learning difficulties of above 40%. A literature review by Crosland et al. (2012) on trends in autism intervention research between 1995 and 2009 reported that most studies employed participants without severe learning and communication difficulties (i.e. 172 and 147 papers, respectively, out of the overall 273 reviewed papers). This has also been identified by Kasari and Smith (2013), who note that research studies

> often exclude children with ASD who test as lower functioning, nonverbal [. . .] and who have multiple disabilities.
>
> (p. 262)

The results of Pellicano et al.'s (2014) study are in agreement with the aforementioned findings. They reported that parents of children with autism feel that autism research tends to focus more on cognitively able individuals. Therefore, the collected evidence on the topic shows that there seems to be a research trend at the expense of people with autism and additional learning difficulties which warrants further investigation.

8.2.3 Sex differences

Arguably, there are some similarities but also many differences in the way autism manifests itself in males and females. Current diagnostic manuals have been criticised for their inability to identify girls as they list symptoms which appear more in males (Kopp and Gillberg, 1992, cited in Hurley, 2014). For example, it is now well known that women with autism tend to be better at masking their autism (Attwood, 2007) and this means that it is more unlikely for them to get a diagnosis. Similarly, Honeybourne (2015) found that women with autism tend to be more passive and keep quiet about their difficulties and, as a result, they are less visible than men.

Studies on sex differences among individuals with autism provide inconsistent findings. Overall, earlier studies tend to report that females have more severe autism especially when severity is defined in terms of lower IQ or greater difficulties in adaptive functioning (Lord et al., 1982; Tsai and Beisler, 1983; Volkmar et al., 1993). More recent studies showed either more difficulties in communication and restricted, repetitive and stereotyped behaviours in males than in females with autism (Hartley and Sikora, 2009; Lai et al., 2011; Park et al., 2012) or no sex differences (Baron-Cohen et al., 2001; Holtmann et al., 2007; Allison et al., 2008). Interestingly Fombonne (2005) claimed that the disparity in male:female ratio among individuals with autism is more prominent for populations without learning difficulties. In reviewing 13 studies which identified their participants as having autism without learning difficulties, the median male:female ratio was 5.5:1. Conversely, in 12 studies which identified their participants as having autism with moderate to severe learning difficulties the median male:female ratio was 1.95:1.

Another important point regarding gender and autism is the unequal representation of males and females in research. In a review by Edwards et al. (2012) on the age of autistic participants receiving intervention. 86% of the participants whose sex was reported were male. This figure exceeds the percentage of people with autism who are male in the general population especially as far as individuals with autism and learning difficulties are concerned. For example, according to the aforementioned Fombonne's (2005) review males with autism and additional learning difficulties represented 66% of the sample whereas males with autism without learning difficulties represented 85% of the sample. If the fact that many women with autism remain undiagnosed is added to this argument, then one can understand how unequal their representation in research is.

Although there is a growing body of research on sex differences among males and females with autism, this is still a topic which merits further investigation. A more equal representation of males and females in research is needed (Edwards et al., 2012; Hurley, 2014). Moreover, there is a call for more rigorous research on issues such as the impact of different interventions on each gender and ways of learning and processing information (Honeybourne, 2015).

8.2.4 Research priorities

Generally speaking, there seems to be a large discrepancy between the priorities identified by the research portfolio and the stakeholders' and beneficiaries' agenda. Indicative is the example of the UK, a country which, after the US, leads autism research, where according to Pellicano et al. (2013), more than half (56%) of the grant expenditure goes towards basic science grants (e.g. neural and cognitive systems, genetics and risk factors). At the same time, little research targets interventions (18%), effective services for autistic people and their families (5%), diagnosis (5%) and societal issues (1%). Another interesting study by Pellicano et al. (2014) involved a number of stakeholders such as people with autism, parents or close family members, practitioners, researchers and others. Among them 1624 completed the online survey and 72 participated in in-depth focus groups and 1:1 interviews. All stakeholders were dissatisfied with the pattern of current funding and especially autistic adults, parents and practitioners, who prioritised research into issues of immediate practical concern. Specifically, they declared that they want '*to see real change and real things happening*' (p. 760). Another interesting finding of this study was the discrepancy of views between researchers, family members and autistic individuals regarding research areas which should be given priority; developing life skills, treatment and thinking and learning were all important research priorities for practitioners and family members but not for autistic individuals who prioritised areas such as their place in society, co-occurring conditions, lifespan issues and gender differences.

8.3 Importance of real-world research

Conducting real-world research or research 'in the wild' (i.e. work in close partnerships with beneficiaries to achieve transformational impact) (Engineering and Physical Sciences Research Council-EPSRC, 2012) is getting increasing attention in the field of autism and special needs. Although there is valid criticism that most autism intervention research is still conducted in clinics and laboratories (e.g. Roos et al., 2008; Crosland et al., 2012; Kasari and Smith, 2013), a number of scholars have argued in favour of conducting research in the child's home, school or wider community (e.g. Parsons et al., 2013; Kossyvaki and Papoudi, 2016) as these are 'natural environments' where the taught skills need to be displayed. It is true that real-world research is becoming more and more popular. For example, Matson and Konst (2014) reviewed 31 studies on early intensive interventions and found that 23 of them were conducted at least partially at either home or school.

Real-world studies may differ from each other on a number of matters but the remainder of this section will focus on two significant elements as identified by Kasari and Smith (2013): the research design and the effectiveness of the study. With regard to research design, real-world studies largely employ Single Subject Design (SSD) in which each participant serves as his or her own control. In this, a baseline condition in which the participants receive no intervention is compared to one or more intervention conditions. These type of studies, although providing valuable information, are weaker than Group Design (GD) studies in which a group of participants goes through an intervention and is then compared to another group who went through a different - or no - intervention. Nevertheless, two points need to be mentioned here for GD studies: (i) they are more often conducted off real world settings and (ii) they use samples that are too small to conduct statistical analyses, in which case a SSD would possibly have been more appropriate. Another interesting point of differentiation is that of 'partial effectiveness' versus 'full effectiveness' trials. In the former case, the researchers conduct the intervention in full at the real-world setting but without involving the stakeholders/beneficiaries. In the latter case, the intervention is conducted by the stakeholders/beneficiaries while the researchers might have designed the study, trained the interventionists and collected fidelity of implementation data (i.e. checks to determine whether the intervention was conducted in the way it was supposed to). The sustainability of full effectiveness studies is much greater when research ceases and they are the only ones which can be considered a truly real-world study. However, they seem to be the exception to the rule.

From an academic's point of view who teaches post-graduate students (most of whom work as full-time teaching staff), doing real-world research can be a great way of evidencing effective practices at school which often go unnoticed because they are not reported and disseminated beyond the school boundaries. Of course, there are procedural and methodological barriers when conducting interventions in children's primary environments such as schools and homes. For example, clinic-based settings may provide a context in which internal validity (findings indicate a causal relationship) is enhanced but external validity (findings can be generalised) and ecological validity (findings are applicable to people's everyday life) are often limited. The following section aims to provide some ideas of how rigour can be enhanced in real-world studies.

8.4 Enhancing rigour in real-world studies

Although the recently published *Rochford Review* (2016) argues in favour of schools being engaged '*in research to support good practice*' (p. 25), it is very difficult to conduct valid, reliable school-based research. Good practice-based research should be well-planned, carefully executed, rigorous, conducted with integrity, meticulously reported, transparent and ethical. Although small-scale studies can provide some insightful accounts of great value, these are often insufficient to promote and support substantial changes (Hallett and Hallett, 2015). Case study, a widely used methodology for educational small-scale studies, is one of the most abused methodologies and can become an unstructured description of randomly chosen features (Swetnam, 1997). Abuse of certain research designs has led to practices of anathematization which has resulted in whole university departments conducting certain types of research to the exclusion of others, with journals publishing only papers using certain methodologies. Some journals have no history of publishing qualitative research which is more likely to be published as books or book chapters. When a qualitative paper is published in a journal, this often describes the methodology of the study instead of reporting findings (Beail and Williams, 2014).

This dichotomy between education (primarily qualitative approaches) and psychology (often use of standardised tests and quantitative statistical analysis) is also obvious among academics working in the field of SEN, an area thoroughly studied by both disciplines. As Bölte (2014) very successfully states in regards to the polemic between quantitative and qualitative research *'inadequate arrogance exists on both sides of the debate'* (p. 67). He goes on arguing that qualitative research can be as important as quantitative if scientific rigour is applied. Few people in either field adopt the pragmatic approach where the philosophical assumptions and methods that work best for a particular piece of research are followed. Further promoting the pragmatic approach, Frost (2011, cited in Beail and Williams, 2014) criticises this notion of 'methodolatry' claiming that research should be driven by questions and curiosity and that researchers should not slavishly follow a particular methodological approach.

The rest of this section provides some hands-on advice (i.e. criteria and quality indicators) on how to increase rigour in real-world research. Denscombe (2002) provides ten criteria or ground rules for conducting good research, which are of great interest for those conducting small-scale projects. To start with, every piece of research needs to have clearly stated aims (criterion 1: purpose). It should also relate to existing knowledge and needs (criterion 2: relevance) while the researcher should acknowledge time, money and opportunity constraints (criterion 3: resources). Another very important element of research projects is that they have to contribute something new to existing knowledge (criterion 4: originality). Using reliable methods to produce valid data (criterion 5: accuracy) while providing an explicit account of the methodology used (criterion 6: accountability) are also substantial. Generalisations or at least tentative suggestions (criterion 7: generalisations) are recommended. The researchers have to disclose the values and beliefs they bring to the research while acknowledging the impact of these on the research questions, methods, analysis and outcomes (criterion 8: objectivity). Denscombe closes his ground rules by underlining the importance of researchers recognising the rights and interests of the participants (criterion 9: ethics) and only making claims based on their findings (criterion 10: proof).

Reichow et al. (2008) provide the following lists of primary and secondary quality indicators for single subject and group intervention research which can apply in real-world research. Studies should provide information on quality indicators '*with operational and replicable precision*' (p. 1314) in order to achieve rigour. For single subject research, they suggest that information on the subsequent primary quality indicators should be given: (i) participant characteristics (age, gender, diagnosis), (ii) independent variable (intervention), (iii) dependent variable (dependent measures/tests), (iv) baseline condition (at least three measurement points, no trend or counter trend), (v) visual analysis (all relevant data for participants to be graphed) and (vi) experimental control (changes in the dependent variables with the manipulation of the independent variable). Secondary quality indicators entail: (i) inter-observer agreement ($\leq$20% of sessions with agreement of $\leq$80%), (ii) Kappa (at $\leq$20% of sessions with a score of $\leq$.60), (iii) fidelity (reliability at $\leq$80%), (iv) blind raters (raters unaware of whether the participants are going through the intervention), (v) generalisation and/or maintenance (measures for generalisation and maintenance to be used) and (vi) social validity (socially important dependent variable/s, time and cost effective intervention, participants satisfied with the results).

For group research, primary quality indicators refer to: (i) participant characteristics (already noted), (ii) independent variable (already noted), (iii) comparison condition (description of any other intervention the participants are to receive), (iv) dependent variable (already noted), (v) link between research question and data analysis (data analysis for all variables) and (vi) use of statistical tests (statistical analysis of the results). Secondary quality indicators entail: (i) random assignment (participants are randomly assigned to groups), (ii) inter-observer agreement (already noted), (iii) blind raters (already noted), (iv) fidelity (already noted), (v) attrition (loss of participants is comparable between groups), (vi) generalisation and/or maintenance (already noted), (vii) ES (to be reported for $\leq$ 75% of the outcome measures and to be $\leq$0.40) and (viii) social validity (already noted).

Based on the aforementioned quality indicators, studies can be rated as having strong, adequate or weak research strength. In order to be classified as strong, a study has to receive high quality ratings on all primary quality indicators and show evidence of at least three (for single subject research) and four (for group research) or more secondary quality indicators. To be classified as having adequate strength, a study has to receive high quality ratings on four or more primary quality indicators (no unacceptable rating on any of the primary quality indicators) and show evidence of at least two secondary quality indicators. Studies to be classified as having weak rigour receive fewer than four high quality ratings on primary quality indicators or show evidence of fewer than two secondary quality indicators.

To sum up, growing attention has been paid to the importance of real-world research, and increasingly, scholars provide detailed guidelines to researchers as to how to enhance rigour. The next three sections highlight the importance of involving stakeholders (practitioners, parents and individuals with autism) in the research process, and suggest ways of doing this.

8.5 Involving stakeholders in research

Involving stakeholders in research is a tendency that is gaining ground in the last few years. This comes not only as a result of the demand expressed by stakeholders themselves but also because universities and research councils (e.g. Economic and Social Research Council (ESRC), EPSRC, Medical Research Council) require more impactful research and engagement with stakeholders. Although for some researchers there has only been one way of doing research, namely that of working closely with stakeholders as opposed to doing research *on* them, more and more scholars comment on the benefits of this process:

> Knowledge is more likely to be useful, applicable, and impactful if the beneficiaries of research were engaged in the research process.
> (Elsabbagh et al., 2014, p. 775)

While stakeholders are likely to be involved at different stages of research, this knowledge development is still felt to be unidirectional, or 'top down', from scientists to research end-users. The tension between unidirectional versus bi-directional engagement of stakeholders in research is very prominent in the field of autism (Elsabbagh et al., 2014) primarily because of the autistic activists and other advocates who push towards a more equal and equitable representation of stakeholders' voice in research projects. This section explores the involvement of different types of stakeholders in autism research.

Despite a gradually increasing interest towards research in schools with practitioners in the role of researchers, a number of scholars have identified a substantial gap between research and practice in real-world classrooms (Reichow et al., 2008) and considerable lack of teacher and practitioner involvement in intervention research (Parsons et al., 2011). However, since children with autism all over the world spend most of their day at school, as opposed to clinics and therapeutic centres, there is a pressing need to conduct better research in schools especially when these studies are related to exploring ways of overcoming barriers to learning (Imray and Hincliffe, 2014). Parsons et al. (2013) claim:

> Building collaborative partnerships between researchers and school practitioners is central to achieving improved understanding of, and outcomes for, pupils on the autism spectrum.
> (p. 269)

This partnership should be among equal contributors as a process of *knowledge exchange* between academics and school staff rather than *knowledge transfer* from the former to the latter (Parsons et al., 2013). However, since sometimes even in knowledge exchange the power and direction of influence still remains primarily with the researchers, a process of *knowledge co-creation* (Parsons et al., 2015) and a shared endeavour which is in line with the theoretical underpinnings of Participatory Action Research should be promoted.

Implications for research

Parsons et al. (2013) outline a number of reasons why strong links between academic researchers and school practitioners should be established. To start with, schools collect a range of data on their pupils for their own purposes; researchers can offer their expertise to help school staff to formulate valid research questions, select and develop appropriate data collection methods and analyse their findings. Working in partnership with universities can also ensure that school-based research is subject to rigorous ethical review and that the results are disseminated to a wider audience. From a practical point of view, schools consist of large cohorts of pupils which means value for money for funding bodies. Last but not least, most children spend many years in the same school offering opportunities for longitudinal studies.

However, thus far, autism intervention research in schools fails to show great outcomes. One reason for this is that practitioners do not achieve high fidelity of implementation (Parsons et al., 2013). Although research needs to determine whether interventions in schools are effective and explore the extent to which interventionists follow fidelity of implementation procedures (Charman et al., 2011), it should also be noted that in these studies, practitioners need to 'fit in' with what is prescribed without having their needs considered (Parsons et al., 2013). Therefore, achieving high fidelity in real-world studies is an issue which is worth further consideration.

The Pan-London Autism Schools Network – Research (PLASN-R) partnership (i.e. a partnership between head teachers of special schools and university researchers in order to meet regularly to discuss challenges and opportunities in school-based research in autism) is an effective way of school practitioner involvement in research. One of the main limitations of the PLASN-R partnership is that it does not involve other stakeholders aside from head teachers. Although this has been done for understandable reasons (senior management teams in schools must be involved in the process if systemic change is to be applied), it has to be acknowledged as a limitation which future studies need to consider.

Nowadays research is tending to become an integral part of the teaching profession. Teachers are expected to be more and more involved in research- related activities. This responsibility is underscored in the Teacher Standards (DfE, 2011) which outline the minimum level of practice expected by teachers in England. According to these standards teachers are expected to

> use relevant data to monitor progress, set targets, and plan subsequent lessons.
>
> (p. 12)

Additionally, practitioner experts with long-standing experience in schools vividly outline the pressing need for school practitioners to develop strong research skills in order to be successful in their jobs:

> Teaching [. . .] needs to be a classroom research-based and a classroom inquiry-based profession.
>
> (Imray and Hincliffe, 2015, p. 49)

154 *Implications for research*

Teachers also need to become more discerning consumers of research in order to improve their skills and practice. A way of achieving this is to pursue postgraduate university studies which aim to teach students critical thinking skills. This is in agreement with Teacher Standards (DfE, 2011) which purport that teachers should

> demonstrate a critical understanding of developments in the subject and curriculum areas, and promote the value of scholarship.
>
> (p. 11)

I have many times challenged my postgraduate students to give me the evidence a study provides in order to support its claim, so that instead of merely embracing the conclusions drawn, they can realise that they often have not looked deep enough to critique the evidence provided.

More research is needed on the effectiveness of the use of TAs in the classroom, as current results on the topic are quite inconsistent and contradictory (see 7.4.3 'The Significant Role of Teaching Assistants' for more details). It is interesting to mention here the findings of two reports which explored the role of TAs. Blatchford et al. (2008) in the *Deployment and Impact of Support Staff project* found that teachers and head teachers tended to report more on the effect TAs had on teachers and teaching than outcomes for pupils. More precisely, they mentioned positive effects on teachers' job satisfaction and decreases in workload and levels of stress. The following *Making a Statement project* (Webster and Blatchford, 2013) reported that TAs tend to be the ones who are responsible for planning and teaching for pupils with SEN and despite good intentions, the support they provide is not enough to increase academic attainment. Another interesting point regarding research on the impact of the role of TAs was made by Saddler (2014), who claims that so far research has narrowly focused on pupils' academic achievement, with little attention paid to how TAs influence pupils' social outcomes. However, the concepts of academic achievement and social inclusion are inextricably linked. To this end, Vincett et al. (2005) suggest the use of detailed case studies to complement the existent large-scale studies on the topic. Lastly, further research needs to incorporate specialist health practitioners, as there is a considerable amount of joint working between teaching staff and SLTs, OTs, psychologists, mental health and social care professionals (Charman et al., 2011).

In all research projects I have participated in so far, teaching staff were involved to a great extent. Teachers, TAs and therapists were asked about ways that technology can be improved and used effectively at school to meet the needs of children with autism (i.e. ECHOES: Avramides et al., 2012; Shape: Parsons et al., 2015; Share-it: Porayska-Pomsta et al., 2013; Monoma: Kossyvaki et al., in preparation) and share strategies and resources for good autism practice (i.e. AISI: Kossyvaki et al., 2012; Kossyvaki et al., 2016; TAE: Guldberg et al., 2016). Therefore, in all the aforementioned cases, school-based stakeholders have determined to a lesser or greater extent the research agenda in collaboration with university researchers.

8.5.1 Involving parents

A number of studies have explored the impact of parents training on certain behaviours of their autistic children. Parents' involvement in intervention research is important for a number of reasons. First of all, since early intervention in autism is highly recommended (Rogers, 1996), parents' involvement is undoubtedly an area worth investment. Training parents as co-therapists means that children will be exposed to a greater number of opportunities to practise the learnt skills, as parents spend considerably more time with their children than anybody else. The benefits of any intervention can therefore be maintained better if they are involved in the process (White et al., 1992). Parent training is of crucial importance not only for their children but also for themselves, as this is likely to reduce stress levels and increase their feeling of competence (Schultz et al., 2011). The cost effectiveness of involving parents in intervention research is an added bonus (White et al., 1992). Parents' involvement is a very sensible thing to achieve; they are the ones who know their child the best and who care about them the most. I will never forget what a mother of a 10-year-old child with autism and limited speech told me regarding how uncomfortable she feels every time her son is about to start a new activity she is not involved in; she is very anxious about how her son will be treated and also worried that he might not be able to make his needs understood to new people. She characteristically told me '*I am his voice, how will he get on without me?*'

There is a number of reviews and meta-analyses on parents' involvement in autism intervention research showing that this is an area which has been well explored. For example, Schultz et al. (2011) reviewed 30 studies on parent education programmes for children with autism but found a number of weaknesses in them. The majority of the studies (70%) employed SSD, none of them reported data on fidelity of implementation and 47% of them did not report using a curriculum or a training manual to teach skills to parents. Additionally, there was no information on frequency or duration in 40% of the papers. This is a common omission in papers conducted in real-world settings.

McConachie and Diggle (2007) conducted a systematic review of parent-implemented early interventions for young children with autism which did not include SSD because of the questionable generalisable power of their findings. They reviewed 12 studies which met their strict inclusion criteria (interestingly there was no date limit for the primary studies), finding that studies tended to suggest that parent training improves the child's social communication, parental performance and parent-child interaction. It is worth mentioning here that in half of the reviewed studies ($n = 6$) the setting in which parents worked with their children (e.g. home, clinic, university laboratory) was not identified.

Matson and Konst (2014) reviewed 31 studies on early interventions for children with autism and found that 16 of these studies used parents as co-therapists whereas in 4 studies parents were the only therapists. This finding is of great importance given that 27 of these studies employed ABA, one of the interventions with most prescriptive manual and intensity (up to 40 hours per week) and traditionally less open to involve non-professionals in therapy. This shows that the landscape is changing and parents are more and more likely to be involved in research.

A recent meta-analysis comparing studies of parent- and clinician-implemented interventions for children with autism found significantly greater improvements in clinician-implemented studies with small to no effects in parent-implemented studies (Nahmias and Mandell, 2014, cited in Stahmer and Pellecchia, 2015). However, Stahmer and Pellecchia (2015) believe that when parents are involved in research there should be a shift in the posed research question in order to move towards a more ecologically valid intervention model. For example, 'How can we best support parents in improving family functioning?' is a more appropriate question to ask. In such cases there needs to be a change of priorities as parents should not be expected to become therapists but they should be assisted by the researchers to succeed in parenting.

The two PACT studies (Green et al., 2010; Pickles et al., 2016) are from the most rigorous studies which involved parents. PACT is a one-year, parent-mediated developmentally focused social communication intervention which aims to optimise naturalistic parent – child social communication at home in order to improve the child's social communication and reduce repetitive behaviours. It consists of 12 therapy sessions (2 hour long each) for six months followed by monthly support for a further 6 months. During this period, parents are expected to work 20–30 minutes per day with their child on planned activities. In the initial study (Green et al., 2010), 152 children with autism (aged 2 to 5 years) were randomly assigned to the PACT intervention ($n = 77$) or treatment as usual ($n = 75$). At the 13-month endpoint, the severity of symptoms was reduced more in the group assigned to PACT rather than in the group assigned to treatment as usual. Parent synchronous responses and child communication initiations were the variables that showed greater increase. Six years later, the PACT follow-up study (Pickles et al., 2016) hit the headlines and caused a lot of discussion within the autism research community but also among lay audiences. 126 parent-child dyads participated in the follow-up study which showed a considerable decrease in autism symptoms and a further increase in child's initiations and parents' synchrony for the PACT group.

An interesting point to make here is the importance of coaching sessions in order to sustain changes in parents' attitudes and behaviours following training. Meadan et al. (2014) showed that training alone might not be enough to bring substantial changes in parents' behaviours as opposed to coaching sessions which seemed more effective. Although their study involved parents of young children (2–5 years old) with Down syndrome to promote their social-pragmatic communication skills parallels can be drawn for training parents of children with autism.

Research so far has involved parents in training to improve their parenting skills but has limitedly explored their potential as co-researchers. Walmsley and Mannan (2009) described how parents of individuals with learning difficulties were trained to facilitate focus groups of parents in Ireland in order to explore avenues of better communication with service providers. A PAR approach was followed. Initially the researchers presented to some parents different ways on how to approach the project and it was agreed that a series of focus groups would be the most accessible way of enabling parents to participate in the specific study. A set of questions was discussed with the advisory group and piloted with a group of parents. More parents were then invited for focus groups which were held in the morning. After the end of the focus groups parents were invited for lunch and a training workshop on focus groups was held in the afternoon for parents who would like to attend. Following the training workshop parents were asked whether they would like to further participate in the study as interviewers themselves. One of the most important findings of this project was the role model that parent co-researchers offered for other participants. For example, one of the co-researchers mentioned a comment they made during a focus group: '*at the moment we're going through pure hell*' which encouraged other parents to acknowledge their own struggles. The co-researchers also reported that non-verbal support facilitated the dialogue as sitting '*in a group of parents who know what you are talking about. [. . .] makes a huge difference*' (p. 273).

Overall, there seems to be extensive research on involving parents of autistic children in research, but not without limitations. As many of the reviews revealed primary studies fail to provide information on the content, duration and frequency of the intervention parents were trained in as well as the setting where the intervention took place. Additionally, there is a dearth of studies employing parents as co-researchers. Ending this section on a more positive note, it seems that more traditionally expert-led interventions such as ABA have become more open to working with parents.

8.5.2 Involving individuals with autism

Broadly speaking there are two ways of involving people with autism in research which this section aims to cover: i) as co-researchers and ii) as research participants. As autism and learning difficulties form the dual focus of this book, I have drawn on literature on both autism and learning difficulties in an attempt to give a more accurate picture of the current situation.

Although participation of people with SEN in doing research is not a new concept or practice (Moore et al., 1998; Nind and Vinh, 2014), it is not until recently that they have a clear presence in research. The social model of disability led to the 'nothing about us without us' movement which increased the involvement of individuals with SEN in research. An indicative example of this transformation is the academic journal the *British Journal of Learning Disabilities* which published in 2012 (volume 40, number 2) the very first special issue in the field that was authored and edited by people with learning difficulties. It has also to be noted that in the specific journal all papers apart from the usual abstract they include an accessible abstract in the form of bullet points so that people with learning difficulties can follow it. This is a growing tendency seen in a number of other academic journals in the field.

158 Implications for research

8.5.2.1 Employing individuals with autism as co-researchers

According to Bigby et al. (2014) there are three distinctive ways people with SEN can participate in research. These are the following: i) the advisory approach, ii) the leading and controlling approach and iii) the collaborative groups. In the first case, individuals with SEN act as advisors or counsellors in research projects. In the leading and controlling approach, people with SEN are the ones who initiate, lead and conduct research on topics that are important to them. In the collaborative groups, people with and without SEN work together on research projects each providing their skills and experience to create new knowledge together. The collaborative approach is congruent with inclusive research postulating that people with SEN should initiate research by determining the topic, its focus and aims (Northway et al., 2014; Puyalto et al., 2016).

A number of scholars have very reasonably challenged the notion of researchers with and without SEN working together in equal partnerships. For example, Kiernan (1999) questions how equal participation can be ensured when the latter support the former in conducting research and McClimens (2008) talks about power relations and their impact. Puyalto et al. (2016) draw the readers' attention to the fine line between NT people supporting individuals with SEN in doing research and crossing the line to make decisions for them. Similarly, Strnadová and Cumming (2014) talk about the blurry boundaries between inclusive research and advocacy.

Despite the challenges of involving people with SEN in academic research, with time being one of the main ones (Stalker, 1998), a number of studies so far have employed people with SEN only for some stages of research. Jivraj et al. (2014) reviewed seven papers which examine research partnerships between academic researchers and individuals with autism or other neurodevelopmental disorders and found some limitations on the latter's involvement in research. More precisely, in five out of the seven studies individuals with SEN were only involved in operational tasks such as data collection rather than in higher-order aspects of the research process such as identifying research questions and informing methodology and methods. In only two studies, individuals with SEN were involved throughout the entire research process.

Nonetheless, numbers of studies have involved people with SEN at stages of research which have been for long recognised as the province of university-based academics, namely data analysis and report/paper writing. Stevenson (2014) reported on a study which involved 2 people with learning difficulties in an exploratory textual data analysis. A NT university-based researcher asked the two people with learning difficulties to go through 3 to 4 transcripts each and highlight and offer comments about what they felt was 'important' or 'interesting'. Then basic themes were negotiated and discussed as a group. Three people with learning difficulties participated as co-researchers in another project about abuse and wrote a paper on their experience (Flood et al., 2012). Ruth Northway, from the University of South Wales, supported them; she asked them about their experience of being researchers, she then wrote their answers up and share the document with them for final approval. Overall, the researchers felt that they acquired a number of new skills related to research (e.g. know what kind of questions to ask, work as a team), independence (e.g. know how to use the bus in order to go to work) and better mental health and well-being (e.g. build up confidence). More precisely, they mentioned that *'working as a researcher has given a reason for getting up in the morning'* (p. 292) and *'we have come across some difficulties, we feel it has been good to be challenged to do new things'* (p. 293).

Nowadays, a number of autistic researchers have obtained the training to produce high quality research and who either work independently or join research teams. Among them I would like to mention here Damian Milton, a sociologist by training and a PhD holder who is active in both community work and academic research and writing (Milton, 2014b). Michelle Dawson is a Canadian autistic researcher who works for the University of Montreal and has produced a number of research papers (Dawson, 2016a). Both Milton and Dawson give lectures around the world and provide reliable, constructive criticism of other people's research through social media (Milton, 2016; Dawson, 2016b).

A growing number of research projects either employ people with autism as researchers or are primarily executed by autistic researchers with some support from NT academics and practitioners. To name a few, TAE (2016a, 2016b) is a project funded by the European commission to develop best autism practices in Greece and Italy based on a model developed in the UK. Autistic individuals are employed in all three countries to support the development and adaptation of the material. AuVision (TAE, 2016c) is a project led by autistic students at the University of Birmingham who explore the experiences of other autistic students, aiming to develop guidelines to ensure that future students are better supported.

Overall, it appears that people with SEN and more precisely autism who participate in research projects are of certain abilities and they have taken specific roles. More specifically, they tend to be more involved in qualitative small exploratory case studies at an advocacy (e.g. development of training materials) rather than full researcher role (e.g. data analysis, dissemination). There is also the issue of the intellectual abilities of people who end up working for research projects as these tend to be people with less severe or no learning difficulties (Kiernan, 1999). Although there are some studies which have researched the views of people with special needs who have participated in research projects as co-investigators, there are no studies exploring the other side of the coin, the views of NT researchers who have worked with them. A study by Puyalto et al. (2016) looked at the experiences of both researchers with and without learning difficulties working together and reported that NT researchers believe that participation of people with learning difficulties resulted in better quality research. More research to explore this issue in detail would be helpful.

8.5.2.2 Getting their views

In order to involve people with SEN in research, there needs to be some understanding of effective ways of getting their views. As far as of people with learning difficulties are concerned, Lewis and Porter (2007) suggest, among others, two effective ways: (i) observations and (ii) individual or small group interviews. Because Chapter 5 explored in great detail how observations can be conducted and recorded, the remainder of this section will explore different ways of getting the views of people and more precisely children with autism and severe learning difficulties.

Although there seems that most of the published papers which involved people with SEN in research report on the findings of these studies rather than the process of engaging the participants, there has been some growing literature on methodological issues when gathering the views of children with autism in interview formats. Some researchers (Mauthner, 1997; Owen et al., 2004) reported that discussing specific events and feelings rather than using direct questions can be more effective. Harrington et al. (2013) suggest that interview questions should focus on present experiences given that most people with autism find it difficult to recall and narrate personal past experiences. Close-ended questions might be more effective (Lewis, 2002; Harrington et al., 2013) as individuals with autism tend to communicate better in structured situations (Lovaas, 1981; Lord and Schopler, 1994). However, Lewis (2002) also suggests mixing open with close-ended questions during interviews as autistic children tend to have a predisposition to confirm what is put to them. A very interesting review on this topic was conducted by Funazaki and Oi (2013) who explored how school-aged children responded to 'yes/no' and 'wh-' (i.e. who, what, where, when, why) questions. Summarising the findings of four studies, they suggested that children displaying high levels of echolalia have difficulty responding to 'yes/no' questions, but those without echolalia, regardless of their cognitive abilities, may find it easier to respond to 'yes/no' questions than 'wh-' questions. Whether questions should be repeated is also debated, as some suggest that by repeating the question children may perceive that their answer has been incorrect (Westcott et al., 2002; Lewis, 2009). Nevertheless, for some children with autism slower processing skills may mean that repetition is helpful if not imperative (Bogdashina, 2005).

Special attention during interviews should be paid to moments in which the child responds with silence. This might be happening for a number of reasons. Children may respond with silence because they require additional time to process what has been asked by the interviewer or because they have not understood the question. However, silence can also be '*the most powerful form of voice*' (Lewis, 2011, p. 55) and '*some children may genuinely and freely prefer silence to voicing their views*' (Lewis and Porter, 2007, p. 224). To denote conscious silence, literature (Beresford et al., 1997; Lewis and Porter, 2007) suggests providing children with a squeaky toy that they can squeeze when they do not know the answer to the question or they would like to give no response. Lewis and Porter (2007) recommend children to be given control of the video/audio recorder or a stop symbol to show the researcher that they would like to finish.

Apart from verbal questioning, there might be other ways of getting children's with autism views. Dockrell et al. (2000) suggest that objects and pictures can be useful in interviews, particularly with children who have limited verbal communication skills. An example of using concrete materials in order to express choice is the 'Talking Mats' intervention (Cameron and Murphy, 2002; Murphy and Cameron, 2008). Talking Mats is an effective tool to assist a person to describe their feelings about a variety of issues by manipulating symbols on a board. It is worth considering though that while helpful in facilitating communication, for some more cognitively able children visual prompts may limit discussion to the range of pictures or symbols available at the time (Lewis, 2002; Preece, 2009; Lewis, 2009). In a similar vein, Williams and Hanke (2007) explored how the views of 15 mainstream pupils with autism (13 males and 2 females/ aged from 7 to 15 years) on what they consider the optimum school features can be obtained via the use of the Drawing the Ideal Self technique (Moran, 2001), based on Personal Construct Psychology (Kelly, 1955); pupils expressed their views using a mixture of drawing, talking and writing.

8.5.2.3 Ethical considerations

Addressing the ethical issues of involving people, and in particular children, with SEN in research can be a particularly challenging issue. The importance of ethics when working with children with autism has also been covered elsewhere in this book (see section 5.13 'Ethical Considerations') but this was done with regard to a specific research project. This section aims to further explore the issue of assent/ consent, as there is considerable debate around it.

The British Psychological Society (BPS, 2010) provides detailed documentation of the basic rules which apply to obtaining consent for participation in research. More precisely, it outlines that researchers should ensure that consent of all participants regardless of age and intellectual capacity is sought by using appropriate means as every person should consent *'freely to the process on the basis of adequate information'* (p. 15). In order to ensure that young children's participation in research is entirely voluntary and not a product of coercion, their assent should be sought. As a general rule (exceptions may apply), assent should be sought from children above 9 years of age who are able to make decisions for themselves and *'reason about the consequences of participation'* (Leikin, 1993, p. 6). For children under 16 years old and people whose capacity to consent might be questioned, the consent of parents or those with legal responsibility for the individual should also be sought. In cases that competence to consent is questionable (e.g. people with severe learning or communication difficulties), researchers are encouraged to engage potential participants in conversation in order to decide whether they have got the capacity to give consent (Mental Capacity Act, 2005; BPS, 2008). However, in the name of protection from potential exploitation and harm, people with SEN, especially the ones with SPMLD, are under the risk of not being represented in relevant research (Iacono, 2006) or even silenced (Ware, 2016).

Although the need to get people's consent for participating in research has been widely acknowledged, relatively little is written on the importance and ways of ensuring ongoing consent. Harrington et al. (2013) advise researchers to check the participants' level of engagement during the first meeting as they might have given consent due to power imbalance with the adult researcher or because their parents think that this was a good idea. In a similar vein, Lloyd (2012) highlights the need to provide people with autism with several opportunities to say 'yes' or 'no' to participating in the research throughout the process. To make it more effective, these opportunities should be presented in different ways, by different people and in different contexts. Participants should always be reminded of and given the right to withdraw if signs of distress are apparent (e.g. upset, high anxiety levels). If the participant is not able to take this decision for themselves, their parents should act on their behalf. If distress continues despite parents' decision to keep their child in the study, the child should automatically withdraw to protect their rights.

After having covered the issue of involving people with autism in research, especially when they have additional learning difficulties, as this is a population which is largely underrepresented in research the chapter will close with an account of the current situation on cross-cultural and cross-country studies. The aim of the following section is to bring light to research gaps in the field and work as a starting point for future research projects of that nature.

8.6 Cross-cultural and cross-country studies

Although the first studies showing differences in the autism prevalence, symptoms and educational priorities across the globe have been around for longer than 30 years, it is not until fairly recently that a reasonable number of studies from different countries and cultures within the same country started to emerge. It is also true that the majority of autism studies so far have been conducted with populations that are predominantly North American and Western European and most research has failed to identify individuals with autism according to culture (Dyches et al., 2004). Therefore, more research needs to be conducted outside the US and Europe and with ethnic minority groups in these countries. Nonetheless, there is some debate as to whether country-specific epidemiological studies on autism prevalence, in order to assess needs and establish educational approaches, should be a priority, especially where resources are limited and current priorities include preventing life-threatening conditions (Elsabbagh et al., 2012). If local bodies decide that this is the way forward, translation and adaptation of existing widely used diagnostic instruments such as Autism Diagnostic Observation Schedule (ADOS, Lord et al., 2000) and Autism Diagnostic Interview-Revised (ADI-R) (Lord et al., 1994) and interventions (e.g. ABA-based therapies, developmental approaches) in other languages and cultures need to be considered. Given that diagnosis of autism still relies on behavioural observation, there is plenty of room for wide variation in clinical judgment especially when different cultural and social variables interfere (Elsabbagh et al., 2012). For example, in ADOS, the examiner has to set up a pretend birthday party. However, this is organised according to how birthdays are celebrated in Western societies; this may be very different from birthday celebrations in a developing country. Therefore, a child from these countries might not do well in ADOS because what the instrument assesses is irrelevant to them.

Implications for research

Guillemin et al. (1993) developed some easily applied standardised guidelines for cross-cultural adaptation of health-related quality of life measures which can be used for autism and SEN research too. Their recommendations consist of five points:

1. There should be high quality translation by at least two independent qualified translators. Translators should preferably translate in their mother tongue and a combination of translators who are aware of concepts involved and some who are unaware of them is preferable.
2. There should be as many back-translations as translations. Back-translation means '*translate back from the final language into the source language*' (p. 1422). Back-translators should also translate into their mother tongue and they should preferably be unaware of the concepts involved to be biases free.
3. The formation of a multidisciplinary and bilingual committee to check final and source documents is recommended. Primary goal of the committee should be to ensure that translation is fully comprehensive which means that language to be used should be understood by a 10- to 12-year-old child.
4. Pre-testing is also necessary. This means that a sample population trials the instrument to identify potential errors and inconsistencies. For immigrant populations there should be an assessment of the language of administration and they should also be given the option to answer in more than one languages.
5. Importantly, the instrument should be checked for cross-cultural validity using mathematical approaches.

In terms of selecting the appropriate intervention, there may be some variations according to countries or cultures. For example, individualistic cultures may be in favour of structured approaches whereas collectivistic societies are likely to choose developmental/child-led approaches (relevant research needs to be conducted). Beyond cultural and country differences, Fleming et al. (2015) compiled a list of principles that should be taken into consideration when choosing intervention for individuals with autism with universal effect. According to them, a good intervention should

1. be based on good understanding of autism (e.g. it is alarming when parental issues or cure of autism are mentioned)
2. be adapted to the needs of the person with autism (e.g. over/hypo sensitivity)
3. be based on a scientific theory
4. be evidence based (however, evidence does not guarantee that the intervention will work with every person with autism)
5. work in the real world
6. consist of a set of instructions/guidance
7. be reviewed on a regular basis
8. provide significant benefits

9 not cause any significant physical or emotional harm
10 stipulate benefits which outweigh any costs
11 be good value for money and time

The interventionists should also

12 know the person with autism well and respect their feelings and views
13 be qualified and experienced professionals
14 seek the person's consent to participate in the intervention

It is interesting to mention here a basic point for people from developed countries doing joint research with colleagues from different cultural backgrounds. Rose and Doveston (2015) recommend that it is essential for the former to recognise that their so-called expertise is often accompanied by an equally significant degree of ignorance, meaning that they often have to spend time in the country to understand national and local conditions and legislation. They witness cases of academics from Western universities make arbitrary judgments about people in other cultures '*based upon the narrow lens of their own national experiences*' (Biggs, 2001, cited in Rose and Doveston, 2015, p. 180). More importantly, they say that working and subsequently doing research in another country should be '*a process of shared learning*' (p. 188), from which all participants can gain new insights into the education of pupils with special needs. In my experience from doing research in different countries and being a foreigner in the UK who is working together with people from different countries, the best way to overcome such difficulties is to work in close and equal partnerships. Respect for each other's differences and ability to actively listen and act upon each other's views are the most valuable skills for effective collaboration. It is interesting to mention here that being Greek and having spent most of my life in Greece was inadequate to conduct research successfully there, as I no longer live there. The TAE project experience taught me that while I might have the cultural understanding to work with Greek practitioners, I am no longer fully aware of how the educational and legislative system works there. Consequently, I concluded that it is crucially important when doing research in a different country not only to work with researchers of the same culture but also with local stakeholders who have established, long-standing links with the authorities in the country in question.

I would like to close this chapter with a quotation which reflects my view on how culture should be viewed in research:

> Culture is not a variable to be controlled for or overcome, rather it is integral to the way in which a condition is experienced, defined, and managed.
> (Grinker et al., 2012, p. 208)

Researching autism through the lens of other countries and cultures can enrich the current picture of the condition, increasing its accuracy, but also make it as diverse and unique as every person, with or without autism, in the world.

8.7 Reflection activities

- Reflecting on the situation of current autism research, which points were new and which striking for you? Can you accommodate one or more of them in your next research project?
- Bearing in mind Denscombe's (2002) and Reichow et al.'s (2008) advice for enhancing rigour in real-world research, can you identify five points which are relevant and you can apply in the next research project (and which you haven't possibly thoroughly consider in previous research)?
- Involving stakeholders (e.g. school practitioners, parents and individuals with autism) in research has been strongly recommended. Which of the stakeholders have not so far participated in research projects which you have conducted? Can they be a priority for a future project and which are the main relevant points you need to bear in mind?
- Are there any elements from the section on cross-cultural research on SEN which are relevant for you to take on board for future research projects involving different countries or researchers from different countries and cultures?

9 Conclusions

9.1 Introduction

In this book, I set out to use my doctoral thesis as an example of conducting real-world research and build on this by providing lessons learnt for practitioners and parents and ideas for future research. To this end, I also reflected on my wider experience as a researcher and practitioner. Part 1 provides a systematic review of the literature on spontaneous communication in individuals with autism and SLD/PMLD and presents the AISI, which I developed alongside school staff. Part 2 focuses on presenting my doctoral study and some findings. In this part I attempted to cover a number of methodological and data analytical issues which should be relevant to people who undertake similar studies. Part 3 aims to address parents, practitioners and researchers and provide them with some hands-on advice on how to work in empowering and reflective ways as well as developing more rigorous and meaningful real-world research projects.

The following section briefly summarises each chapter's main points to refresh the reader's memory before moving on to some brief concluding comments and ways forward.

9.2 Summary points

Chapter 2 starts with defining social communication and giving an overview of the different ways this develops in TD children when compared to children with autism and continues by analysing the concepts of intentionality and spontaneity of communication in the context of autism. The chapter reports that echolalia, echopraxia, pronoun reversal, difficulties with deictic words, extreme literalness, repetitive questioning, endless talking and poor intonation control are some of the issues autistic children may have in initiating social communication. It also presents a number of cognitive, psychological and sensory processing theories such as Theory of Mind, Executive Functioning, Central Coherence, monotropic attention and sensory processing sensitivities which can account for the difficulties individuals with autism have in initiating social communication.

Chapter 3 presents a review of a number of approaches which are widely used in the field of autism to teaching social communication and which are classified into two broad categories: i) behavioural/naturalistic approaches and ii) developmental/relationship-based. It argues that existing developmental/relationship-based approaches focus a lot on adults and the way they interact with children with autism. However, all interventions, even the more structured behavioural/naturalistic ones offer some advice on how adults should behave in order to maximise the chances for children to initiate communication. The advice emerging from the literature is discussed in detail. Additionally, the chapter makes the point that parents' and practitioners' involvement in research aiming at the development of interventions is very limited. Even in research designs, which do explore the impact of adults' interactive style on children's communication, there is often no participants' contribution to the development of the intervention. Researchers-experts usually train adults in a set of principles and measure the children's and adults' behaviour pre- and post-intervention.

Chapter 4 discusses in detail the intervention I developed with school staff for my doctoral thesis (i.e. Adult Interactive Style Intervention- AISI). AISI consists of 13 general principles which relate to the NT adults' body language, speech and timing. These are the following: (i) gain the child's attention; (ii) establish appropriate proximity or touch; (iii) show availability; (iv) wait for initiations; (v) respond to all communicative attempts; (vi) assign meaning to random actions or sounds; (vii) imitate the child; (viii) follow the child's lead or focus of attention; (ix) use exaggerated pitch, facial expression, gestures and body language; (x) use minimal speech; (xi) provide time for the child to process the given information; (xii) expand on communicative attempts; and (xiii) use non-verbal cues. In AISI, adults are also asked to set up situations which are likely to provoke spontaneous communication. These communicative opportunities are: (i) offer choices, (ii) stop part way, (iii) give small portions, (iv) make items inaccessible, (v) give the child material they need help with, (vi) contradict expectations, (vii) give non-preferred items and (viii) 'forget' something vital.

Chapter 5 presents the research design of my doctoral thesis while tackling relevant research methodology issues. More precisely, it argues that research questions should be clear, specific, answerable, interconnected and substantively relevant; they should inform the literature search but also influence the choice of research methodology and methods. Participatory Action Research (PAR) is another topic of the specific chapter. PAR is a practice-driven approach where researchers and practitioners work in close partnership to produce viable improvements to real-world problems. Bridging the gap between academic research and practice, professional and personal development and empowerment, teamwork and the close collaboration between the participants and the researcher are significant advantages of PAR. Criticisms against the rigour of action research and the generalisability of the findings are also frequent. The use of video recordings as a method of data collection and its strengths and limitations is another topic which is covered in Chapter 5. The openness of the data to multiple scrutiny, their objectiveness and their 'longer shelf life' are some of the strengths whereas the camera effect and the likelihood that some participants may be put off by its presence are among the limitations. Additionally, there is reference to focus group interviews as a method to get participants' views and attitudes with the interaction among the participants, the role of the facilitator/moderator and the danger of false consensus being some of the issues the researcher has to pay attention to when conducting focus groups. Last but not least, the chapter talks about ethics. Gaining participants' consent, ensuring confidentiality, involving people with SEN in the research process and acting in the participants' best interests are some of the most significant ethical issues when doing research with vulnerable people in real-world settings. Overall, the chapter aims to give a good theoretical foundation for people who would like to conduct similar type of studies, and it also presents the data collection process of the AISI project.

Chapter 6 outlines some of the results of my PhD study. It shows that all children increased their spontaneous communication after staff were introduced to AISI. This increase was significant for the children both as a group and as individuals. Although both video recordings and focus group interviews evidenced this increase at group level, the two sets of data disagree as to which individual children increased their spontaneous communication the most. The reasons for this discrepancy are explored. With regard to the effect of the type of activity on children's spontaneous communication, only tentative conclusions can be drawn reflecting the discrepancy of findings in previous studies. When pre- and post-intervention group means were calculated snack time and 1:1 work showed the most significant increase post-intervention whereas when the total number of children's initiations per activity was considered, soft play showed the greatest increase. Overall, post-intervention, the children seemed more aware of the presence of staff as they increased the reasons they communicate for and the methods they used for doing so. Regarding the communicative functions, requesting showed the most increase overall. Initiating social games, seeking attention and expressing feelings (all belonging to the social interaction category) also increased for the whole group. Joint attention acts (i.e. commenting or giving and seeking information) were the least coded functions both pre- and post-intervention. With regard to the communicative methods, simple motor actions, vocalisations, use of pictures/symbols, re-enactments, proximity/touch, smile and objects of reference were coded the most post-intervention. Behaviours of concern decreased post-intervention. With regard to staff, the three of them increased, by at least 100, the times they used AISI principles post-intervention. As a group the three of them significantly increased the times they used imitation and minimal speech, responded to all the child's communicative attempts and offered choices post-intervention. Overall, staff found the general AISI principles easier to implement than the communicative opportunities with the specific sample of children.

Chapter 7 is primarily addressed to parents and practitioners and disseminates some lessons for this population resulting from the AISI study and my wider pre- and post-PhD professional career. Reflection is an integral part of both my doctoral study and my career. Therefore, the chapter outlines a number of ways of being reflective, an effective and empowering practice which has gained ground in the last few years. Video Interaction Guidance (VIG) and Video Enhanced Reflective Practice (VERP) are presented as two theoretically sound interventions to support reflection on good practice. The chapter also argues that people with autism and SPMLD are still not often involved in decision making. Parents and practitioners should employ a number of strategies to ensure that the formers' true wishes are communicated. Parents and people who know the individual with autism well can be their best advocates but it should always be borne in mind that these people are likely to express their own preferences as opposed to the individual's views. Therefore, interpretation should be used to a minimal extent. The chapter closes with a section maintaining that autism and SEN are not perceived the same way around the world and within different cultures, as do educational priorities. Although the US and UK lead research in the field, findings from studies originating from these countries cannot apply to other countries and cultures without adaptations. Hence, practitioners in the US and UK working with immigrant populations and practitioners and parents from other parts of the world should be very mindful but also respectful of existing cultural differences.

Chapter 8 gives some general conclusions regarding autism intervention research. More precisely, it shows that autism research so far has overlooked older people and people with learning difficulties. It also makes the claim that females have been underrepresented in autism research and there is inconclusive evidence as far as sex differences are concerned. Moreover, the chapter underscores the importance of conducting rigorous real-world research and provides some criteria and quality indicators in order to enhance research rigour. The need to build close links with schools, parents and individuals with autism in research while providing examples of good practice and limitations of existing research is also emphasised. Chapter 8 concludes that most autism intervention research has involved North American and Western European participants with limited representation of ethnic minority groups from these regions and that adaptations of assessment tools and interventions need to be made when these are used to research different populations.

9.3 Concluding comments and ways forward

I have tried to cover a lot of ground in this book and hope that readers will feel they have gained some knowledge of a number of topics related to autism and SLD/PMLD. I will conclude this chapter with three clear points. My hope is that the readership will remember them long after having read this book and perhaps might even act upon them. These points should be treated as an extended equivalent of the 'take home messages' I tend to close my lectures with, re-stating the most important arguments of the session and linking these to the wider context.

First and foremost, there is an ethical obligation for academics to conduct rigorous real-world research which actively involves a number of stakeholders in all stages (from defining research questions to disseminating findings). At the same time, parents - and even more practitioners - have an ethical obligation to report effective interventions and strategies they use. In this endeavour, academics should support them, as the experts in developing research designs. In order for this to happen, researchers and stakeholders need to work together and listen to each other above and beyond doing research together. Given that people tend to listen more when they trust each other and have developed long lasting relationships, this is when the best research ideas and projects are likely to emerge. In my case, teaching at a university programme in which many practitioners and some parents are students, being a governor in a special school and attending conferences geared towards parents and practitioners gives me the chance to meet and create links and often long lasting relationships with these people who will then develop new research projects with me. Another practice I often use is to support my students to first conduct rigorous research projects and then publish them in order to inform other colleagues and hopefully some parents on effective interventions but also the importance of collecting systematic evidence and drawing conclusions from this. Academics in the field of education should often leave the university premises and work out in the community, as this is where the real-world projects can emerge. At this point, I would like to make clear that education takes place beyond school (e.g. in the afternoon/evening and weekends and when the pupils finish school) especially for people with learning difficulties and it should be within the responsibility of educational academics to conduct research beyond the strict school boundaries (e.g. with parents at home, with play workers at leisure centres, with employers at the workplace).

A second point to make is that more research needs to be done with people with autism and additional SPMLD as this population has been largely ignored in existing literature. In my professional experience, I tend to meet people, more academics than practitioners, who *either* specialise in autism *or* SPMLD. I often sense a polemic between the two camps. Few papers and even fewer books focus specifically on this distinct population. Having experience from both the SPMLD and autism courses at the University of Birmingham I have witnessed that students on the autism courses feel that these do not focus much on individuals with SLD/PMLD and, on the other hand, students on the SPMLD courses often think that their studies do not entail enough autism related material (despite the fact that a great percentage of their pupils have autism). One of the main reasons I decided to write this book was to fight this attitude as there is a substantial number of individuals with autism and SPMLD who need to be taught in certain ways combining elements from both fields. To give a basic example, interventions which are traditionally developed for individuals with SPMLD such as Intensive Interaction and Talking Mats need to incorporate a number of visual cues, a degree of predictability and limited language by the intervener to become effective for individuals with autism. Hence, more people should produce valid naturalistic research focusing on both conditions.

Lastly, teaching spontaneous communication to individuals with autism is of great significance because this is a skill they have difficulty with and because improving spontaneous communication is likely to make them more able to influence their lives to a greater extent and participate in decisions made for them. As was explained in detail in Chapter 2, individuals with autism tend to depend on other people's prompts to initiate communication, and they may not try to communicate a message because (1) they may not know how, (2) they may think that their communication partner already knows or (3) they might not be able to due to sensory overload or confusion from inexplicit social rules. However, the more this skill is taught to them the more independent they can become by choosing what they want in life (e.g. from simple choices such as food to more complicated ones such as who to work with and where to live). Therefore, NT adults, and hopefully peers when it comes to children, should do their best to scaffold communication. AISI gives an easy to follow framework which is also well routed in autism knowledge that they can use by focusing on their body language, speech and timing but also the number and quality of communicative opportunities they provide.

I will end this book with a moving and powerful quote from a person with SEN because this very population was the inspiration for this book. Jonathan Brian, an 11-year-old boy with cerebral palsy and renal failure told his story in the Guardian (2016), describing his experience and growth from a child with no hope for education to a young man who thrives academically and communicatively with the use of an eye gaze computer and a spelling board. He finishes his article by saying:

'Never judge a book by its cover; never look at child like me and assume we are not worth teaching'.

Appendix 1
Questionnaire for Determining Spontaneous Communication in Children

Questionnaire devised by L. Kossyvaki

Please complete the following questionnaire by ticking (√) the relevant box/es or writing where appropriate
  *Note that you are asked about the communication that the child **INITIATES**.*
  Initiation of communication is defined as 'every child's attempt to transmit a message without being verbally prompted by others' (Potter and Whittaker, 2001).

Part A: Respondent's details

1 *Your first name:* _____
2 *Role*

Teacher ☐

Teaching Assistant ☐

Other, please describe ☐
_____

Part B: The child

Child's first name: _____

a. Communicative partners

3 *How often does this child __INITIATE__ contact with others? (tick one box)*
   Not at all ☐ Not often ☐ Often ☐ Very often ☐
4 *How often does this child __INITIATE__ contact with adults? (tick one box)*
   Not at all ☐ Not often ☐ Often ☐ Very often ☐
5 *How often does this child __INITIATE__ contact with children? (tick one box)*
   Not at all ☐ Not often ☐ Often ☐ Very often ☐

b. Communication and activities

6 At school, when is this child most likely and when most unlikely to <u>INITIATE</u> communication?
   - Activities <u>most likely</u> to elicit communicative initiations

   - Activities <u>most unlikely</u> to elicit communicative initiations

c. Methods of communication

7 If this child wants to <u>INITIATE</u> contact with others, how does s/he usually do it? *(tick one box in each row)*

	Not at all	Not often	Often	Very often
Pre-symbolic means				
1. By behaving in an inappropriate way (e.g. challenging behaviour, self-injuries)	☐	☐	☐	☐
2. By looking at you	☐	☐	☐	☐
3. By pointing at objects/ people	☐	☐	☐	☐
4. By approaching or touching you	☐	☐	☐	☐
5. By pushing, pulling you or manipulate your hands	☐	☐	☐	☐
6. By making word-like sounds or partial words (e.g. 'b' for 'biscuit', 'app' for 'apple')	☐	☐	☐	☐
Symbolic means				
7. By using objects of reference	☐	☐	☐	☐
8. By using signs/gestures	☐	☐	☐	☐
9. By using symbols/pictures	☐	☐	☐	☐
10. By using speech				
• Echolalia (i.e. repeats what others have said)	☐	☐	☐	☐
• One or two spoken words (e.g. drink, no)	☐	☐	☐	☐
• Two or three word phrases	☐	☐	☐	☐
• Sentences	☐	☐	☐	☐
11. Other, please describe _____	☐	☐	☐	☐

d. Functions of communication

8 For which of the following reasons does this child usually <u>INITIATE</u> communication with others? *(tick one box in each row)*

	Not at all	Not often	Often	Very often
Behaviour Regulation				
1. To request objects and activities	☐	☐	☐	☐
2. To reject objects and activities	☐	☐	☐	☐
Joint Attention				
3. To comment on objects and other people	☐	☐	☐	☐
4. To ask for information	☐	☐	☐	☐
Social Interaction				
5. To express feelings, personal preferences and dislikes	☐	☐	☐	☐
6. To draw another's person attention to himself/herself	☐	☐	☐	☐
7. To ask for approval of what s/he is doing	☐	☐	☐	☐
8. To perform simple routines of social nature (e.g. say 'hi', 'thank you', wave to somebody)	☐	☐	☐	☐
9. To initiate social games (e.g. tickling, peek-a-boo)	☐	☐	☐	☐
10. Other, please describe _____	☐	☐	☐	☐

9 Would you like to add any other comments about the contact this child <u>INITIATES</u> with you?

Thank you for taking time to fill out this questionnaire.

Appendix 2
AISI protocol

AISI principle	Definition
General principles	
1. Gain child's attention (modified from Prizant et al., 2006)	The adult calls the child's name before addressing them. They may alternatively say something like '*Hello Paul*', '*Where is Paul?*' or '*Paul's turn*'. The adult may also sing gaining attention songs such as '*Hello Paul how are you?*', '*Paul Martin where are you?*', '*What shall we do with Paul now?*'
2. Establish appropriate proximity/touch (modified from Nind and Hewett, 2001)	The adult approaches the child in distance less than 1 metre and may touch them too. NOTE: In sensory room/soft play code appropriate proximity when the adult approaches the child in distance less than 1 metre AND gets down to their level. In snack/work (appropriate proximity is the case most of the time) code it only when the adult comes to the table from far.
3. Show availability (modified from Prizant et al., 2006)	The adult extends their hands towards the child (palms facing up or down). They may also have wide and questioning eyes.
4. Wait for initiations (modified from Prizant et al., 2006)	The adult sets up the stage for interaction (e.g. gets down to the child's level, makes a toy inaccessible, offers the child a communication board with choices of food) and waits for at least 5 seconds for the child to initiate.
5. Respond to all communicative attempts (modified from Prizant et al., 2006)	The adult gives the object the child asks for, takes away the object they protest for, allows them to start and terminate activities when they communicate these. In cases that the child cannot finish their activity or get the object they want, the adult acknowledges the communicative attempt and indicates steps for completion of the present task. When the child makes a choice (e.g. toy, work activity), the adult responds to this choice and engage with them. Adult

AISI principle	Definition
	answering the child's questions belong to this category. When the child chooses an activity and the adult responds by giving them this activity, this principle should be coded. To code responding to the child's communicative attempts, the child should communicate (e.g. five elements for an act to be communicative-Bogdashina, 2005) their desires/choices. If the child does not communicate their request/protest and the adult guesses them, this should be coded as 'assign meaning to random actions or sounds' (next principle).
6. Assign meaning to random actions or sounds (modified from Christie et al., 2009)	The adult reacts as if the child's behaviour is communicative, when it is not. The adult assigns meaning to the child's pre-intentional/ unconventional communicative attempts. (e.g. when the child jumps to get an object out of reach, the adult reacts as if the child asked them to bring it down or if the child just touches a photo or holds it in front of their eyes, the adult gives them the object or food of the photo). This principle is coded when not all the five elements for an act to be communicative (Bogdashina, 2005) are present.
7. Imitate the child (modified from Prizant et al., 2006)	The adult imitates the child's verbal (vocalisations, words) and non-verbal behaviour (actions) (e.g. the child vocalises, taps the floor, uses equipment in an 'unconventional' way and the adult copies the exact same sounds and actions or a close approximation of them).
8. Follow child's lead/ focus of attention (modified from Prizant et al., 2006)	The adult follows what the child is doing or comment on it. In the sensory room, if the child moves away from the interaction with the adult and engages with a piece of equipment, the adult follows them and joins in their game. In the soft play, the child goes up the steps or down the slide and the adult follows. The adult may chant or talk about what the child is attending to or doing.
9. Use exaggerated pitch, facial expression, gestures and body language (modified from Kaufman, 1994; Greenspan and Wieder, 1998)	The adult uses animated pitch (e.g. exclamation words such as '*ah*', '*uh, uh*', words which increase anticipation such as '*aaaaaaaand*', enthusiastic singing, loud laughs), gestures (e.g. wiggle fingers before tickling) and body language (stamping feet, clapping hands or tapping the floor).
10. Use minimal speech (modified from Potter and Whittaker, 2001)	The adult uses up to four concrete words and map them exactly onto aspects of the situation in hand (e.g. '*time for work*', '*first work, then toys*'). Words such as '*good boy*', '*look*', '*well done*', '*good job*' are quite abstract and can be coded as minimal speech only if they are accompanied by gestures (e.g. thumbs up, pointing) or symbols (e.g. 'star' for 'well done').

(*Continued*)

AISI principle	Definition
11. Provide time to process information (modified from Nind and Powell, 2000)	The adult gives the child verbal or non-verbal information and provides them with at least 5 seconds to process the given information (e.g. the adult shows the child the 'finish' symbol when snack is finished or the 'work' photo when it's time for work and gives them time to process this). The difference with the principle of 'wait' is that here the adult has to give a piece of information to the child.
12. Expand on communicative attempts (modified from Rogers and Dawson, 2010)	The adult models the next stage of the child's communication development to build on the child's initiations. When the child is non-verbal, the adult models single words and when the child uses some words to communicate, the adult models two and three word phrases. When the child asks for a toy using the word or an approximation (e.g. 'tars' with or without symbol), the adult may say, '*Paul wants cars*' or '*Give cars*'.
13. Use non-verbal cues (modified from Prizant et al., 2006)	The adult uses non-verbal cues to help the child understand what they are asked to do or not to do. These are symbols/pictures (e.g. showing their timetable, 'finish' or 'wait' symbol), objects of reference (e.g. show their coat when it's time to play outside), gestures (e.g. 'come here', pointing), physical prompts (e.g. adult touches the child's hands to remind them that they are supposed to do something, uses their body to prevent the child from leaving) and Makaton signs. If more than one non-verbal cues are used, 1 tally should be coded. If the adult keeps using non-verbal cues for more than 5 seconds another tally should be coded according to the 5-seconds-rule.

Communicative opportunities

1. Offer choice (modified from Potter and Whittaker, 2001; Prizant et al., 2006)	The adult gives a choice of activity or food without any verbal prompt. The adult might hold out two objects for the child to choose or provide the child with a photo choice board for toys or snacks.
2. Stop part way (modified from Potter and Whittaker, 2001)	The adult stops part way through an activity or social interaction giving the child a chance to request to continue. The adult stops abruptly and may also say '*stop*' or '*uh, uh*'. (e.g. The adult plays a 'rough and tumble' or 'burst and pause' game and suddenly stops).
3. Give small portions (Potter and Whittaker, 2001)	The adult gives the child small portions of food or drink so that the child may ask for more (e.g. when the child asks for a biscuit or a fruit, the adult gives them one or two bits of it instead of the whole thing).

AISI principle	Definition
4. Make items inaccessible (Potter and Whittaker, 2001)	The adult puts items 'in sight but out of reach' so that the child will need to ask for them (e.g. The adult does not put any equipment on as they enter the sensory room and wait for the child to ask what they want).
5. Give material the child will need help with (Potter and Whittaker, 2001)	The adult gives the child materials they will need help with to elicit asking for help (e.g. a box of cars with the lid on, a wind-up toy which the child cannot make work).
6. Contradict expectations (Potter and Whittaker, 2001; Griffin and Sandler, 2010)	The adult does something unexpected or out of routine to elicit a request or comment (e.g. the adult turns a toy animal over to see whether the child will restore it to the original position or reads a book upside down and turns the pages backward).
7. Give non-preferred items (Potter and Whittaker, 2001)	The adult gives the child items they are not interested in to elicit protest or comment (e.g. the adult gives the child a toy that they don't like). Note: The adult gives the child these items when the child has not asked for something else. If the child asks for an item, the adult should either give it or indicate steps for getting it and in no occasion give a non-preferred item instead. In such a case, the child gets confused by being given different items to the ones they asked.
8. 'Forget' something vital (Christie et al., 2009)	The adult sets up a situation where s/he 'forgets' something vital (e.g. the adult helps the child to put the coat on but does not do the zip up or when changing clothes, the adult helps the child to put one shoe on and 'forgets' the other).

References

Adelman, C. (1989) "The practical ethic takes priority over methodology". In: W. Carr (ed.) *Quality in teaching: Arguments for a reflective profession*. London: Falmer, pp. 173–182.

Agius, K. (2009) A Maltese study in patterns of spontaneous and intentional nonverbal communication in young nonverbal children with autistic spectrum disorders. Birmingham: MEd Thesis, University of Birmingham.

Aldred, C., Green, J. and Adams, C. (2004) A new social communication intervention for children with autism: Pilot randomised controlled treatment study suggesting effectiveness. *Journal of Child Psychology and Psychiatry*, 45 (8): 1420–1430.

Aldred, C., Pollard, C., Phillips, R. and Adams, C. (2001) Multidisciplinary social communication intervention for children with autism and pervasive developmental disorder: The child's talk project. *Educational and Child Psychology*, 18 (2): 76–87.

Allen, B. and Matthews, G. (2008) *Team-teach workbook*. East Sussex: Steaming Publishing.

Allison, C., Baron-Cohen, S., Wheelwright, S., Charman, T., Richler, J., Pasco, G. and Brayne, C. (2008) The Q-CHAT (Quantitative Checklist for Autism in Toddlers): A normally distributed quantitative measure of autistic traits at 18–24 months of age: Preliminary report. *Journal of Autism and Developmental Disorders*, 38 (8): 1414–1425.

American Psychiatric Association-APA (2013) *Diagnostic and statistical manual of mental disorders (DSM-5®)*. American Psychiatric Pub.

Ametepee, L. and Chitiyo, M. (2009) What we know about autism in Africa: A brief research synthesis. *Journal of the International Association of Special Education*, 10: 11–13.

Ashton, P., Hunt, P., Jones, S. and Watson, G. (1980) *Curriculum in action*. Milton Keynes: Open University Press.

Association for Video Interaction Guidance UK-AVIGUK (2016) [online]. Available from: www.videointeractionguidance.net (accessed 1st September 2016).

Attard, K. (2008) Uncertainty for the reflective practitioner: A blessing in disguise. *Reflective Practice: International and Multidisciplinary Perspectives*, 9 (3): 307–317.

Attwood, T. (2007) *The complete guide to Asperger syndrome*. London: Jessica Kingsley Publishers.

Autism Society of America (2000) What is autism? *Advocate: The Newsletter of the Autism Society of America*, 33: 3.

Autism Treatment Center of America (2008) *Autism solution: Getting started with the Son-Rise program* [DVD]. Sheffield, MA: The Option Institute.

Avramides, K., Bernardini, S., Foster, M.E., Frauenberger, C., Kossyvaki, L. and Mademtzi, M. (2012) State of-the-art in TEL to support social communication skill development in children with autism: a multi-disciplinary review. *International Journal of Technology Enhanced Learning*, 4 (5/6): 359–372.

Ayres, A.J. (1998) *Sensory integration and praxis tests: Manual*. Los Angeles: Western Psychological Services.

Baggs, A. (2007) *In my language*. Available from: www.youtube.com/watch?v=JnylM1hI2jc (accessed 8th November 2016).

Baird, G., Simonoff, E., Pickles, A., Chandler, S., Loucas, T., Meldrum, D. and Charman, T. (2006) Prevalence of disorders of the autism spectrum in a population cohort of children in south Thames: The special needs and autism project (SNAP). *Lancet*, 368 (9531): 210–215.

Bandura, A. (1977) *Social learning theory*. Englewood Cliffs, NJ: Prentice Hall.

Barney, A., Choi, S., Clarke, C., Davies, W., Davis, H., Fill, K., Gobbi, M., Halnan, A., Maier, P., Moloney, J., Morris, D., Price, J., Smith, H., Swabey, C., Treves, R., Warner, J., Warren, A. and Williams, I. (n.d.) *University of Southampton e-research methods* [online]. Available from: www.erm.ecs.soton.ac.uk/theme4/aims_and_objectives.html (accessed 1st March 2016).

Baron-Cohen, S. (1995) *Mindblindness: An essay on autism and theory of mind*. Cambridge, MA: MIT Press.

Baron-Cohen, S., Allen, J. and Gillberg, C. (1992) Can autism be detected at 18 months? The needle, the haystack, and the CHAT. *The British Journal of Psychiatry*, 161 (6): 839–843.

Baron-Cohen, S., Wheelwright, S., Skinner, R., Martin, J. and Clubley, E. (2001) The Autism-Spectrum Quotient (AQ): Evidence from Asperger syndrome/high-functioning autism, males and females, scientists and mathematicians. *Journal of Autism and Developmental Disorders*, 31: 5–17.

Barry, T., Grofer Klinger, L., Lee, J., Palardy, N., Gilmore, T. and Bodin, D. (2003) Examining the effectiveness of an outpatient clinic-based social skills group for high functioning children with autism. *Journal of Autism and Developmental Disorders*, 33 (6): 685–701.

Bauminger, N., Shulman, C. and Agam, G. (2003) Peer interaction and loneliness in high-functioning children with autism. *Journal of Autism and Developmental Disorders*, 33 (5): 489–507.

Beail, N. and Williams, K. (2014) Using qualitative methods in research with people who have intellectual disabilities. *Journal of Applied Research in Intellectual Disabilities*, 27 (2): 85–96.

Beresford, B., Tozer, R., Rabiee, P. and Sloper, P. (1997) Developing an approach to involving children with autistic spectrum disorders in a social care research project. *British Journal of Learning Disabilities*, 32: 180–185.

Bettelheim, B. (1967) *The empty fortress: Infantile autism and the birth of the self*. London: Collier-Macmillan.

Bigby C., Frawley P. and Ramcharan P. (2014) Conceptualizing inclusive research with people with intellectual disability. *Journal of Applied Research in Intellectual Disabilities*, 27: 3–12.

Birmingham City Council (2013) *Census 2011 KS201: Ethnic groups* [online]. Available from: www.birmingham.gov.uk/downloads/file/220/census_2011_ks201_ethnic_groups (accessed 5th October 2016).

Blackburn, R. (2007) Logically illogical: The perspective of an adult with autism. In: *Lectures for Masters Students* (M.Ed. autism). Birmingham, 6 February 2007.

Blackburn, R. (2011) Logically illogical: The perspective of an adult with autism. In: *Autism Residential Weekend*, University of Birmingham, Birmingham, 23–25 September 2011.

Blatchford, P., Bassett, P., Brown, P., Martin, C., Russell, A., Webster, R., Babayigit, S. and Haywood, N. (2008) *Deployment and impact of support staff in schools and the impact of the national agreement: Results from strand 2 wave 1, 2005/06*. London: Institute of Education.

Bloor, M., Frankland, J., Thomas, M. and Robson, K. (2001) *Focus group in social research*. London: SAGE Publications Ltd.

Blubaugh, N. and Kohlmann, J. (2006) TEACCH model and children with autism. *Teaching Elementary Physical Education*, 17 (6): 16–19.

Bogdashina, O. (2003) *Sensory perceptual issues in autism and Asperger syndrome*. London: Jessica Kingsley Publishers.

Bogdashina, O. (2005) *Communication issues in autism and Asperger syndrome*. London: Jessica Kingsley Publishers.

Bölte, S. (2014) The power of words: Is qualitative research as important as quantitative research in the study of autism? *Autism*, 18 (2): 67–68.

Bondy, A. and Frost, L. (2002) *A picture's worth: PECS and other visual communication strategies in autism*. Bethesda, MD: Woodbine House.

Borg, J. (2008) *Body language: 7 easy lessons to master the silent language*. Upper Saddle River, NJ: Pearson Education.

British Association for Music Therapy-BAMT (2012) [online]. Available from: www.bamt.org/ (accessed 12th February 2012).

British Education Research Association-BERA (2011) *Ethical guidelines for educational research* [online]. Available from: www.bera.ac.uk/files/2011/08/BERA-Ethical-Guidelines-2011.pdf (accessed 9th April 2012).

British Psychological Society (BPS) (2008) *Conducting research with people not having the capacity to consent to their participation a practical guide for researchers* [online]. Available from: www.ed.ac.uk/files/atoms/files/bps_guidelines_for_conducting_research_with_people_not_having_capacity_to_consent.pdf (accessed 2nd November 2016).

British Psychological Society (BPS) (2010) *Code of human research ethics* [online]. Available from: www.bps.org.uk/sites/default/files/documents/code_of_human_research_ethics.pdf (accessed 2nd November 2016).

Brown, F., Belz, P., Corsi, L. and Wenig, B. (1993) Choice diversity for people with severe disabilities. *Education and Training in Mental Retardation*, 28 (4): 318–326.

Brown, J.R. and Rogers, S.J. (1997) "Cultural issues in autism". In: S. Ozonoff, S. Rogers and R. Hendren (eds.) *Autism spectrum disorders: A research review for practitioners*. Washington, DC: American Psychiatric Publishing, Inc., pp. 209–226.

Bruner, J. (1981) The social context of language acquisition. *Language and Communication*, 1 (2–3): 155–178.

Brunner, D. L. and Seung, H. (2009) Evaluation of the Efficacy of Communication-Based Treatments for Autism Spectrum Disorders A Literature Review. *Communication Disorders Quarterly*, 31 (1): 15–41.

Bryan, J. (2016) Experience: I talk with my eyes [online]. *The Guardian*, 27th January 2017. Available from: www.theguardian.com/lifeandstyle/2017/jan/27/experience-i-talk-with-my-eyes (accessed 10th February 2017).

Bryman, A. (2008) *Social research methods*. 3rd ed. Oxford: Oxford University Press.
Buckley, B. (2003) *Children's communication skills: From birth to five years*. London: Routledge.
Burns, R. (2000) *Introduction to research methods*. London: SAGE Publication Ltd.
Burrell, G. and Morgan, G. (2005) *Sociological paradigms and organisational analysis*. Burlington: Ashgate Publishing Co.
Caldwell, P. (2006) Speaking the other's language: Imitation as a gateway to relationship. *Infant and Child Development*, 15 (3): 275–282.
Caldwell, P. (2008) *Using intensive interaction and sensory integration: A handbook for those who support people with severe autistic spectrum disorder*. London: Jessica Kingsley Publishers.
Camaioni, L., Perucchini, P., Muratori, F., Parrinini, B. and Cesari, A. (2003) The communicative use of pointing in autism: Developmental profile and factors related to change. *European Psychiatry*, 18 (1): 6–12.
Cameron, L. and Murphy, J. (2002) Enabling young people with a learning diability to make choices at a time of transition. *British Journal of Learning Disabilities*, 30: 105–112.
Carr, E. (1982) "Sign language". In: R.L. Koegel, A. Rincover and A.L. Egel (eds.) *Educating and understanding autistic children*. New York: College Hill Press, pp. 142–157.
Carter, M. and Hotchkis, G.D. (2002) A conceptual analysis of communicative spontaneity. *Journal of Intellectual and Developmental Disability*, 27 (3): 168–190.
Chambers, W. and R. Ltd. (1998) *The chambers dictionary*. Edinburgh: Chambers Harrap Publishers Ltd.
Chan, A.S., Cheung, J., Leung, W.W., Cheung, R. and Cheung, M.C. (2005) Verbal expression and comprehension deficits in young children with autism. *Focus on Autism and Other Developmental Disabilities*, 20 (2): 117–124.
Chandler, S., Christie, P., Newson, E. and Prevezer, W. (2002) Developing a diagnostic and intervention package for 2- to 3-year-olds with autism: Outcomes of the frameworks for communication approach. *Autism*, 6 (1): 47–69.
Charlop, M.H. and Trasowech, J.E. (1991) Increasing autistic children's daily spontaneous speech. *Journal of Applied Behavior Analysis*, 24 (4): 747–761.
Charlop-Christy, M.H., Carpenter, M., Le, L., LeBlanc, L.A. and Kellet, K. (2002) Using the Picture Exchange Communication System (PECS) with children with autism: Assessment of PECS acquisition, speech, social-communicative behavior, and problem behaviour. *Journal of Applied Behavior Analysis*, 35 (3): 213–231.
Charman, T., Dockrell, J., Peacey, N., Peacey, L., Forward, K. and Pellicano, L. (2011) *What is good practice in autism education?* London: Centre for Research in Autism and Education (CRAE), Department of Psychology and Human Development, Institute of Education, University of London.
Chiang, C.H., Soong, W.T., Lin, T.L. and Rogers, S. (2008) Nonverbal communication skills in young children with autism. *Journal of Autism and Developmental Disorders*, 38 (10): 1898–1906.
Chiang, H.M. (2008a) Communicative spontaneity of children with autism: A preliminary analysis. *Autism*, 12 (1): 9–21.
Chiang, H.M. (2008b) Expressive communication of children with autism: The use of challenging behaviour. *Journal of Intellectual Disability Research*, 52 (11): 966–972.
Chiang, H.M. (2009a) Differences between spontaneous and elicited expressive communication in children with autism. *Research in Autism Spectrum Disorders*, 3 (1): 214–222.

Chiang, H.M. and Lin, W.T. (2008) Expressive communication of children with autism. *Journal of Autism and Developmental Disorders*, 38 (3): 538–545.

Christie, P., Newson, E., Prevezer, W. and Chandler, S. (2009) *First steps in intervention with your child with autism: Frameworks for communication.* London: Jessica Kingsley Publishers.

Chung, K.M., Jung, W., Yang, J.W., Ben-Itzchak, E., Zachor, D.A., Furniss, F., Heyes, K., Matson, J.L., Kozlowski, A.M. and Barker, A.A. (2012) Cross cultural differences in challenging behaviors of children with autism spectrum disorders: An international examination between Israel, South Korea, the United Kingdom, and the United States of America. *Research in Autism Spectrum Disorders*, 6: 881–889.

Clements, J. (2005) *People with autism behave badly: Helping people with ASD move on from behavioral and emotional challenges.* London: Jessica Kingsley Publishers.

Clifford, S., Hudry, K., Brown, L., Pasco, G., Charman, T. and the PACT Consortium (2010) The Modified-Classroom Observations Schedule to Measure Intentional Communication (M-COSMIC): Evaluation of reliability and validity. *Research in Autism Spectrum Disorders*, 4 (3): 509–525.

Cohen, J. (1988) *Statistical power analysis for the behavioral sciences.* London: Academic Press.

Cohen, L., Manion, L. and Morrison, K. (2007) *Research methods in education.* 6th ed. London: Routledge/Falmer.

Coles, J. (2014) Transition to secondary school: A comparison of parents' and pupils' concerns. *Good Autism Practice*, 15 (1): 70–80.

Connors, J.L. and Donnellan, A.M. (1998) "Walk in beauty: Western perspectives on disability and Navajo family/cultural resilience". In: H.I. McCubbin, E.A. Thompson, A.I. Thompson and J.E. Fromer (eds.) *Resiliency in native American and immigrant families.* Thousand Oaks, CA: SAGE Publications Ltd., pp. 159–182.

Coolican, H. (2006) *Introduction to research methods in psychology.* 3rd ed. London: Hodder Arnold.

Cooper, J.O., Heron, T.E. and Heward, W.L. (2007) *Applied behavior analysis.* 2nd ed. Upper Saddle River, NJ: Pearson Education.

Cordingley, P., Bell, M., Rundell, B., Evans, D. and Curtis, A. (2005) *The impact of collaborative continuing professional development (CPD) on classroom teaching and learning.* London: EPPI-Centre, University of London.

Corke, M. (2002) *Approaches to communication through music.* London: David Fulton Publishers.

Couper, J.J. and Sampson, A.J. (2003) Children with autism deserve evidence-based intervention: The evidence for behavioural therapy. *The Medical Journal of Australia*, 178 (9): 424–425.

Courchesne, E., Townsend, J., Akshoomoff, N.A., Saitoh, O., Yeung-Courchesne, R., Lincoln, A.J., James, H.E., Haas, R.H., Schreibman, L. and Lau, L. (1994) Impairment in shifting attention in autistic and cerebellar patients. *Behavioral Neuroscience*, 108 (5): 848–865.

Creswell, J. (2003) *Research design: Qualitative, quantitative and mixed methods approaches.* 2nd ed. London: SAGE Publications Ltd.

Creswell, J. and Plano Clark, V. (2007) *Designing and conducting mixed methods research.* London: SAGE Publications Ltd.

Creswell, J. W. and Tashakkori, A. (2007) Editorial: Differing perspectives on mixed methods research. *Journal of Mixed Methods Research*, 1 (4): 303–308.

References

Crosland, K.A., Clarke, S. and Dunlap, G.A. (2013) Trend Analysis of Participant and Setting Characteristics in Autism Intervention Research. *Focus on Autism and Other Developmental Disabilities*, 28 (3): 159–165.

Cross, J. and Kennedy, H. (2011) How and Why does VIG Work. In H. Kennedy, M. Landor and L. Todd (Eds.) *Video Interaction Guidance: A Relationship-based Intervention to Promote Attunement, Empathy and Wellbeing*. London: Jessica Kingsley Publishers (pp. 58–81).

Dahlgren, S.O. and Trillingsgaard, A. (1996) Theory of mind in non-retarded children with autism and Asperger's syndrome: A research note. *Journal of Child Psychology and Psychiatry*, 37 (6): 759–763.

Dancey, C. and Reidy, J. (2002) *Statistics without maths for psychology*. 2nd ed. Harlow, England: Pearson.

DARL (Development in Areas Related to Learning) assessment (unpublished). Provided by the school.

Dawson, G., Hill, D., Spencer, A., Galpert, L. and Watson, L. (1990) Affective exchanges between young autistic children and their mothers. *Journal of Abnormal Child Psychology*, 18 (3): 335–345.

Dawson, M. (2016a) *Autismcrisis: Papers & presentations*. Available from: https://sites.google.com/site/autismcrisis/papers-presentations (accessed 14th December 2016).

Dawson, M. (2016b) @autismcrisis [Twitter account]. Available from: https://twitter.com/autismcrisis (accessed 14th December 2016).

Denscombe, M. (2002) *Ground rules for good research*. Milton Keynes: Open University Press.

Denscombe, M. (2010) *The good research guide for small-scale research projects*. 4th ed. Berkshire: Open University Press.

Department for Children, Schools and Families (DCSF) (2008a) *Early Support Developmental Journal* [online]. Available from: www.education.gov.uk/publications/eOrderingDownload/ES54.pdf (accessed 8th February 2012).

Department for Children, Schools and Families (DCSF) (2008b) *Early Years Foundation Stage (EYFS) pack* [online]. Available from: www.education.gov.uk/publications/eOrderingDownload/eyfs_practiceguid_0026608.pdf (accessed 8th February 2012).

Department for Education (DfE) (2011) *Teachers' standards*. London: Department for Education.

Department for Education (DfE) (2015) *Induction for newly qualified teachers (England)* [online]. Available from: www.gov.uk/government/uploads/system/uploads/attachment_data/file/458233/Statutory_induction_guidance_for_newly_qualified_teachers.pdf (accessed 10th June 2016).

Department for Education (DfE) and Department of Health (DoH) (2014) *Special educational needs and disability code of practice: 0 to 25 years* [online]. Available from: www.gov.uk/government/publications/send-code-of-practice-0-to-25 (accessed 24th April 2016).

Dewart, H. and Summers, S. (1988) *The pragmatics profile of early communication*. Windsor, Berkshire: NFER-NELSON.

Divan, G., Vajaratkar, V., Desai, M.U., Strik-Lievers, L. and Patel, V. (2012) Challenges, coping strategies, and unmet needs of families with a child with autism spectrum disorder in Goa, India. *Autism Research*, 5: 90–200.

Dobson, S., Upadhyaya, S., McNeil, J., Venkateswaran, S. and Gilderdale, D. (2001) Developing an information pack for the Asian carers of people with autism spectrum disorders. *International Journal of Language and Communication Disorders*, 36 (1): 216–221.

Dockrell, J., Lewis, A. and Lindsay, G. (2000) "Researching children's perspectives: A psychological dimension". In: A. Lewis and G. Lindsay (eds.) *Researching children's perspectives*. Buckingham: Open University Press, pp. 46–58.

Doussard-Roosevelt, J., Joe, C., Bazhenova, O. and Porges, S. (2003) Mother-child interaction in autistic and nonautistic children: Characteristics of maternal approach behaviors and child social responses. *Development and Psychopathology*, 15 (2): 277–295.

Drain, S. and Engelhardt, P.E. (2013) Naturalistic observations of nonverbal children with autism: A study of intentional communicative acts in the classroom. *Child Development Research*, 2013: Article ID 296039, 10 pages.

Drew, A., Baird, G., Taylor, E., Milne, E. and Charman, T. (2007) The Social Communication Assessment for Toddlers with Autism (SCATA): An instrument to measure the frequency, form and function of communication in toddlers with autism spectrum disorder. *Journal of Autism and Developmental Disorders*, 37 (4): 648–666.

Dunn, W., Saiter, J. and Rinner, L. (2002) Asperger syndrome and sensory processing: A conceptual model and guidance for intervention planning. *Focus on Autism and Other Developmental Disabilities*, 17 (3): 172–185.

Dyches, T.T., Wilder, L.K., Sudweeks, R.R., Obiakor, F.E. and Algozzine, B. (2004) Multicultural issues in autism. *Journal of Autism and Developmental Disorders*, 34 (2): 211–222.

Education Endowment Foundation (2016). *Teaching Assistants* [online]. Available from: https://educationendowmentfoundation.org.uk/evidence/teaching-learning-toolkit/teaching-assistants/ (accessed 14 April 2016).

Edwards, T.L., Watkins, E.E., Lotfizadeh, A.D. and Poling, A. (2012) Intervention research to benefit people with autism: How old are the participants? *Research in Autism Spectrum Disorders*, 6 (3): 996–999.

Eikeseth, S., Smith, T., Jahr, E. and Eldevik, S. (2007) Outcome for children with autism who began intensive behavioral treatment between ages 4 and 7: A comparison control study. *Behavior Modification*, 31 (3): 264–278.

Elliot, J. (1991) *Action research for educational change*. Milton Keynes: Open University Press.

Elsabbagh, M., Divan, G., Koh, Y.-J., Kim, Y.S., Kauchali, S., Marcín, C., Montiel-Nava, C., Patel, V., Paula, C.S., Wang, C., Taghi Yasamy, M. and Fombonne, E. (2012) Global prevalence of autism and other pervasive developmental disorders. *Autism Research*, 5: 160–179.

Elsabbagh, M., Yusuf, A., Prasanna, S., Shikako-Thomas, K., Ruff, C.A. and Fehlings, M.G. (2014) Community engagement and knowledge translation: Progress and challenge in autism research. *Autism*, 18 (7): 771–781.

Emerson, E. (2001) *Challenging behaviour: Analysis and intervention in people with severe intellectual disabilities*. 2nd ed. Cambridge: Cambridge University Press.

Emerson, E. and Baines, S. (2010) The estimated prevalence of autism among adults with learning disabilities in England. In: *Improving Health and Lives: Learning Disabilities Observatory*, Durham.

Engineering and Physical Sciences Research Council-EPSRC (2012) *Research in the wild 2012*. Available from: www.epsrc.ac.uk/funding/calls/researchinthewild/ (accessed 17th November 2016).

Escalona, A., Field, T., Singer-Strunck, R., Cullen, C. and Hartshorn, K. (2001) Brief report: Improvements of children with autism following massage therapy. *Journal of Autism and Developmental Disorders*, 31 (5): 513–516.
Farrell, P., Balshaw, M.H. and Polat, F. (1999) *The management, role and training of learning support assistants.* London: DfEE.
Fey, M.E. (1986) *Language intervention with young children.* Needham Height, MA: Allyn and Bacon.
Field, A. (2005) *Discovering statistics using SPSS.* 2nd ed. London: SAGE Publication Ltd.
Filbey, L. (2016) The most valuable resource you have is other people's ideas: The role of informal knowledge sharing and collaboration in supporting teachers working in a special school. In: *Assignment Submitted for the Completion of the Module Special Studies in Special Education*, University of Birmingham, Birmingham.
Fisher, C. (2006) "Interventions in general education classrooms: One boy's story as seen by his mother". In: R.L. Koegel and L.K. Koegel (eds.) *Pivotal response treatments for autism: Communication, social and academic development.* London: Paul Brookes Publishing Co., pp. 53–79.
Fleischmann, C. (2012) *Carly's Café: Experience Autism through Carly's Eyes.* Available from: www.youtube.com/watch?v=KmDGvquzn2k (accessed 8th November 2016).
Fleming, B., Hurley, E. and the Goth (2015) *Choosing autism interventions: A research-based guide.* Hove: Pavilion Publishing and Media Ltd.
Floeter, M.K. and Greenough, W.T. (1979) Cerebellar plasticity: Modification of purkinje cell structure by differential rearing in monkeys. *Science*, 206 (4415): 227–229.
Flood, S., Bennett, D., Melsome, M. and Northway, R. (2012) Becoming a researcher. *British Journal of Learning Disabilities*, 41: 288–295.
Flores, G., Bauchner, H. and Feinstein, A.R. (1999) The impact of ethnicity, family income, and parental education on children's health and use of health services. *American Journal of Public Health*, 89: 1066–1071.
Fombonne, E. (1998) "Epidemiological surveys of autism". In: F.R. Volkmar (ed.) *Autism and pervasive developmental disorders.* Cambridge: Cambridge University Press, pp. 32–63.
Fombonne, E. (2005) "Epidemiological studies of pervasive developmental disorder". In: F.R. Volkmar, R. Paul, A. Klin and D. Cohen (eds.) *Handbook of autism and pervasive developmental disorders, Volume 1: Diagnosis, development, neurobiology and behavior.* 3rd ed. Hoboken, NJ: Wiley, pp. 42–69.
Freeman, N.L., Perry, A. and Bebko, J.M. (2002) Behaviour is communication: Nonverbal communicative behaviour in students with autism and instructors' responsivity. *Journal on Developmental Disabilities*, 9 (2): 145–155.
Frith, U. (2003) *Autism: Explaining the enigma.* 2nd ed. Oxford: Blackwell.
Frost, L. and Bondy, A. (2002) *PECS: The Picture Exchange Communication System: Training manual.* Newark, DE: Pyramid Educational Consultants Inc.
Funazaki, Y. and Oi, M. (2013) Factors affecting responses of children with autism spectrum disorder to yes/no questions. *Child Language Teaching and Therapy*, 29 (2): 245–259.
Gallardo, M. and Gallardo, M. (n.d.) *Maria and I* (translated from Spanish). English copy was sent to me by M.Gallardo.
Georgiades, S., Szatmari, P. and Boyle, M. (2013) Importance of studying heterogeneity in autism. *Neuropsychiatry*, 3 (2): 123–125.

Gerland, G. (2000) *Finding out about Asperger syndrome, high functioning autism and PDD*. London: Jessica Kingsley Publishers.

Ghaye, A. and Ghaye, K. (1998) *Teaching and learning through critical reflective practice*. London: David Fulton Publishers.

Giallo, R., Wood, C.E., Jellett, R. and Porter, R. (2013) Fatigue, wellbeing and parental self-efficacy in mothers of children with an autism spectrum disorder. *Autism*, 17 (4): 465–480.

Gibson, K.A. (2014) Appreciating the world of autism through the lens of video interaction guidance: An exploration of a parent's perceptions, experiences and emerging narratives on autism. *Disability & Society*, 29 (4): 568–582.

Gillett, J.N. and LeBlanc, L.A. (2007) Parent-implemented natural language paradigm to increase language and play in children with autism. *Research in Autism Spectrum Disorders*, 1 (3): 247–255.

Goodwin, M. (2013) Listening and responding to children with PMLD – towards a framework and possibilities. *SLD Experience*, 65: 21–27.

Goodwin, M. and Edwards, C. (2009) I am creative too. *PMLD Link*, 21 (1): 11–17.

Goodwin, M., Miller, J. and Edwards, C. (2015) *Communicate with me: A resource to enable effective communication and involvement with people who have a learning disability*. London: Speechmark.

Grandin, T. (1984) My experiences as an autistic child. *Journal of Orthomolecular Psychiatry*, 13 (3): 144–174.

Grandin, T. (2006) *Thinking in pictures*. London: Bloomsbury.

Gray, C. (2000) From both sides now: How to teach social understanding. In: *6th Autism-Europe Congress*, Glasgow, 19–21 May 2000.

Green, J. and Aldred, C. (2012) On the right track: Can early intervention change the trajectory of communication development for children who have autism? In: *3rd Professional Conference National Autistic Society*, Manchester, 28–29 February 2012.

Green, J., Charman, T., McConachie, H., Aldred, C., Slonims, V., Howlin, P., Le Couteur, A., Leadbitter, K., Hudry, K., Byford, S., Barrett, B., Temple, K., Macdonald, W., Pickles, A. and the PACT Consortium (2010) Parent-mediated Communication-focused Treatment in Children with Autism (PACT): A randomised controlled trial. *Lancet*, 375 (9732): 2152–2160.

Greenspan, S. and Wieder, S. (1998) *The child with special needs*. Reading, MA: Perseus.

Greenspan, S. and Wieder, S. (1999) A functional developmental approach to autism spectrum disorders. *Journal of the Association for Persons with Severe Handicaps*, 24 (3): 147–161.

Griffin, S. and Sandler, D. (2010) *Motivate to communicate! 300 games and activities for your child with autism*. London: Jessica Kingsley Publishers.

Grinker, R.R. (2007) *Unstrange minds: Remapping the world of autism*. New York: Basic Books.

Grinker, R.R. (2009) *Isabel's world: Autism and the making of a modern epidemic*. London: Icon Books Ltd.

Grinker, R.R., Chambers, N., Njongwe, N., Lagman, A.E., Guthrie, W., Stronach, S., Richard, B.O., Kauchali, S., Killian, B., Chhagan, M., Yucel, F., Kudumu, M., Barker-Cummings, C., Grether, J. and Wetherby, A.M. (2012) 'Communities' in community engagement: Lessons learned from autism research in South Korea and South Africa. *Autism Research*, 5: 201–210.

Grove, N., Bunning, K., Porter, J. and Morgan, M. (2000) *See what I mean: Guidelines to aid understanding of communication by people with severe and profound learning disabilities.* Kidderminster, Worcestershire: Bild/Mencap.

Guba, E.G. and Lincoln, Y.S. (1994) "Competing paradigms in qualitative research". In: N.K. Denzin and Y.S. Lincoln (eds.) *Handbook of qualitative research.* Thousand Oaks, CA: Sage. pp. 105–117.

Guillemin, F., Bombardier, C. and Beaton, D. (1993) Cross-cultural adaptation of health-related quality of life measures: Literature review and proposed guidelines. *Journal of Clinical Epidemiology*, 46 (12): 1417–1432.

Guldberg, K., Bradley, R., Laskaridou, K., Molteni, P., Kossyvaki, L., Angelidi, E., D'Alonzo, L., Hadjipateras-Giannoulis, K. and Sala, R. (2016) Inclusion in practice: European perspectives on educating and empowering pupils with autism. In: *XI Autism-Europe International Congress*, Edinburgh, Scotland.

Hall, D. and Hall, I. (1996) *Practical social research: Project work in the community.* London: Macmillan.

Halle, J.W. (1987) Teaching language in the natural environment: An analysis of spontaneity. *Journal of the Association for Persons with Severe Handicaps*, 12 (1): 28–37.

Hallett, G. and Hallett, F. (2015) Editorial: Evidence-based practice. *British Journal of Special Education*, 42 (1): 2–121.

Happé, F.G.E. (1997) Central coherence and theory of mind in autism: Reading homographs in context. *British Journal of Developmental Psychology*, 15 (1): 1–12.

Harding, C.G. (1982) Development of the intention to communicate. *Human Development*, 25: 140–151.

Harrington, C., Foster, M., Rodger, S. and Ashburner, J. (2013) Engaging young people with Autism Spectrum Disorder in research interviews. *British Journal of Learning Disabilities*, 42: 153–161.

Hartley, S.L. and Sikora, D.M. (2009) Sex differences in autism spectrum disorder: An examination of developmental functioning, autistic symptoms, and coexisting behavior problems in toddlers. *Journal of Autism and Developmental Disorders*, 39 (12): 1715–1722.

Hauck, M., Fein, D., Waterhouse, L. and Feinstein, C. (1995) Social initiations by autistic children to adults and other children. *Journal of Autism and Developmental Disorders*, 25 (6): 579–595.

Heath, C., Hindmarsh, J. and Luff, P. (2010) *Video in qualitative research: Analysing social interaction in everyday life.* London: SAGE Publication Ltd.

Hewitt, J., Satariano, S. and Todd, L. (2015) "Making sure that teaching assistants can make a difference to children: Training that uses Video Enhanced Reflective Practice (VERP)". In: H. Kennedy, M. Landor and L. Todd (eds.) *Video enhanced reflective practice: Professional development through attuned interactions.* London: Jessica Kingsley Publishers, pp. 94–103.

Higashida, N. (2013) *The reason I jump: One boy's voice from the silence of autism.* London: Sceptre Books.

Hill, E. (2004) Executive dysfunction in autism. *Trends in Cognitive Sciences*, 8 (1): 26–32.

Hobson, P. (2002) *The cradle of thought: Exploring the origins of thinking.* London: Macmillan.

Hodge, N. and Chantler, S. (2010) It's not what you do: It's the way that you question: That's what gets results. *Support for Learning*, 25 (1): 11–14.

Hodges, L. (2003) *First choice eye contact supplement.* RNIB.

Holtmann, M., Bolte, S. and Poustka, F. (2007) Autism spectrum disorders: Sex differences in autistic behaviour domains and coexisting psychopathology. *Developmental Medicine & Child Neurology*, 49: 361–366.

Honeybourne, V. (2015) Girls on the autism spectrum in the classroom: Hidden difficulties and how to help. *Good Autism Practice*, 16 (2): 11–20.

Hopkins, D. (2002) *A teacher's guide to classroom research*. 3rd ed. Buckingham: Open University Press.

Howlin, P., Baron-Cohen, S. and Hadwin, J. (1999) *Teaching children with autism to mind-read: A practical guide*. Chisester: John Wiley and Sons Ltd.

Hudry, K., Leadbitter, K., Temple, K., Slonims, V., McConachie, H., Aldred, C., Howlin, P., Charman, T. and the PACT Consortium (2010) Preschoolers with autism show greater impairment in receptive compared with expressive language abilities. *International Journal of Language and Communication Disorders*, 45 (6): 681–690.

Hurley, E. (2014) *Ultraviolet voices: Stories of women on the autism spectrum*. Birmingham: Autism West Midlands.

Hwang, B. and Hughes, C. (2000) Increasing early social-communicative skills of preverbal preschool children with autism through social interactive training. *The Association of Persons with Severe Handicaps*, 25 (1): 18–28.

Iacono, T.A. (2006) Ethical challenges and complexities of including people with intellectual disability as participants in research. *Journal of Intellectual and Developmental Disability*, 31 (3): 173–179.

Imray, P. and Hinchcliffe, V. (2014) *Curricula for teaching children and young people with severe or profound and multiple learning difficulties: Practical strategies for educational professionals*. Abingdon, Oxon: Routledge.

Ingersoll, B. (2008) The social role of imitation in autism: Implications for the treatment of imitation deficits. *Infants & Young Children*, 21 (2): 107–119.

Ingersoll, B. (2010a) Teaching social communication: A comparison of naturalistic behavioral and development, social pragmatic approach for children with autism spectrum disorders. *Journal of Positive Behavior Interventions*, 12 (1): 33–43.

Ingersoll, B. (2010b) Brief report: Pilot randomized controlled trial of reciprocal imitation training for teaching elicited and spontaneous imitation to children with autism. *Journal of Autism and Developmental Disorders*, 40 (9): 1154–1160.

Ingersoll, B. (2011) The differential effect of three naturalistic language interventions on language use in children with autism. *Journal of Positive Behavior Interventions*, 13 (2): 109–118.

Ingersoll, B. and Dvortcsak, A. (2006) Including parent training in early childhood special education curriculum for children with autism spectrum disorders. *Journal of Positive Behavior Intervention*, 8 (2): 79–87.

Ingersoll, B., Dvortcsak, A., Whalen, C. and Sikora, D. (2005) The effects of a developmental, social-pragmatic language intervention on rate of expressive language production in young children with autistic spectrum disorders. *Focus on Autism and Other Developmental Disabilities*, 20 (4): 213–222.

Ingersoll, B. and Schreibman, L. (2006) Teaching reciprocal imitation skills to young children with autism using a naturalistic behavioral approach: Effects on language, pretend play and joint attention. *Journal of Autism and Developmental Disorders*, 36 (4): 487–505.

Institute of Consumer Rights (2012) *Focus group research: Features, advantages and disadvantages* [online]. Available from: http://myics.org/marketing/focus-group-research-features-advantages-and-disadvantages/ (accessed 29th February 2016).

Jackson, L. (2002) *Freaks, geeks and Asperger syndrome: A user guide to adolescence.* London: Jessica Kingsley Publishers.

James, D.M., Hall, A., Phillipson, J., McCrossan, G. and Falck, C. (2012) Creating a person-centered culture within the North East Autism Society: Preliminary findings. *British Journal of Learning Disabilities*, 41: 296–303.

James, K. and Fletcher, R. (2011) *Initial Tutor Training on ABA*, Manchester, 30–31 March 2011. Peach.

Jang, J., Matson, J.L., Adams, H.L., Konst, M.J., Cervantes, P.E. and Goldin, R.L. (2014) What are the ages of persons studied in autism research: A 20-year review. *Research in Autism Spectrum Disorders*, 8 (12): 1756–1760.

Jarrold, C. and Russell, J. (1997) Counting abilities in autism: Possible implications for central coherence theory. *Journal of Autism and Developmental Disorders*, 27 (1): 25–37.

Jarvis, J. and Lamb, S. (2001) Interaction and development of communication in the under twos: Issues for practitioners working with young children in groups. *Early Years*, 21 (2): 129–138.

Jarvis, J. and Lyon, S. (2015) "What makes Video Enhanced Reflective Practice (VERP) successful for system change?" In: H. Kennedy, M. Landor and L. Todd (eds.) *Video enhanced reflective practice: Professional development through attuned interactions.* London: Jessica Kingsley Publishers, pp. 35–46.

Jivraj, J., Sacrey, L.-A., Newton, A., Nicholas, D. and Zwaigenbaum, L. (2014) Assessing the influence of researcher – partner involvement on the process and outcomes of participatory research in autism spectrum disorder and neurodevelopmental disorders: A scoping review. *Autism*, 18 (7): 782–793.

Johnson, B., Onwuegbuzie, A. and Turner, L. (2007) Toward a definition of mixed methods research. *Journal of Mixed Methods Research*, 1 (2): 112–133.

Jones, E.A., Carr, E.G. and Feeley, K.M. (2006) Multiple effects of joint attention intervention for children with autism. *Behavior Modification*, 30 (6): 782–834.

Jones, G. (2002) *Educational provision for children with autism and Asperger syndrome.* London: David Fulton Publishers.

Jordan, R. (1993) "The nature of linguistic and communication difficulties of children with autism". In: D.J. Messer and G.J. Turner (eds.) *Critical influences on child language acquisition and development.* London: Macmillan, pp. 229–249.

Jordan, R. (1999) *Autistic spectrum disorders: An introductory handbook for practitioners.* London: David Fulton Publishers.

Jordan, R. (2001) *Autism with severe learning difficulties.* London: Souvenir Press (EandA) Ltd.

Jordan, R., Jones, G. and Murray, D. (1998) *Educational interventions for children with autism: A literature review of recent and current research.* London: DfEE.

Kaczmarek, L.A. (1990) Teaching spontaneous language to individuals with severe handicaps: A matrix model. *Journal of the Association for Persons with Severe Handicaps*, 15 (3): 160–169.

Kai, J., Loudon, R. and Beavan, J. (2006) "The nature of culture-valuing diversity and the individual". In: J. Kai (ed.) *Valuing diversity.* 2nd ed. London: Royal College of General Practitioners, pp. 97–118.

Kaiser, A.P., Yoder, P.J. and Keetz, A. (1992) "Evaluating milieu teaching". In: S.F. Warren and J. Reichle (eds.) *Causes and effects in communication and language intervention.* Baltimore: Brooks, pp. 9–48.

Kalyva, E. (2011) *Autism: Educational and therapeutic approaches.* London: SAGE Publications Ltd.

Kanner, L. (1943) Autistic disturbances of affective contact. *Pathology*, 217–250.
Kanner, L. (1946) Irrelevant and metaphorical language in early infantile autism. *American Journal of Psychiatry*, 103: 242–245.
Kasari, C. (2002) Assessing change in early intervention programs for children with autism. *Journal of Autism and Developmental Disorders*, 32 (5): 447–461.
Kasari, C., Freeman, S. and Paparella, T. (2006) Joint attention and symbolic play in young children with autism: A randomized controlled intervention study. *Journal of Child Psychology and Psychiatry*, 47 (6): 611–620.
Kasari, C. and Smith, T. (2013) Interventions in schools for children with autism spectrum disorder: Methods and recommendations. *Autism*, 17 (3): 254–267.
Kashinath, S., Woods, J. and Goldstein, H. (2006) Enhancing generalized teaching strategy use in daily routines by parents of children with autism. *Journal of Speech, Language, and Hearing Research*, 49 (3): 466–485.
Kaufman, B.N. (1994) *Son-rise: The miracle continues*. Novato, CA: New World Library.
Kaufman, R.K. (2002) "Building the bridges: Strategies for reaching our children". In: G. Jones (ed.) *Autism early intervention: A supplement for Good Autism Practice Journal*. Kidderminster, Worcestershire: Bild Publications, pp. 10–16.
Kearney, A.J. (2008) *Understanding applied behaviour analysis: An introduction to ABA for parents, teachers and other professionals*. London: Jessica Kingsley Publishers.
Keen, D., Woodyatt, G. and Sigafoos, J. (2002) Verifying teacher perceptions of the potential communicative acts of children with autism. *Communication Disorders Quarterly*, 23 (3): 131–140.
Keenan, M., Henderson, M., Kerr, K.P. and Dillenburger, K. (2006) *Applied Behaviour Analysis and Autism, Building a Future Together*. London: Jessica Kingsley Publishers.
Kelly, G. (1955) *The Psychology of Personal Constructs*. New York: Norton.
Kemmis, K. and McTaggart, R. (1992) *The action research planner*. 3rd ed. Geelong, Victoria: Deakin University Press.
Kemmis, K. and McTaggart, R. (2000) "Participatory action research". In: N. Denzin and Y. Lincoln (eds.) *Handbook of qualitative research*. London: SAGE Publications Ltd, pp. 567–605.
Kennedy, H. (2011) "What is Video Interaction Guidance (VIG)?" In: H. Kennedy, M. Landor and L. Todd (eds.) *Video interaction guidance: A relationship-based intervention to promote attunement, empathy and wellbeing*. London: Jessica Kingsley Publishers, pp. 20–42.
Kennedy, H. and Landor, M. (2015) "Introduction". In: H. Kennedy, M. Landor and L. Todd (eds.) *Video enhanced reflective practice: Professional development through attuned interactions*. London: Jessica Kingsley Publishers, pp. 18–34.
Kennedy, H. and Sked, H. (2008) "Video interaction guidance: A bridge to better interactions with individuals with communication impairments". In: M.S. Zeedyk (ed.) *Promoting social interaction for individuals with communicative impairments: Making contact*. London: Jessica Kingsley Publishers, pp. 139–154.
Kiernan, C. (1999) Participation in research by people with learning disability: Origins and issues. *British Journal of Learning Disabilities*, 27: 43–47.
Kim, H.U. (2012) Autism across cultures: Rethinking autism. *Disability & Society*, 27 (4): 535–545.
Kitahara, K. (1984) *Daily life therapy: A method of educating autistic children: Record of actual education at Musashino Higashi Gakuen School, Japan, Volume 1*. Boston, MA: Nimrod Press.

Klin, A. (1991) Young autistic children's listening preferences in regard to speech: A possible characterization of the symptom of social withdraw. *Journal of Autism and Developmental Disorders*, 21 (1): 29–42.

Koegel, L.K. (2000) Interventions to facilitate communication in autism. *Journal of Autism and Developmental Disorders*, 30 (5): 383–391.

Koegel, R.L., Openden, D., Fredeen, R. and Koegel, L.K. (2006) "The basics of pivotal response treatment". In: R.L. Koegel and L.K. Koegel (eds.) *Pivotal response treatments for autism: Communication, social and academic development*. London: Paul Brookes Publishing Co., pp. 4–30.

Koshy, V. (2005) *Action research for improving practice: A practical guide*. London: Paul Chapman Publishing.

Kossyvaki, L. (2010) The effect of adult style on the communication of young children on the autism spectrum. In: *9th Research Student Conference Entitled Education Researchers: Research for Change*, School of Education, University of Birmingham, Birmingham, 10th July 2010.

Kossyvaki, L. (2011) Using action research in special education: Advantages and challenges. In: *10th Research Student Conference Entitled Curiosity Driven or Improving Policy and Practice: What's the Point of University Research in an Age of Austerity?*, School of Education, University of Birmingham, Birmingham, 19th November 2011.

Kossyvaki, L. and Curran, S. (in preparation) *Using music through new technologies to enhance engagement, expression of positive emotions and social communication in children with autism and SLD/PMLD*.

Kossyvaki, L., Jones, G. and Guldberg, K. (2012) The effect of adult interactive style on the spontaneous communication of young children with autism at school. *British Journal of Special Education*, 39 (4): 173–184.

Kossyvaki, L., Jones, G. and Guldberg, K. (2016) Training teaching staff to facilitate spontaneous communication in children with autism: Adult Interactive Style Intervention (AISI). *Journal of Research in Special Educational Needs*, 16 (3): 156–168.

Kossyvaki, L. and Papoudi, D. (2016) A review of play interventions for children with autism at school. *International Journal of Disability, Development and Education*, 63 (1): 45–63.

Kuhn, T.S. (1962) *The structure of scientific revolutions*. Chicago: University of Chicago Press.

Lacey, P. (1998) Interdisciplinary training for staff working with people with profound and multiple learning disabilities. *Journal of Interprofessional Care* 12 (1): 43–52.

Lacey, P. (2012) "Meeting complex needs through collaborative multidisciplinary teamwork". In: P. Lacey and C. Ouvry (eds.) *People with profound and multiple learning disabilities: A collaborative approach to meeting complex needs*. London: Routledge, pp. ix–xvii.

Lacey, P. (2014) *Reflective practice*. Course material. Unpublished. Birmingham: University of Birmingham.

Lacey, P. and Oyvry, C. (2013) *People with profound & multiple learning disabilities: A collaborative approach to meeting complex needs*. Oxon: Routledge.

Lai, M.C., Lombardo, M.V., Pasco, G., Ruigrok, A.N., Wheelwright, S.J., Sadek, S.A., Chakrabarti, B., Baron-Cohen, S. and MRC AIMS Consortium (2011) A behavioral comparison of male and female adults with high functioning autism spectrum conditions. *PLoS One*, 6 (6): p. e20835.

Landor, M. (2015) How and Why Video Enhanced Reflective Practice (VERP) works. In H. Kennedy, M. Landor and L. Todd (Eds.) *Video Enhanced Reflective*

Practice: Professional Development through Attuned Interactions. London: Jessica Kingsley Publishers (pp. 60–70).

Lankshear, C. and Knobel, M. (2004) *A handbook for teacher research: From design to implementation*. Maidenhead, Berkshire: Open University Press.

Latham, C. and Miles, A. (1997) *Assessing communication*. London: David Fulton Publishers.

Lava, V., Recchia, S. and Giovacco-Johnson, T. (2004) Early childhood special educators reflecton their preparation and practice. *Teacher Education and Special Education*, 27 (2): 190–201.

Lawson, H., Fergusson, A., Brookes, M., Duffield, T. and Skipworth, A. (2015) "Citizenship, participation and voice". In: P. Lacey, R. Ashdown, P. Jones, H. Lawson and M. Pipe (eds.) *The routledge companion to severe, profound and multiple learning difficulties*. Abingdon, Oxon: Routledge, pp. 102–111.

Lawson, W. (1998) *Life behind glass: A personal account of autism spectrum disorder*. London: Jessica Kingsley Publishers.

Lawson, W. (2001) *Understanding and working with the spectrum of autism: An insider's view*. London: Jessica Kingsley Publishers.

Lawson, W. (2003) *Build your own life: A self-help guide for individuals with Asperger's syndrome*. London: Jessica Kingsley Publishers.

Lawson, W. (2011) *The passionate mind: How people with autism learn*. London: Jessica Kingsley Publishers.

Lee, B. and Mawson, C. (1998) *Survey of classroom assistants*. Slough: NFER and UNISON.

Leech, N. and Onwuegbuzie, A. (2009) A typology of mixed methods research designs. *Quality and Quantity*, 43 (2): 265–275.

Leikin, S. (1993) Minors' assent, consent, or dissent to medical research. *IRB: Ethics & Human Research*, 15 (2): 1–7.

Leko, M.M., Kiely, M.T., Brownell, M.T., Osipova, A., Dingle, M.P. and Mundy, C. (2015) Understanding special educators' learning opportunities in collaborative groups: The role of discourse. *Teacher Education and Special Education*, 38 (2): 138–157.

Leonard, L. and Leonard, P. (2003) The continuing trouble with collaboration: Teachers talk. *Current Issues in Education*, 6 (15): 1–10.

Lewin, K. (1946) Action research and minority problems. *Journal of Social Issues*, 2 (4): 34–46.

Lewis, A. (2002) Accessing, through research interviews, the views of children with difficulties in learning. *Support for Learning*, 17 (3): 110–116.

Lewis, A. (2009) Methodological issues in exploring the ideas of children with autism concerning self and spirituality. *Religion, Disability and Health*, 13: 64–76.

Lewis, A. (2011) "The importance of silence when hearing the views of children and young people with speech, language and communication needs". In: S. Roulstone and S. McLeod (eds.) *Listening to children and young people with speech, language and communication needs*. Guildford: J & R Press, pp. 55–62.

Lewis, A. and Porter, J. (2007) "Research and pupil voice". In: L. Florian (ed.) *The SAGE handbook of special education*. London: SAGE Publications Ltd., pp. 22–232.

Limbrick, P. (2001) *The team around the child: Multi-agency service co-ordination for children with complex needs and their families: A manual for service development*. Interconnections.

Litosseliti, L. (2003) *Using focus groups in research*. London: Continuum.

Llaneza, D.C., DeLuke, S.V., Batista, M., Crawley, J.N., Christodulu, K.V. and Frye, C.A. (2010) Communication, interventions, and scientific advances in autism: A commentary. *Physiology and Behavior*, 100 (3): 268–276.

Lloyd, D. (2012) Obtaining consent from young people with autism to participate in research. *British Journal of Learning Disabilities*, 41: 133–140.

Lonergan, J. (1990) *Technology in language learning: Making the most of your video camera*. London: CiLT.

Longhorn, F. (1993) *Prerequisites to learning for very special people*. Wootton, Bedfordshire: Catalyst Education Resources Ltd.

Lord, C., Risi, S., Lambrecht, L., Cook Jr, E.H., Leventhal, B.L., DiLavore, P.C., Pickles, A. and Rutter, M. (2000) The autism diagnostic observation schedule – Generic: A standard measure of social and communication deficits associated with the spectrum of autism. *Journal of Autism and Developmental Disorders*, 30 (3): 205–223.

Lord, C., Rutter, M. and Le Couteur, A. (1994) Autism diagnostic interview-revised: A revised version of a diagnostic interview for caregivers of individuals with possible pervasive developmental disorders. *Journal of Autism and Developmental Disorders*, 24 (5): 659–685.

Lord, C. and Schopler, E. (1994) "TEACCH services for preschool children". In: S.L. Harris and J.S. Handleman (eds.) *Preschool education programs for children with autism*. Austin, TX: Pro-Ed., pp. 87–106.

Lord, C., Schopler, E. and Revicki, D. (1982) Sex differences in autism. *Journal of Autism and Developmental Disorders*, 12: 317–330.

Lovaas, O.I. (1981) *Teaching developmentally disabled children: The me book*. Baltimore, MD: University Park Press.

Lowe, M. and Costello, A. (1988) *Symbolic play test*. 2nd ed. Windsor, Berkshire: NFER-NELSON.

Luke, L., Clare, I., Ring. H., Redley, M. and Watson, P. (2012) Decision-making difficulties experienced by adults with autism spectrum conditions. *Autism*, 16 (6): 612–621.

Lundeby, H. and Tossebro, J. (2008) Family structure in Norwegian families of children with disabilities. *Journal of Applied Research in Intellectual Disabilities*, 21: 246–256.

Mahoney, G. and MacDonald, J. (2007) *ASD and developmental delays in young children: The responsive teaching curriculum for parents and professionals*. Austin, TX: Pro-Ed.

Mahoney, G. and Perales, F. (2003) Using relationship-focused intervention to enhance the social emotional functioning of young children with autism spectrum disorders. *Topics in Early Childhood Special Education*, 23 (2): 74–86.

The Makaton Charity. Available from: www.makaton.org/ (accessed 17th March 2012).

Male, D.B. (2015) "Leaners with SLD and PMLD: Provision, policy and practice". In: P. Lacey, R. Ashdown, P. Jones, H. Lawson and M. Pipe (eds.) *The Routledge companion to severe profound and multiple learning difficulties*. London: Routledge, pp. 9–18.

Male, D.B. and May, D. (1997) Stress, burnout and workload in teachers of children with special educational needs. *British Journal of Special Education*, 24 (3): 133–140.

Manchester, H. (ed.) (2012) *Creative approaches to improving participation: Giving learners a say*. Oxon: Routledge.

Manolson, A. (1992) *It takes two to talk: A parent's guide to helping children communicate*. Toronto, Canada: The Hanen Centre.

Martin, T. and Alborz, A. (2014) Supporting the education of pupils with profound intellectual and multiple disabilities: The views of teaching assistants regarding their own learning and development needs. *British Journal of Special Education*, 41 (3): 309–327.

Matson, J.L. and Konst, M.J. (2014) Early intervention for autism: Who provides treatment and in what settings. *Research in Autism Spectrum Disorders*, 8 (11): 1585–1590.

Matson, J.L., Sevin, J.A., Box, M.L. and Francis, K.L. (1993) An evaluation of two methods for increasing self-initiated verbalizations in autistic children. *Journal of Applied Behavior Analysis*, 26 (3): 389–398.

Matson, J.L., Worley, J.A., Fodstad, J.C., Chung, K.M., Suh, D., Jhin, H.K., Ben-Itzchak, E., Zachor, D.A. and Furniss, F. (2011) A multinational study examining the cross cultural differences in reported symptoms of autism spectrum disorders: Israel, South Korea, the United Kingdom, and the United States of America. *Research in Autism Spectrum Disorders*, 5: 1598–1604.

Mauthner, M. (1997) Methodological aspects of collecting data from children: Lessons from three research projects. *Children and Society*, 11: 16–28.

McAteer, M. and Wilkinson, M. (2009) Adult style: What helps to facilitate interaction and communication with children on the autism spectrum. *Good Autism Practice*, 10 (2): 57–63.

McClimens, A. (2008) This is my truth, tell me yours: Exploring the internal tensions within collaborative learning disability research. *British Journal of Learning Disabilities*, 36: 271–276.

McConachie, H. and Diggle, T. (2007) Parent implemented early intervention for young children with autism spectrum disorder: A systematic review. *Journal of Evaluation in Clinical Practice*, 13 (1): 120–129.

McCray, E.D. (2012) Learning while teaching: A case study of beginning special educators completing a master of arts in teaching. *Teacher Education and Special Education*, 35 (3): 166–184.

McGee, G.G., Daly, T. and Jacobs, H.A. (1994) "The walden preschool". In: S.L. Harris and J.S. Handleman (eds.) *Preschool education programs for children with autism*. Austin, TX: Pro-Ed., pp. 126–162.

McGee, G.G., Feldman, R.S. and Morrier, M.J. (1997) Benchmarks of social treatment for children with autism. *Journal of Autism and Developmental Disorders*, 27 (4): 353–364.

McIntyre, D. (2005) Bridging the gap between research and practice. *Cambridge Journal of Education*, 35 (3): 357–382.

McNiff, J. and Whitehead, J. (2006) *All you need to know about action research*. London: SAGE Publications Ltd.

Meadan, H., Angell, M.E., Stoner, J.B. and Daczewitz, M.E. (2014) Parent-implemented social-pragmatic communication intervention: A pilot study. *Focus on Autism and Other Developmental Disabilities*, 29 (2): 95–110.

Meadan, H., Halle, J., Ostrosky, M.M. and DeStefano, L. (2008) Communicative behavior in the natural environment: Case studies of two young children with autism and limited expressive language. *Focus on Autism and Other Developmental Disorders*, 23 (1): 37–48.

The Mental Capacity Act (2005) [online]. Available from: www.legislation.gov.uk/ukpga/2005/9/section/3 (accessed 18th February 2016).

Merriam-Webster (1988) *Webster collegiate dictionary.* Springfield, MA: Merriam-Webster.
Mertens, D. (1998) *Research methods in education and psychology: Integrating diversity with quantitative and qualitative approaches.* London: SAGE Publications Ltd.
Mesibov, G.B. (2007) *Three day TEACCH training course.* Kettering, 6–8 June 2007. Autism Independent UK.
Mesibov, G.B., Adams, L. and Klinger, L. (1997) *Autism: Understanding the disorder.* New York: Plenum Press.
Messer, D.J. (1994) *The development of communication: From social interaction to language.* Chichester, West Sussex: John Wiley and Sons.
Methley, A. and Wimpory, D. (2010) *Music interaction therapy for children with autism* [DVD]. Bangor: Bangor University.
Milton, D.E. (2012) Personal communication via email on the 17th May 2012.
Milton, D.E. (2014a) So what exactly are autism interventions intervening with? *Good Autism Practice*, 15 (2): 6–14. Chapter 7.
Milton, D.E. (2014b) *Publications.* Available from: http://damianmiltonsociol.wixsite.com/dmilton-autism/publications (accessed 14th December 2016).
Milton, D.E. (2016) @milton_damian [Twitter account]. Available from: https://twitter.com/milton_damian (accessed 14th December 2016).
Moore, M., Beazley, S. and Maelzer, J. (1998) *Research disability issues.* Maidenhead, Berkshire: Open University Press.
Moran, H. (2001) Who do you think you are? Drawing the Ideal Self: a technique to explore a child's sense of self. *Clinical Psychology and Psychiatry*, 6 (4): 599–604.
Morgan, D.L. (1988) *Focus groups as qualitative research.* London: SAGE Publications Ltd.
Murdock, L.C., Cost, H.C. and Tieso, C. (2007) Measurement of social communication skills of children with autism spectrum disorders during interactions with typical peers. *Focus on Autism and Other Developmental Disabilities*, 22 (3): 160–172.
Murphy, K. and Cameron, L. (2008) The effectiveness of talking mats with people with intellectual disability. *British Journal of Learning Disabilities*, 36: 232–41.
Myles, B.S., Cook, K.T., Miller, N.E., Rinner, L. and Robbins, L.A. (2000) *Asperger syndrome and sensory issues: Practical solutions for making sense of the world.* Shawnee Mission, KS: Autism Asperger Publishing Co.
Naoi, N., Tsuchiya, R., Yamamoto, J.I. and Nakamura, K. (2008) Functional training for initiating joint attention in children with autism. *Research in Developmental Disabilities*, 29 (6): 595–606.
National Autistic Society (NAS) (n.d.) *SPELL* [online]. Available from: www.autism.org.uk/spell (accessed 29th February 2016).
National Foundation for Educational Research (NFER) (2014) *A randomised trial of catch up: Numeracy evaluation report and executive summary November 2013.* London: Education Endowment Foundation.
National Institute for Health and Care Excellence (NICE) (2012) Social and emotional wellbeing: early years [online]. Available from: www.nice.org.uk/guidance/ph40/chapter/8-glossary (accessed 1st September 2016).
National Research Council, Division of Behavioral and Social Sciences and Education, Committee on Educational Interventions for Children with Autism (NRC) (2001) *Educating children with autism.* Washington, DC: National Academies Press.
Natt, S. (2015) Views of adult interactive style: A study exploring the views of children with autism using semi-structured interviews. Birmingham: MEd Thesis, University of Birmingham.

Nind, M. (1999) Intensive interaction and autism: A useful approach? *British Journal of Special Education*, 26 (2): 96–102.
Nind, M. (2014) *What is inclusive research?* London: Bloomsbury.
Nind, M. and Hewett, D. (1994) *Access to communication*. London: David Fulton Publishers.
Nind, M. and Hewett, D. (2001) *A practical guide to intensive interaction*. Kidderminster, Worcestershire: Bild Publications.
Nind, M. and Powell, S. (2000) Intensive interaction and autism. *Children and Society*, 14 (2): 98–109.
Nind M. and Vinha H. (2014) Doing research inclusively: bridges to multiple possibilities in inclusive research. *British Journal of Learning Disabilities*, 42: 102–109.
Noens, I. and Van Berckelaer-Onnes, I. (2004) Making sense in a fragmentary world: Communication in people with autism and learning disability. *Autism*, 8 (2): 197–218.
Norbury, C.F. and Sparks, A. (2012) Difference or disorder? Cultural issues in understanding neurodevelopmental disorders. *Developmental Psychology*, 49 (1): 45–58.
Nordoff, P. and Robbins, C. (1977) *Creative music therapy*. New York: John Day.
Northway, R., Hurley, K., O'Connor, C., Thomas, H., Bale, S., Howarth, J. and Langley, E. (2014) Deciding what to research: An overview of a participatory workshop. *British Journal of Learning Disabilities*, 42: 323–327.
NVivo (2012) *Qualitative data analysis software*. QSR International Pty Ltd. Version 10.
Odom, S.L., Brantlinger, E., Gerstein, R., Horner, R.H., Thompson, B. and Harris, K.R. (2005) Research in special education: Scientific methods and evidence-based practices, *Council for Exceptional Children*, 71 (2): 137–148.
Ofsted Reports (2007, 2010, 2014).
Ogletree, B.T., Pierce, K., Harn, W.E. and Fischer, M.A. (2002) Assessment of communication and language in classical autism: Issues and practices assessment for effective intervention. *Assessment for Effective Intervention*, 27 (1): 61–71.
Ollerton, M. (2008) "Moving from reflective practitioner to practitioner research". In: S. Elton-Chalcraft, A. Hansen and S. Twiselton (eds.) *Doing classroom research: A step by step guide for student teachers*. New York: Open University Press, pp. 11–24.
Olson, S., Bayles, K. and Bates, J. (1986) Mother-child interaction and children's speech progress: A longitudinal study of the first two years. *Merrill-Palmer Quarterly*, 32 (1): 1–20.
Onwuegbuzie, A. and Leech, N. (2005) On becoming a pragmatic researcher: The importance of combining quantitative and qualitative research methodologies. *International Journal of Social Research Methodology*, 8 (5): 375–387.
O'Reilly, M., Sigafoos, J., Lancioni, G., Edrisinha, C. and Andrews, A. (2005) An examination of the effects of a classroom activity schedule on levels of self-injury and engagement for a child with severe autism. *Journal of Autism and Developmental Disorders*, 35 (3): 305–311.
Ospina, M.B., Seida, J.K., Clark, B., Karkhaneh, M., Hartling, L., Tjosvold, L., Vandermeer, B. and Smith, V. (2008) Behavioural and developmental interventions for autism spectrum disorder: A clinical systematic review. *PLoS One*, 3 (11): e3755.
Owen, R., Hayett, L. and Roulstone, S. (2004) Children's views of speech and language therapy in school: Consulting children with communication difficulties. *Child Language Teaching and Therapy*, 20 (1): 55–73.

Ozonoff, S., Pennington, B.F. and Rogers, S. (1990) Are there emotion perception deficits in young autistic children? *Journal of Child Psychology and Psychiatry*, 31 (3): 343–361.
Ozonoff, S., Pennington, B.F. and Rogers, S. (1991) Executive function deficits in high-functioning autistic individuals: Relationship to theory of mind. *Journal of Child Psychology and Psychiatry*, 32 (7): 1081–1105.
Park, S., Cho, S.C., Cho, I.H., Kim, B.N., Kim, J.W., Shin, M.S., Chung, U.S., Park, T.W., Son, J.W. and Yoo, H.J. (2012) Sex differences in children with autism spectrum disorders compared with their unaffected siblings and typically developing children. *Research in Autism Spectrum Disorders*, 6 (2): 861–870.
Parsons, S., Charman, T., Faulkner, R., Ragan, J., Wallace, S. and Wittemeyer, K. (2013) Bridging the research and practice gap in autism: The importance of creating research partnerships with schools. *Autism*, 17 (3): 268–280.
Parsons, S., Guldberg, K., MacLeod, A., Jones, G., Prunty, A. and Balfe, T. (2011) International review of the evidence on best practice in educational provision for children on the autism spectrum. *European Journal of Special Needs Education*, 26 (1): 47–63.
Parsons, S., Guldberg, K., Porayska-Pomsta, K. and Lee, R. (2015) Digital stories as a method for evidence-based practice and knowledge co-creation in technology-enhanced learning for children with autism. *International Journal of Research & Method in Education*, 38 (3): 247–271.
Peeters, T. and Jordan, R. (1999) "What makes a good practitioner in the field of autism?" In: G. Jones (ed.) *GAP: Celebrating the first 10 years of the journal*. Location: Publisher, pp. 85–90.
Pelios, L.V. and Lund, S.K. (2001) A selective overview on issues on classification, causation, and early intensive behavioral intervention for autism. *Behavior Modification*, 25 (5): 678–697.
Pellicano, E., Dinsmore, A. and Charman, T. (2013) *A future made together: Shaping autism research in the UK*. London: Institute of Education.
Pellicano, E., Dinsmore, A. and Charman, T. (2014) What should autism research focus upon? Community views and priorities from the United Kingdom. *Autism*, 18 (7): 756–770.
Pelphrey, K.A., Morris, J.P. and McCarthy, G. (2005) Neural basis for eye gaze processing deficits in autism. *Brain*, 128 (5): 1038–1048.
Pennington, B.F. and Ozonoff, S. (1996) Executive functions and developmental psychopathology. *Journal of Child Psychology and Psychiatry*, 37 (1): 51–87.
Pennington, L. and Thomson, K. (2007) It takes two to talk: The Hanen program and families of children with motor disorders: A UK perspective. *Child Care Health Development*, 33 (6): 691–702.
Perepa, P. (2014) Cultural basis of social 'deficits' in autism spectrum disorders. *European Journal of Special Needs Education*, 29 (3): 313–326.
Pickles, A., Le Couteur, A., Leadbitter, K., Salomone, E., Cole-Fletcher, R., Tobin, H., Gammer, I., Lowry, J., Vamvakas, G., Byford, S. and Aldred, C. (2016) Parent-mediated social communication therapy for young children with autism (PACT): long-term follow-up of a randomised controlled trial. *The Lancet*, 388 (10059): 2501–2509.
Pilnick, A. and James, D. (2013) 'I'm thrilled that you see that': Guiding parents to see success in interactions with children with deafness and autistic spectrum disorder. *Social Science & Medicine*, 99: 89–101.

Pittman, M. (2007) *Helping pupils with autistic spectrum disorders to learn*. London: Paul Chapman Publishing.

Pollard, A. (2008) *Reflective teaching*. 3rd ed. London: Continuum.

Porayska-Pomsta, K., Anderson, K., Bernardini, S., Guldberg, K., Smith, T., Kossyvaki, L., Hodgings, S. and Lowe, I. (2013) Building an intelligent authorable serious game for autistic children and their carers. In: *Proceedings of the 10th International Conference on Advances in Computer Entertainment* (ACE 2013). Boekelo, The Netherlands

Potter, C. and Whittaker, C. (2001) *Enabling communication in children with autism*. London: Jessica Kingsley Publishers.

Preece, D. (2009) Obtaining the views of children and young people with autism spectrum disorders about their experience of daily life and social care support. *British Journal of Learning Disabilities*, 38: 10–20.

Preece, D. and Jordan, R. (2010) Obtaining the views of children and young people with autism spectrum disorders about their experience of daily life and social care support. *British Journal of Learning Disabilities*, 38 (1): 10–20.

Preece, D., Symeou, L., Stošić, J., Troshansk, J., Mavrou, K., Theodorou, E. and Frey Škrinjar, J. (2016) Accessing parental perspectives to inform the development of parent training in autism in southeastern Europe. *European Journal of Special Needs Education*, 32 (2): 252–269.

Prizant, B.M. and Duchan, J. (1981) The functions of immediate echolalia in autistic children. *Journal of Speech and Hearing Disorders*, 46 (3): 241–249.

Prizant, B.M. and Rydell, P.J. (1984) Analysis of functions of delayed echolalia in autistic children. *Journal of Speech and Hearing Research*, 27 (2): 183–192.

Prizant, B.M., Wetherby, A.M., Rubin, E., Laurent, A. and Rydell, P. (2006) *The SCERTS model: A comprehensive educational approach for children with autism spectrum disorders, Volume 1: Assessment*. Baltimore, MD: Paul H. Brookes Publishing.

Prizant, B.M., Wetherby, A.M. and Rydell, P.J. (2000) "Communication intervention issues for children with autism spectrum disorders". In: A.M. Wetherby and B.M. Prizant (eds.) *Autism spectrum disorders: A transactional developmental perspective, Volume 9*. London: Paul Brookes Publishing Co., pp. 1993–224.

Puyalto, C., Pallisera, M., Fullana, J. and Vilà, M. (2016) Doing Research Together: A Study on the Views of Advisors with Intellectual Disabilities and Non-Disabled Researchers Collaborating in Research. *Journal of Applied Research in Intellectual Disabilities*, 29 (2): 146–159.

Reason, P. and Bradbury, H. (2001) "Introduction: Inquiry and participation in search of a world worthy of human aspiration". In: P. Reason and H. Bradbury (eds.) *Handbook of action research: Participative enquiry and practice*. London: SAGE Publications Ltd., pp. 1–14.

Reed, J. (2005) Using action research in nursing practice with older people: Democratizing knowledge. *Journal of Clinical Nursing*, 14 (5): 594–600.

Reeve, D. (2004) "Psycho-emotional dimensions of disability and the social model". In: C. Barnes and G. Mercer (eds.) *Implementing the social model of disability: Theory and research*. Leeds: The Disability Press, pp. 83–100.

Reichow, B., Volkmar, F. and Cicchetti, D. (2008) Development of the evaluative method for evaluating and determining evidence-based practices in autism. *Journal of Autism and Developmental Disorders*, 38 (7): 1311–1319.

Remington, B., Hastings, R., Kovshoff, H., Espinosa, F., Jahr, E., Brown, T., Alsford, P., Lemaic, M. and Ward, N. (2007) Early intensive behavioral intervention:

Outcomes for children with autism and their parents after two years. *American Journal of Mental Retardation*, 112 (6): 418–438.

Richman, S. (2001) *Raising a child with autism: A guide to applied behavior analysis for parents*. London: Jessica Kingsley Publishers.

Riege, A. (2003) Validity and reliability tests in case study research: A literature review with 'hands-on' applications for each research phase. *Qualitative Market Research: An International Journal*, 6 (2): 75–86.

Rieser, R. and Mason, M. (1990) *Disability equality in the classroom: A human rights issue*. London: Disability Equality in Education.

Risdal, D. and Singer, G.H.S. (2004) Marital adjustment in parents of children with disabilities: A historical review and meta-analysis. *Research and Practice for Persons with Severe Disabilities*, 29 (2): 95–103.

Roberts, J. (1989) Echolalia and comprehension in autistic children. *Journal of Autism and Developmental Disorders*, 19 (2): 271–281.

Robertson, J., Hatton, C., Felce, D., Meek, A., Carr, D., Knapp, M., Hallam, A., Emerson, E., Pinkney, L., Caesar, E. and Lowe, K. (2005) Staff stress and morale in community based settings for people with intellectual disabilities and challenging behaviour: A brief report. *Journal of Applied Research in Intellectual Disabilities*, 18: 271–277.

Robison, J.E. (2007) *Look me in the eye*. New York: Three Rivers Press.

Robson, C. (2002) *Real word research*. 2nd ed. Oxford: Blackwell.

Rodriguez, B.L. and Olswang, L.B. (2003) Mexican-American and Anglo-American mothers' beliefs and values about child rearing, education, and language impairment. *American Journal of Speech Language Pathology*, 12: 452.

Roeyers, H., Buysse, A., Ponnet, K. and Pichal, B. (2001) Advancing advanced mind-reading tests: Empathetic accuracy in adults with pervasive developmental disorder. *Journal of Child Psychology and Psychiatry*, 42 (2): 271–278.

Rogers, J. (2007) *Adult learning*. Maidenhead: Open University Press.

Rogers, S.J. (1996) Brief report: Early intervention in autism. *Journal of Autism and Developmental Disorders*, 26 (2): 243–246.

Rogers, S.J. and Dawson, G. (2010) *Early start denver model for young children with autism: Promoting language, learning and engagement*. London: The Guilford Press.

Rogers, S.J., Hepburn, S.L., Stackhouse, T. and Wehner, E. (2003) Imitation performance in toddlers with autism and those with other developmental disorders. *Journal of Child Psychology and Psychiatry*, 44 (5): 763–781.

Roos, E., McDuffie, A., Ellis Weismer, S., Gernsbacher, M.A. and Eisenband, L. (2008) A comparison of contexts for assessing joint attention in toddlers on the autism spectrum. *Autism*, 12 (3): 275–291.

Rose, R. and Doveston, M. (2015) Collaboration across cultures: Planning and delivering professional development for inclusive education in India. *Support for Learning*, 30 (3): 177–191.

Ruble, L., McDuffie, A., King, A. and Lorenz, D. (2008) Caregiver responsiveness and social interaction behaviors of young children with autism. *Topics in Early Childhood Special Education*, 28 (3): 158–170.

Rutter, M., Andersen-Wood, L., Beckett, C., Bredencamp, D., Castle, J., Groothues, C., Kreppner, J., Keaveney, L., Lord, C., O'Connor, G.T. and the English and Romanian Adoptee (ERA) Study Team (1999) Quasi-autistic patterns following severe early global privation. *Journal of Child Psychology and Psychiatry*, 40 (4): 537–549.

Rydell, P.J. and Mirenda, P. (1994) Effects of high and low constraint utterances on the production of immediate and delayed echolalia in young children with autism. *Journal of Autism and Developmental Disorders*, 24: 112–149.

Sabbeth, B.F. and Leventhal, J.M. (1984) Marital adjustment to chronic childhood illness: A critique of the literature. *Pediatrics*, 73: 762–768.

Saddler, H. (2014) Researching the influence of teaching assistants on the learning of pupils identified with special educational needs in mainstream primary schools: Exploring social inclusion. *Journal of Research in Special Educational Needs*, 14 (3): 145–152.

Saini, M., Stoddart, K.P., Gibson, M., Morris, R., Barrett, D., Muskat, B., Nicholas, D., Rampton, G. and Zwaigenbaum, L. (2015) Couple relationships among parents of children and adolescents with Autism Spectrum Disorder: Findings from a scoping review of the literature. *Research in Autism Spectrum Disorders*, 17: 142–157.

Sainsbury, C. (2009) *Martian in the playground*. London: SAGE Publications Ltd.

Salmon, C.M., Rowan, L.E. and Mitchell, P.R. (1998) Facilitating prelinguistic communication: Impact of adult prompting. *Infant-Toddler Intervention*, 8 (1): 11–27.

Salter-Ainsworth, M.D.S. and Bell, S.M. (1974) "Mother-infant interaction and the development of competence". In: K.J. Connolly and J. Bruner (eds.) *The growth of competence*. London: Academic Press, pp. 97–118.

Sanua, V.D. (1981a) Autism, childhood schizophrenia and culture: A critical review of the literature. *Transcultural Psychiatric Research Review*, 18: 165–181.

Sanua, V.D. (1981b) Cultural changes and psychopathology in children: With special reference to infantile autism. *Acta Paedopsychiat*, 47: 133–142.

Sanua, V.D. (1984) Is infantile autism a universal phenomenon? An open question. *International Journal of Social Psychiatry*, 30: 163–177.

Scherer, N. and Olswang, L. (1984) Role of mothers' expansions in stimulating children's language production. *Journal of Speech and Hearing Research*, 27 (3): 387–396.

Schertz, H.H. and Odom, S.L. (2004) Joint attention and early intervention with autism: A conceptual framework and promising approaches. *Journal of Early Intervention*, 27 (1): 42–54.

Scheuffgen, K., Happé, F., Anderson, M. and Frith, U. (2000) High "intelligence", low "IQ"? Speed of processing and measured IQ in children with autism. *Development and Psychopathology*, 12 (1): 83–90.

Schlosser, R.W., Arvidson, H.H. and Lloyd, L.L. (2003) *The efficacy of alternative and augmentative communication: Toward evidence-based practice*. Boston: Academic Press.

Schopler, E., Reichler, R. and Rochen Renner, B. (1988) *The Childhood Autism Rating Scale (CARS)*. Los Angeles: Western Psychological Services.

Schultz, T.R., Schmidt, C.T. and Stichter, J.P. (2011) A review of parent education programs for parents of children with autism spectrum disorders. *Focus on Autism and Other Developmental Disabilities*, 26 (2): 96–104.

Scott, D. and Usher, R. (1999) *Researching education: Data, methods and theory in educational enquiry*. London: Cassell.

Seligman, M.E.P. (2002) Positive Psychology, Positive Prevention, and Positive Therapy. In C.R. Snyder and S.J. Lopez (Eds.) *The Handbook of Positive Psychology*. New York: Oxford University Press (pp. 3–12).

Seligman, M.E.P. (2011) *Flourish: A visionary new understanding of happiness and wellbeing*. New York: Free Press.

Seligman, M.E.P. and Pawelski, J.O. (2003) Positive psychology: FAQS. *Psychological Inquiry*, 14 (2): 159–163.

Shakespeare, T. (2004) Social models of disability and other life strategies. *Scandinavian Journal of Disability Research*, 6 (1): 8–21.

Sheridan, M. (2008) *From birth to five years: Children's developmental progress*. 3rd ed. London: Routledge.

Sigafoos, J. (2000) Communication development and aberrant behavior in children with developmental disabilities. *Education and Training in Mental Retardation and Developmental Disabilities*, 35 (2): 168–176.

Siller, M. and Sigman, M. (2002) The behaviors of parents of children with autism predict the subsequent development of their children's communication. *Journal of Autism and Developmental Disorders*, 32 (2): 77–89.

Simpson, R.L. (2005) *Autism spectrum disorders: Interventions and treatments for children and youth*. Thousand Oaks, CA: Corwin Press.

Sinclair, J. (1992) "Bridging the gaps: An inside-out view of autism". In: E. Schopler and G.B. Mesibov (eds.) *High-functioning individuals with autism*. New York: Plenum Press, pp. 294–302.

Sked, H. (2006) Learning their language: A comparative study of social interactions between children with autism and adults, using imitation and video interaction guidance as interventions. Thesis submitted in part fulfilment of the Master of Science Degree in Educational Psychology. Dundee: University of Dundee.

Sloman, M. (2003) *Training in the age of the learner*. London: Chartered Institute of Personnel and Development.

Sloper, P. (1999) Models of service support for parents of disabled children: What do we know? What do we need to know? *Child Care Health and Development*, 25 (2): 85–99.

Smith, C. (1999) The development and evaluation of additional training for Portage Workers in addressing the needs of children with complex social and communication difficulties/autistic spectrum disorders. London: EdD thesis, University of East London.

Smith, J.A. and Osborn, M. (2008) "Interpretative phenomenological analysis". In: J.A. Smith (ed.) *Qualitative psychology: A practical guide to research methods*. 2nd ed. London: SAGE Publications Ltd., pp. 53–80.

Smith, K., Kenner, C. and Barton-Hide, D. (1998) *Research project: Career adder for classroom assistants*. Southampton: University of Southampton/Hampshire City Council.

Somekh, B. (1995) The contribution of action research to development in social endeavours: A position paper on action research methodology. *British Educational Research Journal*, 21 (3): 339–355.

Sonders, S. (2003) *Giggle time: Establishing the social connection*. London: Jessica Kingsley Publishers.

Stahmer, A.C. and Pellecchia, M. (2015) Moving towards a more ecologically valid model of parent-implemented interventions in autism. *Autism*, 19 (3): 259–261.

Stalker, K. (1998) Some ethical and methodological issues in research with people with learning difficulties. *Disability & Society*, 13 (1): 5–19.

Standards and Testing Agency (2016) *The Rochford review: Final report* [online]. Available from: www.gov.uk/government/uploads/system/uploads/attachment_data/file/561411/Rochford_Review_Report_v5_PFDA.pdf (accessed 27th October 2016).

Stevenson, M. (2014) Participatory data analysis alongside co-researchers who have down syndrome. *Journal of Applied Research in Intellectual Disabilities*, 27: 23–33.

Stigler, J.W., Gallimore, R. and Hierber, J. (2000) Using video surveys to compare classrooms and teaching across cultures: Examples and lessons from the TIMSS video studies. *Educational Psychologist*, 35 (2): 87–100.

Stone, W.L. and Caro-Martinez, L.M. (1990) Naturalistic observations of spontaneous communication in autistic children. *Journal of Autism and Developmental Disorders*, 20 (4): 437–453.

Stone, W.L., Ousley, O., Yoder, P., Hogan, K. and Hepburn, S. (1997) Nonverbal communication in two- and three-year-old children with autism. *Journal of Autism and Developmental Disorders*, 27 (6): 677–696.

Strathie, S., Strathie, C. and Kennedy, H. (2011) "Video enhanced reflective practice". In: H. Kennedy, M. Landor and L. Todd (eds.) *Video interaction guidance: A relationship-based intervention to promote attunement, empathy and wellbeing*. London: Jessica Kingsley Publishers, pp. 170–180.

Strnadová, I. and Cumming, T.M. (2014) People with intellectual disabilities conducting research: New directions for inclusive research. *Journal of Applied Research in Intellectual Disabilities*, 27: 1–2.

Sussman, F. (1999) *More than words: Helping parents promote communication and social skills in children with autism spectrum disorder*. Toronto: Hanen Centre.

Swetnam, D. (1997) *Writing your dissertation, how to plan, prepare and present your work successfully*. 2nd ed. Oxford: How to Books LTD.

Sylva, K., Roy, C. and Painter, M. (1980) *Childwatching at playgroup and nursery school*. London: Grant McIntyre.

Teddlie, C. and Tashakkori, A. (2003) "Major issues and controversies in the use of mixed methods in the social and behavioral sciences". In: A. Tashakkori and C. Teddlie (eds.) *Handbook of mixed methods in social and behavioural research*. Thousand Oaks, CA: SAGE Publications Ltd., pp. 3–50.

Thiemann, K. and Goldstein, H. (2004) Effects of peer training and written text cueing on social communication of school-age children with pervasive developmental disorder. *Journal of Speech, Language, and Hearing Research*, 47 (1): 126–144.

Transform Autism Education (TAE) (2016a) *Simone Knowing Simon, S.* [blog] 1st May. Available from: https://transformautismeducation.wordpress.com/2016/05/01/simone-knowing-simon-s/ (accessed 14th December 2016).

Transform Autism Education (TAE) (2016b) *Interview with Katerina Mpakopoulou* [blog] 16th June. Available from: https://transformautismeducation.wordpress.com/2016/06/16/interview-with-katerina-mpakopoulou/ (accessed 14th December 2016).

Transform Autism Education (TAE) (2016c) *AuVision: Led by and for autistic students* [blog] 24th July. Available from: https://acertheblog.wordpress.com/2016/07/24/auvision-led-by-and-for-autistic-students/ (accessed 14th December 2016).

Tregaskis, C. (2002) Social model theory: The story so far. . .*Disability and Society*, 17 (24): 457–470.

Trevarthen, C., Aitken, K., Papoudi, D. and Robarts, J. (1996) *Children with autism: Diagnosis and interventions to meet their needs*. London: Jessica Kingsley Publishers.

Tsai, L.Y. and Beisler, J.M. (1983) The development of sex differences in infantile autism. *British Journal of Psychiatry*, 142: 373–378.

Tsang, H.W.H., Tam, P.K.C., Chan, F. and Cheung, W.M. (2003) Stigmatizing attitudes towards individuals with mental illness in Hong Kong: Implications for their recovery. *Journal of Community Psychology*, 31 (4): 383–396.

Tsao, L. and Odom, S. (2006) Sibling-mediated social interaction intervention for young children with autism. *Topics in Early Childhood Special Education*, 26 (2): 106–123.
United Nations (1989) *Convention on the rights of the child*. New York: UN.
United Nations (2006) *Convention on the rights of persons with disabilities*. New York: UN.
Vanvuchelen, M., Roeyers, H. and De Weerdt, W. (2011) Do imitation problems reflect a core characteristic in autism? Evidence from a literature review. *Research in Autism Spectrum Disorders*, 5 (1): 89–95.
Vasilopoulou, E. and Nisbet, J. (2016) The quality of life of parents of children with autism spectrum disorder: A systematic review. *Research in Autism Spectrum Disorders*, 23: 36–49.
Vincett, K., Cremin, H. and Thomas, G. (2005) *Teachers and assistants working together*. Maidenhead, Berkshire: Open University Press.
Volkmar, F.R. (2016) Autism today-what we do and don't know. In: *Paper Presented at XI Autism-Europe International Congress*, Edinburgh, UK, 16–18 September 2013.
Volkmar, F.R., Szatmari, P. and Sparrow, S.S. (1993) Sex differences in pervasive developmental disorders. *Journal of Autism and Developmental Disorders*, 23: 579–591.
Vygotsky, L. (1978) *Mind in society: The development of higher psychological processes*. Cambridge, MA: Harvard University Press.
The Waldon Association. Available from: www.waldonassociation.org.uk (accessed 25th January 2009).
Walker, M. (1976) *Manual of language programmes for use with the revised Makaton vocabulary*. Camberley, Surrey: Makaton Vocabulary Development Project.
Wall, K. (2004) *Autism and early years practice: A guide for early years professionals, teachers and parents*. London: Paul Chapman Publishing.
Walmsley, J. and Mannan, H. (2009) Parents as co-researchers: A participatory action research initiative involving parents of people with intellectual disabilities in Ireland. *British Journal of Learning Disabilities*, 37 (4): 271–276.
Wantanbe, M. and Sturmey, P. (2003) The effect of choice-making opportunities during activity schedules on task engagement of adults with autism. *Journal of Autism and Developmental Disorders*, 33 (5): 535–538.
Ware, J. (2003) *Creating a responsive environment for people with profound and multiple learning difficulties*. 2nd ed. London: David Fulton Publishers.
Ware, J. (2004) Ascertaining the views of people with profound and multiple learning disabilities. *British Journal of Learning Disabilities*, 32: 175–179.
Ware, J. (2016) Personal face-to-face conversation at the University of Birmingham.
Warwick, A. (2001) "I have a song-let me sing: Relating part of a journey through Music Therapy with an autistic boy". In: J. Richer and S. Coates (eds.) *Autism: The search for coherence*. London: Jessica Kingsley Publishers, pp. 199–204.
Watkins, M.W. and Pacheco, M. (2000) Interoberver agreement in behavioural research. *Journal of Behavioral Education*, 10 (4): 205–212.
Watson, L.R. (1998) Following the child's lead: Mothers' interactions with children with autism. *Journal of Autism and Developmental Disorders*, 28 (1): 51–59.
Watson, L.R., Lord, C., Schaffer, B. and Schopler, E. (1989) *Teaching spontaneous communication to autistic and developmentally handicapped children*. New York: Irvington.

Webster, R. and Blatchford, P. (2013) *The making a statement project final report: A study of the teaching and support experienced by pupils with a statement of special educational needs in mainstream primary schools*. London: Institute of Education.

Webster, R., Blatchford, P., Bassett, P., Brown, P., Martin, C. and Russell, A. (2010) Double standards and first principles: Framing teaching assistant support for pupils with special educational needs. *European Journal of Special Needs Education*, 25 (4): 319–336.

Weisz, J. (2000) Agenda for child and adolescent psychotherapy research: On the need to put science into practice. *Archives of General Psychiatry*, 57 (9): 837–838.

Wellington, J.J. (2000) *Educational research: Contemporary issues and practical approaches*. London: Continuum.

Wels, P.M.A. (2002) *Helping with a camera: The use of video for family intervention*. Nijmegen: Nijmegen University Press.

Westcott, H., Davies, G. and Bull, R. (2002) *Children's testimony: Psychological research and forensic practice*. Chichester: Wiley.

Wetherby, A.M. (1986) Ontogeny of communicative functions in autism. *Journal of Autism and Developmental Disorders*, 16 (3): 295–316.

Wetherby, A.M. and Prizant, B.M. (2000) "Introduction to autism spectrum disorders". In: A. Wetherby and B. Prizant (eds.) *Autism spectrum disorders: A transactional developmental perspective, Volume 9*. London: Paul Brookes Publishing Co., pp. 1–7.

Wetherby, A.M. and Prizant, B.M. (2002) *Communication and symbolic behaviour scales-developmental profile*. Baltimore, MD: Paul H. Brookes Publishing.

Wetherby, A.M., Prizant, B.M. and Schuler, A.L. (2000) "Understanding the nature and language impairments". In: A.M. Wetherby and B.M. Prizant (eds.) *Autism spectrum disorders: A transactional developmental perspective*. Baltimore, MD: Brookes, pp. 109–141.

Wetherby, A.M., Watt, N., Morgan, L. and Shumway, S. (2007) Social communication profiles of children with autism spectrum disorders late in the second year of life. *Journal of Autism and Developmental Disorders*, 37 (5): 960–975.

Whitaker, P., Joy, H., Edwards, D. and Harley, D. (2001) *Challenging behaviour and autism: Making sense – making progress: A guide to preventing and managing challenging behaviour for parent and teachers*. London: The National Autistic Society.

White, K.R., Taylor, M.J. and Moss, V.D. (1992) Does research support claims about the benefits of involving parents in early intervention programs? *Review of Educational Research*, 62 (1): 91–125.

White, M. and Cameron, R.J. (1987) *Portage early education programme: A practical manual*. Windsor, Berkshire: NFER-NELSON.

Whitehead, J. (1989) Creating a living educational theory from questions of the kind, 'how do I improve my practice?' *Cambridge Journal of Education*, 19 (1): 137–153.

Whitehead, J. and McNiff, J. (2006) *Action research living theory*. London: SAGE Publications Ltd.

Wieder, S. and Greenspan, S. (2003) Climbing the symbolic ladder in the DIR model through floor time/interactive play. *Autism*, 7 (4): 425–435.

Wilcox, M. and Shannon, M. (1998) "Facilitating the transition from prelinguistic to linguistic communication". In: S. Warren, J. Reichle and A. Wetherby (eds.) *Communication and language series, Volume 5: Prelinguistic communication*. Baltimore: Paul H. Brookes, pp. 385–416.

Wilkinson, S. (2008) "Focus groups". In: J.A. Smith (ed.) *Qualitative psychology: A practical guide to research methods*. London: SAGE Publications Ltd., pp. 186–206.

Williams, D. (1994) *Somebody somewhere*. Moorebank, NSW: Transworld.

Williams, D. (1996) *Autism: An inside-out approach*. London: Jessica Kingsley Publishers.

Williams, J. and Hanke, D. (2007) Do you know what sort of school I want?: Optimum features of school provision for pupils with autistic spectrum disorder. *Good Autism Practice*, 8 (2): 51–63.

Williams, J.H., Whitten, A. and Singh, T. (2004) A systematic review of action imitation in autistic spectrum disorder. *Journal of Autism and Developmental Disorders*, 34 (3): 285–299.

Willis, J. and Robinson, J. (2011) *Portage basic workshop*. Redditch, UK 7th–10th February 2011. Worcestershire Portage Service.

Wilson, E. (2009) *School-based research: A guide for education students*. London: SAGE Publications Ltd.

Wing, L. (2012) *The Autistic Spectrum*. Revised Edition. Hachette UK.

Wood, D., Bruner, J.S. and Ross, G. (1976) The role of tutoring in problem solving. *Journal of Child Psychology and Psychiatry*, 17 (2): 89–100.

Woodcock, L. and Page, A. (2010) *Managing family meltdown: The low arousal approach and autism*. London: Jessica Kingsley Publishers.

World Health Organisation (WHO) (1993) *Mental disorders: A glossary and guide to their classification in accordance with the 10th revision of the International Classification of Diseases (ICD-10)*. Geneva: WHO.

Yin, R. (2003a) *Case study research: Design and methods*. 3rd ed. London: SAGE Publications Ltd.

Yin, R. (2003b) *Applications of case study research*. London: SAGE Publications Ltd.

Yoder, P.J., Kaiser, A.P., Goldstein, H., Alpert, C., Mousetis, L. and Kaczmareck, L. (1995) An exploratory comparison of milieu teaching and responsive interaction in classroom applications. *Journal of Early Intervention*, 19 (3): 218–242.

Yoder, P.J. and McDuffie, A.S. (2006) "Treatment of responding to and initiating joint attention". In: T. Charman and W. Stone (eds.) *Social and communication development in autism spectrum disorders*. London: The Guilford Press, pp. 117–142.

Yoder, P.J. and Stone, W. (2006) Randomized comparison of two communication interventions for preschoolers with autism spectrum disorders. *Journal of Consulting and Clinical Psychology*, 74 (3): 426–435.

Zanolli, K., Daggett, J. and Adams, T. (1996) Teaching preschool autistic children to make spontaneous initiations to peers using priming. *Journal of Autism and Developmental Disorders*, 26 (4): 406–422.

Zeichner, K. (2001) "Educational action research". In: P. Reason and H. Bradbury (eds.) *Handbook of action research: Participative inquiry and practice*. London: SAGE Publications Ltd., pp. 273–283.

Zeuli, J.S. (1994) How do teachers understand research when they read it? *Teaching and Teacher Education*, 10 (1): 39–55.

Zuber-Skerritt, O. (1996) *New directions in action research*. London: Falmer.

Index

Note: Page numbers in *italic* indicate a figure and page numbers in **bold** indicate a table on the corresponding page. Indexing has been conducted by Routledge.

academic research: accessible for all manner of 1–2; bridging gap between school practice and 1, 167
action research: advantages of 69–70; challenges of 71; definition of 68; empowerment 70; ethics and 71; features of 68–69; personal development and 70; professional development and 70; sequence 79; teamwork 70
Adult Interactive Style Coding Checklist (AISCC) 84, 85–87, **87**
adult interactive style intervention (AISI): based on development/relationship-based approaches 25; communicative opportunities 56–60; in drawings 60–64; overview of 46; study 3; *see also* AISI principles; AISI study
Agius, K. 19–20, 84, 102–103, 107
AISI *see* adult interactive style intervention (AISI)
AISI principles: assign meaning to random actions/sounds 51, *61*, 177; child materials they need help with 58, 118; communication opportunities **45**; communicative opportunities 178–179; contradict expectations 59, 179; establish appropriate proximity/touch 48, *60*, *63*, 176; exaggerated/animated pitch 53, *63*, 113, 177; expand communicative attempts 54–55, *63*, 112, 178; follow child's lead/focus of attention 52, *61*, 177; forget something vital 60, *61*, 115–116, 118, 179; gain child's attention 47, *62*, 176; general principles **44**, 176–178; give material child needs help with 179; give non-preferred items 59, 115, 179; give small portions 57–58, 178; imitate the child 51–52, *61*, 177; make items inaccessible 58, *62*, 118, 179; offer choice 56–57, *61*, 178; provide time for information processing 54, *64*, 178; respond to communicative attempts 50, *64*, 176–177; show availability 48–49, *60*, *62*, 176; small portions *63*; stop part way 57, *63*, 178; used in pre- and post-interventions *108*, 108–112, **110–111**; use minimal speech 53–54, *64*, 112, 177; use non-verbal cues 55–56, *64*, 112, 178; wait for initiations 49–50, *60*, *62*, 176
AISI study: action research 73; activity types **82**; adult:child ratio 82–83; children selected for 75–78, **76–77**; confidentiality of 91; design 67–68, 73–74; development of 89–90; ethical issues 90–92; focus group interviews 88–89, 109–112; implementation of 108–109; methodology 68–71; observation coding 84–88; philosophical underpinnings of 66–67; reflexivity 73; reliability 72; research aims of 65–66; sampling 74–78; school selected for 74–75; staff members selected for 78, 79; validity 71–72; video recordings of staff/children *see* video recordings of staff/children

Index

AISI study, data analysis: activity type, effect of 98–101; communicative functions 101–105, **103**; communicative methods 105–108, **106**; communicative opportunities 114–116; effect size 94–95; focus group interview data 96–97, 98–100; frequency of spontaneous communication 95–98; general notes 93–95; protests, as communicative function 102–104; requesting, as communicative function 102–104; social routines 104; total initiations 95, **95**, *96*, **99**
Aldred, C. 37, 40
American Psychiatric Association (APA) 94
Ametepee, L. 141
analytical skills 122
Applied Behavior Analysis (ABA) 26
Ashton, P. 122
assign meaning to random actions/sounds (AISI principle) 51, *61*, 177
attention-switching problems 18
Augmentative and Alternative Communication (AAC) 20
autism: comorbid with learning difficulties 146; definition of 4; intentional spontaneous social communication in 11–15; medical model to interpret 2; social communication in 9–11; SPMLD and 3; theories 16–18; *see also* global perspective of autism
Autism Diagnostic Interview-Revised (ADI-R) 162
Autism Diagnostic Observation Schedule (ADOS) 162
autism research: of autism with additional SPMLD 170; case studies 150; close-ended questions 160; cross-cultural studies 162–164; enhancing rigor in 149–151; gender differences 147–148; importance of 148–149; intellectual functioning 146–147; involving individuals with autism 157–162; of older people 146, 169; partial effectiveness vs. full effectiveness trials 149; participant age 145–146; primary and secondary quality indicators in 150–151; qualitative vs. quantitative 150; research priorities 148; school-based research 149–150; stakeholders in 152
Autism Society of America 139
autism spectrum disorder (ASD), definition of 4
availability 48–49, *60*, *62*

Baines, S. 146
Bandura, A. 126
Beadle, Dean 133
behavioural/naturalistic interventions: adult style, role of 26–31; benefits of 25; definition of 24; developmental/relationship-based vs. 25; Early Intensive Behavior Intervention 26–27; Early Start Denver Model (ESDM) 28; home-based programme 31; Incidental Teaching 27; Milieu Teaching 28–29; modelling 29; one-up rule 28; Picture Exchange Communication System 29–30, 39; Pivotal Response Training (PRT) 27–28, 39; Portage programme 31; Reciprocal Imitation Training (RIT) 29, 39; reciprocity 29; Treatment and Education of Autistic and related Communication handicapped CHildren 30–31
behaviour regulation 104–105
being reflective *see* reflection/reflective practice
Bettelheim, B. 141
Biemans, Harrie 124
binary model of spontaneity 87–88
Blackburn, R. 10, 20, 46, 48, 59
Blatchford, P. 154
Bloor, M. 88
body language 55
Bogdashina, O. 7, 85
Bölte, S. 150
Bondy, A. 30, 135
Bradbury, H. 68
British Education Research Association (BERA) 91–92
British Journal of Learning Disabilities 157
British Psychological Society (BPS) 161
British Sign Language (BSL) 55
Brown, F. 134–135
Bruner, J. 12, 104, 118
Burns, R. 71, 72
Burrell, G. 67

Caldwell, P. 51–52, 117
Cameron, L. 135
caregiver-infant interaction model 31
Caro-Martinez, L.M. 12–13, 19–21, 83, 97, 102, 104–107
CARS diagnostic rating scale 78
Carter, M. 19
Central Coherence 17
Challenging Behaviour (CB) 4, 20, 22, 49, 85, **86**, 98, 105, 107, 141
Chan, A.S. 11
Chandler, S. 40
Charlop-Christy, M.H. 39
Checklist for the Initiation of Communication in Children with Autism (CICCA) 84–85, **86**, 87–88
Chiang, H.M. 19–22, 83, 97, 100–102, 107–108
child-adult interactions 83
child development: social communication and 8; transactional model of 3
child materials they need help with (AISI principle) 58, 118
children with development delay (DD) 10, 19–20, 22
child's attention, gaining 47
Chitiyo, M. 141
choice diversity model 134–135
choice making 134–135
Christie, P. 47, 52, 53, 56
Clifford, S. 97
close-ended questions 160
Cohen, L. 71, 73, 84, 94
Cohen's d 94, 101
Coles, J. 137
collaborative multidisciplinary teamwork 130
collectivist orientation 141
communication: building blocks of 125; children with autism initiating 13–15; echolalia 13; echopraxia 13; by eye contact 20–21; initiation checklist 86; intentionality of 11–12; personal pronouns and 14; responding to child's attempts at 50; spontaneity of 12–13; un-cued 12–13; *see also* social communication; spontaneous communication
communicative functions 101–105, **103**, 168
communicative methods 105–108, **106**, 168

continuum model 19, 88
contradict expectations (AISI principle) 59
Cordingley, P. 132
Corke, M. 35, 52
Courchesne, E. 18
Crosland, K.A. 145–146
culture, definition of 138; *see also* global perspective of autism
Cumming, T.M. 158

DARL rating scale 78
data generalisability 71
Dawson, G. 54–55
Dawson, Michelle 159
DCSF *see* Department for Children, Schools and Family (DCSF)
decision making 135–136, 169
declarative pointing 21
deficit model of disability 2
deictic words 11, 14, 166
delayed echolalia 13
Denscombe, M. 73, 74, 80–81
Department for Children, Schools and Family (DCSF) 8
Deployment and Impact of Support Staff project 154
Developmental, Individual difference, Relationship-based (DIR) model-Floortime 33–34, 59
developmental/relationship-based interventions: behavioural/naturalistic vs. 25; benefits of 25; caregiver-infant interaction model 31; definition of 24; Giggle Time 33–34; goals of 40; Hanen approach 37; Intensive Interaction 31–32; 'More than Words' approach 37, 40; Musical Interaction 34–36, 40; Music Therapy 35–36; Observe, Wait and Listen (OWL) technique 37; Option Program 36–37; Preschool Autism Communication Trial 37–38, 40; responsiveness 32; Responsive Teaching curriculum 38–39, 40; Social Communication Emotional Regulation Transactional Support 32–33; Son-Rise Program 36–37
Developmental, Social-Pragmatic approach 43–44
Diggle, T. 155
DIR-Floortime model 33–34, 59
Discrete Trial Teaching/Training (DTT) 26, 39

divorce 133–134
Dockrell, J. 160–161
Doussard-Roosevelt, J. 42, 117
Doveston, M. 143, 164
Drain, S. 19, 22
Drawing the Ideal Self technique 161
Drew, A. 42
Dvortcsak, A. 24

Early Intensive Behavior Intervention (EIBI) 26–27
Early Start Denver Model (ESDM) 28
Early Support Developmental Journal 8
echolalia, types of 13
echopraxia 13–14
ecological validity 72
Edwards, T.L. 145, 147
Elliot, J. 69
Emerson, E. 20, 146
empirical skills 122
empowerment 70
endless talking 15
Engelhardt, P.E. 19, 22
epistemology, definition of 67
Escalona, A. 42
establish appropriate proximity/touch (AISI principle) 48, *60*, 63, 176
ethics 71, 90–92, 161–162, 168, 169
evaluative skills 122
exaggerated/animated pitch (AISI principle) 53, *63*, 113, 177
Executive Functioning 16–17
expand communicative attempts (AISI principle) 54–55, *63*, 112, 178
expressive communication 7, 11
external validity 72
extreme literalness 14–15
eye contact 20–21, 107

face-to-face interactions 48
false consensus in focus group interviews 89
fatalism 141–142
females with autism 147
Filbey, L. 132
Fleming, B. 163
focus group interviews 88–89, 167–168
follow child's lead/focus of attention (AISI principle) 52, *61*, 177
Fombonne, E. 140, 147
forget something vital (AISI principle) 60, *61*, 115–116, 118

Freeman, N.L. 104
Frost, L. 30, 135, 150
Funazaki, Y. 160

gain child's attention (AISI principle) 47, *62*, 176
gender and autism 147–148
Gerland, G. 21
Ghaye, A. 121
Ghaye, K. 121
Gibson, K.A. 128
Giggle Time intervention 33–34, 48
Gillett, J.N. 49, 117
give non-preferred items (AISI principle) 59, 115
give small portions (AISI principle) 57–58
global perspective of autism: collectivist orientation 141; cross-cultural studies 162–164; cultural differences in 138–139; educational approaches 141–142; fatalism 141–142; general views on 140–141; immigrant populations 140; individualism 141; parents' training 142; prevalence rates 139–140; symptom diversity 141
Goodwin, M. 55, 137
Grandin, Temple 10, 15, 18, 136
Gray, C. 46
Greenspan, S. 51, 59, 117
Grinker, R.R. 139
Group Design (GD) studies 149
group learning 127
Grove, N. 12, 50
Guba, E.G. 66
Guillemin, F. 163

Hall, D. 69, 73
Hall, I. 69, 73
Halle, J.W. 12
Hanen intervention 37, 40
Hanke, D. 161
Harding, C.G. 12
Harrington, C. 160, 161–162
Hauck, M. 83
Hewett, D. 32, 48, 50, 52
Hewitt, J. 129
Higashida, N. 1, 2, 47
Hincliffe, V. 153
Hodges, L. 135
Honeybourne, V. 147
Hopkins, D. 84
Hotchkis, G.D. 19

Hudry, K. 11
Hughes, C. 43
Hwang, B. 43

ideographic methodology 67
idiosyncratic communication signals 15, 51
imitate the child (AISI principle) 51–52, 61, 177
imitation 29, 117
imperative pointing 21
'inaccessible items' principle *see* make items inaccessible (AISI principle)
Incidental Teaching 27
individualism 141
individuals with autism: as co-researchers 158–159; effectively getting their views 159–161; ethical considerations 161–162; involving in real-world research 157–162
individuals with special education needs (SEN) 134–138, 141, 157–160, 168
Ingersoll, B. 24, 29, 39, 41, 43–44, 116–117
intellectual functioning 146–147
Intensive Interaction intervention 31–32, 48
intentional communication 11–12
inter-disciplinary model 130–134
internal validity 72
International Classification of Diseases and Related Health Problems (ICD-10) 9–10
interpretivism 67, 72
inter-rater reliability 72
intonation 15, 38

Jackson, Luke 2, 20–21
James, D. 128, 129
Jang, J. 145
Jarvis, J. 129
Jivraj, J. 158
Johnson, B. 66
joint attention acts 104–105, 168
Jones, E.A. 39
Jones, Glenys 1
Jordan, R. 13, 131, 133, 137

Kanner, L. 9, 14, 17, 141
Kasari, C. 40, 146
Kashinath, S. 42
Kaufman, B.N. 36, 48
Kennedy, H. 125, 130

Kiernan, C. 158
Kim, H.U. 139
Konst, M.J. 148–149, 155–156
Kuhn, T.S. 66

Lacey, P. 130–131
language development theory 118
Latham, C. 55
Lava, V. 132
Lawson, W. 136–137
learned helplessness 118
Learning Support Assistants 132–133; *see also* teaching assistants (TAs)
LeBlanc, L.A. 49, 117
Leventhal, J.M. 134
Lewin, Kurt 68
Lewis, A. 160
Lin, W.T. 19, 20, 21, 83, 102
Lincoln, Y.S. 66
Litosseliti, L. 88
Llaneza, D.C. 2
Lloyd, D. 162
Lonergan, J. 83
Longhorn, F. 48, 50, 53
Luke, L. 136
Lundeby, H. 133–134
Lyon, S. 129

Mahoney, G. 40
Makaton 55
make items inaccessible (AISI principle) 58, 62, 118
Making a Statement project 154
Mannan, H. 156–157
Manolson, A. 37
Matson, J.L. 141, 148–149, 155–156
McAteer, M. 44
McClimens, A. 158
McConachie, H. 155
McCray, E.D. 132
McGee, G.G. 10–11
McIntyre, D. 1
Meadan, H. 156
mediated learning theory 126
medical model of disability 2
medical tragedy model 2
Mental Capacity Act 135, 161
Mesibov, G.B. 18, 30–31
methodolatry 150
methodology, definition of 67
Miles, A. 55
Milieu Teaching 28–29, 40–41
Milton, D.E. 51, 159

mind-blindness 16
minimal speech 53–54, 112, 116
Mitchel, David 1
mixed-methods research design 68
modelling 29, 55, 126
Moore, M. 91
'More than Words' programme *see* Hanen intervention
Morgan, G. 67, 88
motoric acts 105–107
Murdock, L.C. 10
Murphy, J. 135
Musical Interaction therapy 34–36, 40
Music Therapy 35–36

National Institute for Health and Care Excellence (NICE) 124
Natt, S. 43
negative reinforcement 26
neologisms 15
neurotypical (NT) adults: autism understanding of 46; communication breakdown with 3
Newly Qualified Teachers (NQTs) 132
Nind, M. 32, 48, 50, 52
nomothetic methodology 67
non-preferred items *see* give non-preferred items (AISI principle)
non-probability sampling 74
non-verbal cues 55–56, *64*, 112, 117
Norbury, C.F. 139
Northway, Ruth 158–159
NVivo 94, 95, 119

objects of reference 55
observation coding 84–88
Observe, Wait and Listen (OWL) technique 37
offer choice (AISI principle) 56–57, *61*, 178
Oi, M. 160
one-up rule 28
ontology, definition of 66–67
Operant Conditioning theory 26
Option Program 36–37
O'Reilly, M. 22, 100
orphanages, social deprivation in 9
Osborn, M. 89
Oyvry, C. 130

Page, A. 49, 54
Pan-London Autism Schools Network-Research (PLASN-R) partnership 153
Papadopoulos, Nikos 60
paradigms 66
parent-child interactions 9, 41–44
Parsons, S. 152, 153
Participatory Action Research (PAR) 65, 69, 167
Pawelski, J.O. 126
peer network 132
Peeters, T. 131, 133
Pellecchia, M. 156
Pellicano, E. 146, 147, 148
Perales, F. 40
percentage agreement 72
Perepa, P. 142
PERMA model 126
personal pronouns 14
persons with special education needs (SEN) 134–138, 141, 157–160, 168
physical prompts 26
physical proximity, establishing appropriate 48
Picture Exchange Communication System (PECS) 29–30, 39–41, 135
Pilnick, A. 128
Pivotal Response Training (PRT) 27–28, 39
Pollard, A. 122
Portage programme 31
Porter, J. 160
positive psychology 126
positive reinforcement 26
positivism 67
Potter, C. 13, 19, 20, 43, 83, 85, 100, 102, 116
practical skills 122
Preece, D. 137, 142
Preschool Autism Communication Trial (PACT) 37–38, 40, 156
primary intersubjectivity theory 125–126
Prizant, B.M. 7, 12
probability sampling 74
prompts, EIBI use of 26
pronoun reversal 14
protests, as communicative function 102–104
provide time for information processing (AISI principle) 54, *64*, 178
proximity/touch 107, 113
purism 67
purposive sampling 74
Puyalto, C. 158, 159

qualitative impairments in communication 9–10
qualitative research 150
quantitative (fixed) research design 68, 150

Randomised Control Trial (RCT) study 40
Reason, P. 68
receptive communication 7, 11
Reciprocal Imitation Training (RIT) 29, 39
reciprocity 29
Reeve, D. 3
reflection/reflective practice 120–124, 168
reflective teamwork model 131
reflexivity 73
Reichow, B. 72, 150–151
reinforcement: in Early Start Denver Model 28; EIBI use of 26–27; in TEACCH approach 30
reliability 72
repetitive questioning 15
requesting, as communicative function 102–104, 168
research design: definition of 67–68; in real-world setting 149; types of 68
research paradigms 66
research questions 65–66, 167
research relationship 69
respond to communicative attempts (AISI principle) 50, 64, 176–177
Responsive Education and Prelinguistic Milieu Teaching (RPMT) 40–41
responsiveness 32
Responsive Teaching intervention curriculum 38–41
Risdal, D. 133
Roberts, J. 13
Robison, John Elder 20
Robson, C. 71
Rochford Review 134, 143, 150
Rogers, J. 127
Rogers, S.J. 14, 54–55
room management model 131
Rose, R. 143, 164
Ruble, L. 42
rules of conduct 90
Rutter, M. 9

Sabbeth, B.F. 134
Saddler, H. 154

Saini, M. 134
Sainsbury, Clare 16
Schlosser, R.W. 6–7
school practice, bridging gap between academic research and 1, 167
school staff, interactive style of 43–44
Schreibman, L. 39
Schultz, T.R. 155
Scott, D. 67
secondary intersubjectivity theory 125–126
self-confrontation model 126
self-modelling 126
Seligman, M.E.P. 126
sensory processing 18
severe, profound and multiple learning difficulties (SPMLD) 2–4, 12, 14, 50, 55–56, 93–94, 118, 124, 130–131, 135, **144**, 169–170
Shakespeare, T. 3
Sheridan, M. 8
show availability (AISI principle) 48–49, 60, 62, 176
Sigman, M. 42
sign language 13–14, 55–56
Siller, M. 42
Sinclair, J. 10
Singer, G.H.S. 133
Single Attention and Associated Cognition in Autism (SAACA) 17–18
Single Subject Design (SSD) 149
Sked, H. 125, 128
Skinner, B.F. 26
small portions (AISI principle) 57–58, 63
Smith, J.A. 89
Smith, T. 146
social communication: acts of 7, 16; approaches to 23–25; in autism 9–11; as continuous dynamic interplay 3; definition of 6–7; difficulties in 10; means of 7; qualitative impairments in 9–10; types of 7; in typical development 8–9; *see also* communication
Social Communication Emotional Regulation Transactional Support (SCERTS) 32–33, 81, 83
social communication skills 6, 10–11
social disablism 2–3
social games 104–105, 168
social interactions 104–105
social learning theory 126

Index

social model of disability 2–3
social reinforcement 30
social routines 104
Sonders, S. 33–34, 48, 53, 57
Son-Rise Program 36–37
Sparks, A. 139
Special Educational Needs and Disability (SEND) 130, 134
SPMLD *see* severe, profound and multiple learning difficulties (SPMLD)
spontaneous communication: across activities 22; categorising and coding 84–88; definition of 12–13; difference between adults vs. peers 21–22; effect of type of activity on 98–101; frequency of 95–98; functions of 19; methods children use 19–21; minimal speech and 116; motoric acts 19–20; partners in 21–22; physical manipulation 20; questionnaire to determine 173–175; studies on adult style 41–44; teaching 170; *see also* communication; social communication
Stahmer, A.C. 156
stakeholders: benefits of 152; parents 155–157; as process of knowledge exchange 152–153; in research 152; teachers 154; teaching assistants 154
Stevenson, M. 158
Stone, W.L. 12–13, 19–22, 40, 83, 97, 102, 104–107
stop part way (AISI principle) 57, *63*
strategic skills 122
Strnadová, I. 158
Studio III 49
Sturmey, P. 136
Sussman, F. 40
Sylva, K. 83
symbolic methods 105, 107–108

'Talking Mats' intervention 161, 170
teaching assistants (TAs) 70, 132–133, 154
Team Around the Child (TAC) model 130
teamwork 70; among teachers 132; with parents 133–134; at schools 131; teaching assistants 132–133
Theory of Mind 12, 16
Tossebro, J. 134
transactional model of child development 3
trans-disciplinary collaboration model 130–134
Transform Autism Education (TAE) 159
Treatment and Education of Autistic and related Communication handicapped CHildren (TEACCH) 30–31
Trevarthen, Colwyn 125–126
typical development (TD), child, social communication in 8–11

un-cued communication 12–13
University of Birmingham Code of Practice for Research 90
use minimal speech (AISI principle) 53–54, *64*, 112, 177
use non-verbal cues (AISI principle) 55–56, *64*, 112, 178
Usher, R. 67
utterances, use of 54–55

validity 71–72
verbal prompts 26
Video Enhanced Reflective Practice (VERP) method 126–127, 129–130, 168–169
Video Interaction Guidance (VIG) intervention 90, 124–126, 128–130, 168–169
video recordings of staff/children: action research sequence 79; activity types to record 81–82; camera use 83–84; disadvantages to 80; effects on behavior 80–81; length of 83; microphones 84; researcher's role in 81; strengths of 80
Vincett, K. 121, 131, 133
vocalisations 107
Vygotsky, L. 118, 126

wait for initiations (AISI principle) 49–50, *60, 62*, 176
Walmsley, J. 156–157
Wantanbe, M. 136
Ware, J. 46, 47, 49, 51, 52, 59, 135
Warwick, A. 35
Watson, L.R. 12, 42
Wetherby, A.M. 10, 12
Whitehead, J. 69, 73
Whittaker, C. 13, 19, 20, 43, 83, 85, 100, 102, 116

Wieder, S. 51, 59, 117
Wilkinson, M. 44, 89
Williams, Donna 14, 17
Williams, J. 161
women with autism 147
Woodcock, L. 49, 54

Yin, R. 67–68, 71–72
Yoder, P.J. 25, 40

Zanolli, K. 13
zone of proximal development 118, 126
zoning model 131